THEORY AND INTERPRETATION OF NARRATIVE

JAMES PHELAN, PETER J. RABINOWITZ, AND ROBYN WARHOL, SERIES EDITORS

THE WRITER IN THE WELL

ON MISREADING AND
REWRITING LITERATURE

GARY WEISSMAN

THE OHIO STATE UNIVERSITY PRESS • COLUMBUS

Copyright © 2016 by The Ohio State University.
All rights reserved.

Library of Congress Cataloging-in-Publication Data
Names: Weissman, Gary, author.
Title: The writer in the well : on misreading and rewriting literature / Gary Weissman.
Other titles: Theory and interpretation of narrative series.
Description: Columbus : The Ohio State University Press, [2016] | Series: Theory and interpretation of narrative | Includes bibliographical references and index.
Identifiers: LCCN 2016033663 | ISBN 9780814213193 (cloth ; alk. paper)
Subjects: LCSH: Literature—History and criticism—Theory, etc. | Criticism—Authorship. | Authors and readers. | Narration (Rhetoric)
Classification: LCC PN45 .W358 2016 | DDC 809—dc23
LC record available at https://lccn.loc.gov/2016033663

Cover design by Susan Zucker
Text design by Juliet Williams
Type set in Palatino and Franklin Gothic

9 8 7 6 5 4 3 2 1

CONTENTS

	Acknowledgments	vii
	An Introduction to Misreading and Rewriting Literature	1
	"The Man in the Well" *Ira Sher*	31
CHAPTER 1	Misreadings	37
CHAPTER 2	Authorities	81
CHAPTER 3	Genres	131
	An Afterword in Two Voices	190
	Works Cited	209
	Index	215

ACKNOWLEDGMENTS

This book is an outgrowth of my experiences teaching in the Department of English and Comparative Literature at the University of Cincinnati. I thank the faculty and staff of this great department and its students for providing such a vibrant and enriching community. I am particularly thankful to the students in my Human Values in Literature courses who generously granted me permission to quote from their work and from whom I have learned so much; my indebtedness to them shows throughout this book. I am also grateful to the writers whose excellent scholarship on reading, writing, and interpreting has proven so inspirational to my own thinking and scholarship; much of their work is cited in these pages. My interest in integrating critical theory and writing pedagogy owes much to my experiences as a graduate student teaching composition courses at the University of Wisconsin–Milwaukee in the 1990s under the guidance of Charles Schuster, Alice Gillam, and Margie Mika.

I am grateful for the extraordinary support I have received from the Charles Phelps Taft Research Center at the University of Cincinnati, under the directorships of Jana Braziel and Adrian Parr, in the form of fellowships that gave me the time and mental space to draft much of this book. I thank Eric Hayot and Michael Rothberg for supporting this project in its infancy; Jay Twomey, with whom I shared many pleasurable and productive days of writing at the Iris BookCafé when I was getting this book going; and the many people who engaged my work and offered valuable feedback or support along the way, including Jonathan Alexander, Beth Ash, Chris Bachelder, Michael Bernard-Donals, Dick Blau, Isaac Campos, Julia Carlson, Bruce Chadwick, Stan Corkin, Garrett Cummins, Patricia Donahue, Lance Duerfahrd, Russel Durst, Grace Epstein, Paul Fleming, Adam Frelin, Jane Gallop, Fredrick Gensler, Michelle Gibson, Jenn Glaser, Charlie Green, Michael Griffith, Jenn Habel, Wayne Hall, Joe Harris, Charley Henley, Trish Thomas Henley, Mike Hennessey, Emily Houh, Ken Jacobson, Jon Kamholtz, Jim Knippling, Andrew Lehman, Jennifer Malat, Joyce Malek, John Martin, Dan Martinico, Nicola Mason, Deb Meem, Thérèse Migraine-George, Janine Morris, Lee Person, Donna Qualley, Maria Romagnoli, Mariolina Salvatori, Jim Schiff, John Schilb, Steve Scipione, Michael Staub, Steve Vogl, Matt Weber, and Robby Wright, among others.

The seed of this book is my essay "The Virtue of Misreadings: Interpreting 'The Man in the Well,'" which was published in *College English* (copyright 2010 by the National Council of Teachers of English [NCTE]). I thank the journal and NCTE for permission to reprint material from this essay. I am grateful to Jim Phelan, Peter Rabinowitz, and Robyn Warhol for giving this book a dream home in the Theory and Interpretation of Narrative series. Jim, Peter, and an anonymous third reader provided extremely perceptive and helpful responses to the manuscript. Words cannot express my gratitude to Jim and Peter, whose challenging and thought-provoking engagement with my writing greatly improved the final product. Their willingness to discuss issues of literary interpretation with me as I worked on revising the manuscript is indicative of their tremendous generosity and intellectual spirit. I am grateful to Lindsay Martin, Malcolm Litchfield, Sandy Crooms, and the editorial board and staff of The Ohio State University Press for their support of this book. I thank Lindsay, Laurie Avery, Tara Cyphers, Rebecca Sullivan, and Juliet Williams for all of their work in seeing it published. I thank Rebecca S. Bender for copyediting the manuscript.

I am deeply thankful to Ira Sher for granting me permission to reprint "The Man in the Well," which first appeared in *Chicago Review,* and for his exceptional willingness to engage with me in dialogue that has lasted longer than either of us could have expected. Happily, my fascination with his captivating short story has led not only to this book but also to a lasting friendship with the story's wonderfully thoughtful author. Finally, I thank my family for sustaining my work over the years. I am grateful for the loving community formed by my mother and stepfather, Elaine and Hewitt Rubel, and my brothers and sisters-in-law and nieces and nephew, and for the caring hearts of my in-laws. Most of all, I am grateful to my wife, Laura

Micciche, who has provided both top-notch feedback to my writing and loving support despite my efforts to complete this book in the most drawn-out and stress-inducing ways possible, and to our brilliant and hilarious children Giovanni and Lou, who make the everyday thrilling.

AN INTRODUCTION TO MISREADING AND REWRITING LITERATURE

PUTTING THEORY INTO PRACTICE

The work of interpreting literature is typically understood in terms of critical *reading* practices, the assumption being that it is by becoming better readers that we come to write more perceptive and persuasive analyses of literary texts. While recognizing the tremendous importance of reading, this book proposes that literary analysis is better understood as an activity conducted largely in and through *writing*. As such, it treats writing as central to how students and scholars alike may best engage works of literature and come to complex understandings of them. Donna Qualley describes the first reading of a text as a "draft" we revise through a process of rereading and writing. That, as she puts it, "writing can help people to discover, learn, and clarify the texts they read" has long been understood in composition studies ("Using" 102). This is far less the case in literary studies, where teachers commonly regard students' written analyses of the literature they have been assigned to read, and most likely have read only once, as evidence of the time, effort, and quality of thought that has been put into "doing the reading." This book makes a case for treating such writings not as the end products of students' interpretive efforts, and not even as reliable indicators of students' reading experiences, but rather as first steps in an ongoing, collaborative process of literary analysis.

In literature courses there is typically just one person who learns from engaging with and responding to multiple written responses to an assigned work of literature, and that person, the great beneficiary of the students' work, is the teacher. The teacher has a uniquely enriched perspective, an understanding expanded not only through rereading literature he or she has taught before but also through exposure to myriad students' writings on that literature. This book seeks to open up and broaden this perspective by involving its readers—teachers and students, scholars and laypersons—as participants in the process of analyzing a single remarkable short story in collaboration with others who have read and written on it.

This short story, "The Man in the Well," was the first piece published by novelist and short story writer Ira Sher. Though it appeared in the *Chicago Review* in 1995, I discovered it not as a reader of that journal but as a listener to the wonderful public radio program *This American Life*. Although the program's website states that the stories in most episodes "are journalism, with an occasional comedy routine or essay" ("About"), works of short fiction are occasionally featured as well. Upon hearing the broadcast of "The Man in the Well," I knew I wanted to assign the story to students taking my undergraduate course Human Values in Literature.

The inclusion of courses with such titles in the English curriculum has roots in the belief that works of great literature serve a civilizing or humanizing function, teaching readers "*universal human values,* the most important values that apply to all people at all times and in all places" (Eaglestone 54; italics in original). This belief has diminished since the late 1980s, when scholars seeking to broaden the literary canon charged that it was less indicative of timeless values and the intrinsic quality of Great Books than of the vested interests of generations of white male scholars. When teaching the course (which my department has since renamed Ethics and Literature, on the basis that "human values" is an outmoded term), I have assigned readings that upset traditional notions of literature's humanizing function. "The Man in the Well" struck me as one such work: not a time-tested Great Book but a contemporary short story by a first-time author, it does not demonstrate universal human values so much as test our belief in them.

This book originates in my experience of teaching "The Man in the Well" in the Human Values in Literature courses I offered in 2006 and 2007. More specifically, its origin lies in my students' written responses to the short story, each a single-spaced one-page paper. More specifically still, it lies in those responses I took to be misreadings. These were responses that misinterpreted the short story, whether by neglecting much of the text, referring to narrative elements that have little or no basis in it, or both. These flawed responses presented me with a problem: how was I to convey to my students that their interpretations were largely *wrong* without imposing my own *right* interpretation on the class? I found this to be a particularly thorny problem because I believe that there is no single correct interpretation of a text.

I was introduced to this belief in college over twenty-five years ago, when discussing Roland Barthes's famous essay "The Death of the Author." The 1967 essay denounces efforts to explain—that is, impose a single meaning on—a literary text by attributing that meaning to the text's author. I recall asking, as a puzzled undergraduate in the habit of granting authors say over their work, "But what if the author has written down exactly what the work means?" And I recall the immediate response of Andy, a more informed classmate: "That would be another text," a separate text with no absolute claim upon the meaning of the first. For Barthes, the chief offenders are critics who authorize their own interpretations under the aegis of the Author—the capital A signifying not the flesh-and-blood author but an imagined authority figure, "the Author-God" evoked by critics (146). That said, Barthes also holds that the flesh-and-blood author of a literary text cannot define its meaning. This is because a text has no singular message, no "ultimate meaning" (147). The meaning of writing cannot be fixed: "words [are] only explainable through other words, and so on indefinitely" (146), and a line of words means both more and less than whatever specific meaning a writer might intend it to convey to readers.

While subscribing to these views in theory, I have found that putting them into practice in the classroom can be a challenge. How, as a teacher, was I to respond to writings by student readers of "The Man in the Well" when the meanings they made of the text struck me as unwarranted and erroneous? My solution was to present a handful of excerpts from their papers to the class and have my students evaluate each in turn, distinguishing interpretations based on textual evidence—words and passages that can be cited to support a claim—from those based on presumptions and personal associations that, having little or no basis in the text, lack support. All but one of those excerpts represented, to my mind, clear instances of misreading; the one exception struck me as notably astute. Not surprisingly, of all the student responses I received, it presented an interpretation of the short story closest to my own.

To some extent, my strategy worked: in our discussion, students identified the unsupported assumptions and flawed reasoning displayed by each excerpt, save the one I had included as a kind of corrective. In this way I succeeded at having my students do the dirty work for me of disqualifying what their classmates had written. Still, I was left with an uneasy feeling. What exactly had been learned from this exercise? Over time, as I continued teaching the short story, I grew still more uneasy. The very interpretations I had encouraged my students to reject as misreadings—and had enlisted them in rejecting—stayed with me, and not only because I found them repeated time and again in the writings of other students. They also stayed with me because, slowly but surely, they drew my attention to the limits of my own thinking about "The Man in the Well."

Misreadings can be interpreted as creative responses to troublesome or curious aspects of a text that other readers—particularly those more versed in literature and literary analysis—disregard in order to write cohesive and compelling interpretations. In directing attention to these unobserved or suppressed textual aspects, students' misreadings have something to teach us about the literature to which they respond. To learn from them, though, we would do well to regard these written responses not as finished portraits of what students made of a text when *reading* it, but as first steps in what they may come to understand about a text through *writing* about it.

WRITING AS METAPHOR

In addition to proclaiming the death of the author, Barthes's essay champions "the birth of the reader" (148), contending that a text's meaning is authored by those who read it. This theorizing is lost on readers who assume that the meaning of a literary work resides "in" the text, as if hidden by the author for canny readers to find "behind the words" or "between the lines." Many students make this assumption, although prevailing thought in literary studies since the 1970s has held that meaning is not fixed in the text but produced or made by its readers. Literary scholars and critics have frequently used writing as a metaphor to express this distinction, stating that meaning is not embedded in a text, waiting there to be read, but is something readers "write" into it. At the same time, these commentators hold that some works of fiction afford readers greater opportunity to make meaning than do others, complicating the idea that literary meaning is not a property of texts but a creation of their readers.

In *How Fiction Works,* for example, James Wood tells the following story:

> Years ago, my wife and I were at a concert given by the violinist Nadja Salerno-Sonnenberg. At a quiet, difficult passage of bowing, she frowned.

Not the usual ecstatic moue of the virtuoso, it expressed sudden irritation. At the same moment, we invented entirely different readings. Claire later said to me: "She was frowning because she wasn't playing that bit well enough." I replied: "No, she was frowning because the audience was so noisy." A good novelist would have let that frown alone, and would have let our revealing comments alone, too: no need to smother this little scene in explanation.

Detail like this—that enters a character but refuses to explain that character—makes us the writer as well as the reader; we seem like co-creators of the character's existence. (91–92)

This anecdote reflects a view widely held among scholars and critics, that better, more "literary" works of fiction provide less in the way of explanation, stimulating readers to make their own meanings—to be "the writer as well as the reader." An irony of this view is that the reader is said to act like a writer when doing exactly what the good writer knows not to do—that is, when providing the missing explanation.

In stating that a good novelist would leave his and his wife's "revealing comments alone," Wood indicates that their "entirely different readings" are revealing only to a certain point, past which the novelist should not stray. But if the novelist should say no more, the same does not hold for the reader. No sooner have Claire and Wood offered their interpretations (she faults the artist, he faults the audience) than they too become characters whose expressions I, as a reader, am left to explain. If an interpretation is another text to be interpreted, it follows that any explanation of their "revealing comments" I might offer (e.g., Claire is as prone to self-criticism as Wood is to blaming others) could be interpreted in turn by *my* readers—that is, by you. A good novelist would let this little scene alone, but the interpretive task it elicits is open-ended and cumulative, occasioning layer upon layer of explanation.

Wood's view that a good novelist writes in a way that "refuses to explain" and thus moves readers to "write" their own explanations suggests the influence of Barthes's conception of the author and the reader, including his notion that reading is, at its best, a kind of writing. In his book *S/Z*, Barthes evokes writing to describe both reading in its most active and dynamic form and literary texts that call to be read in this way. Countless scholars have taken up the distinction made there between *readerly* texts, which offer passive readers a story they may "'throw away' . . . once it has been consumed" (15), and *writerly* texts that "make the reader no longer a consumer, but a producer" who, in actively producing his or her own experience and understanding of the text, accesses "the pleasure of writing" (4). Wood's anecdote basically states that good novelists write writerly texts.

In opposing readerly texts that "can be read, but not written" to writerly texts that "can be written (rewritten)" (S/Z 4), Barthes evokes writing as an imaginative activity freed from the material practice of writing. What he calls "the pleasure of writing" exists apart from the actual work of composing sentences and paragraphs and drafting, revising, and editing whole texts. This book moves beyond such metaphoric evocations of writing to explore literary interpretation as an actual writing-based process through which texts come to be rewritten. This is not to say that we will be leaving the act of reading behind. In fact, approaching literary interpretation as an act of writing involves being more, not less, attentive to how we read literature, because it entails recognizing that written responses are not clear indicators of how a text has been read. In other words, the literary work a person mentally "writes" in the process of making his or her way through a text line by line, paragraph by paragraph, page by page, is only distantly related to the interpretation he or she might produce in writing on that text. Written interpretations are nevertheless commonly called *readings*, indicating that just as writing often serves as a metaphor for reading, so reading commonly serves as a metaphor for writing.

If I refer to my written interpretation of, say, Austen's *Pride and Prejudice* as my "reading" of the novel, I am not gesturing to the time I spent holding the book in my hand, scanning the words on its pages and forming from them a story. Nor am I referring to the time I spent rereading the text, annotating passages, formulating ideas, and making connections; nor to the time I spent reading other scholars' analyses of it; nor to the time I spent with the novel beside me as I wrote about it, intermittently leafing through its pages for passages I might reference. No, my "reading" is my written response itself, the story I tell in writing about the novel, what it means, and how it conveys or allows for those meanings. Moreover, this written "reading" is predicated upon what Ellen J. Esrock aptly describes as "a hypothetical, complete reading, which synthesizes knowledge from all possible readings of a text" (152). In fact, my written "reading" is far less indicative of my reading experience—the private and largely unshareable cognitive process of constructing a meaningful story from written words—than of how I have come to think about Austen's novel in the course of composing an argument about it *in writing*.

When reading and writing are treated metaphorically, these metaphors tend to misrepresent reading and marginalize the work of writing—an act that, though certainly interconnected with that of reading, differs from it substantially. Simply put, in reading a work of literary fiction, one seeks to construct and understand a story written by someone else, the author of that text; in writing an interpretive analysis of that work, one seeks to construct one's own story about the text and its meaning. This is no less the case when one's story concerns a uniquely personal experience of a text or when it addresses how a text has been designed by its author to affect readers in a certain way. Instead of regarding literary analyses as readings, then, I will argue for conceiving of them as rewritings, though not in the metaphoric sense suggested by Barthes and other literary theorists.

INTERPRETATION AS REWRITING

For a less metaphoric, more practical conception of rewriting, I turn to Joseph Harris's *Rewriting: How to Do Things with Texts*, a work predicated on the idea that academic writing is distinguished by the use writers make of other writers' work. One sees this use of other people's writing most clearly in the many references to critical essays and books that appear as quotations, citations, notes, and bibliographies in works of scholarship. But, as Harris makes clear, these are only the most obvious signs of how academic writers "engage with and rewrite the work of other thinkers" (2). At its most basic level, academic writing involves drawing from and commenting on what others have written in order "to keep the conversation going, *to add to* what other writers and intellectuals have thought and said about a subject" by contributing something new (121; italics in original).

Harris contends that we rewrite what others have written when we take up their words and ideas to develop our own lines of thought (as I have been doing in using Barthes's and Wood's writings, and now Harris's, to formulate and present my arguments). Moreover, we rewrite the work of other writers simply by describing their work in our own words. "In a sense, this is rewriting in its clearest form," states Harris. "For as soon as you begin to say what you think a text is 'about' you are involved in rewriting it, in translating its language into your own" (5). Oftentimes writers will summarize a text before presenting their interpretations of it, so as to provide readers unacquainted with that text some understanding of its form and content. Yet, in doing so, writers are already interpreting it—presenting what they make of a text in place of the text itself, rewriting it in their own words.

Arguably, the fairest way to incorporate a text into one's own writing is to quote it in full, thus enabling readers to compare what the writer makes of it to the text as they experience it themselves. The inclusion of "The Man in the Well" in this book, and its placement before the chapters that discuss various interpretations of it, is intended to allow you to experience and interpret the short story independently of how I and others have rewritten it. Of course, this incorporation of the full text is unusual for practical and legal reasons. Except in the case of short poems, academic writers commonly quote only bits and pieces of the texts they discuss, and readers unfamiliar with those texts depend on the writers to provide them with a sense of what the absent texts are "like" and "about."

Though Harris is chiefly concerned with how academic writers utilize the critical writings of other academics or intellectuals, rewriting occurs no less when the texts being discussed are poems, plays, short stories, or novels. In writing on works of literature we also rewrite them, crafting our own versions of the texts we analyze. This hardly means that we are free to make whatever we want of these texts. As Harris notes, in rewriting others' texts you need to "be fair" by endeavoring to represent them accurately, but at the same time you need to make "the work of others . . . useful to your own aims in writing" (5). Ideally, these aims include writing something that is worth reading in its own right, using other texts to arrive at ideas that are interesting in themselves. For this reason, Harris tells student writers: "You want the focus of your readers . . . to be on your ideas, to draw their attention not to the texts you're quoting but to the work you're doing *with* those texts" (20; italics in original).

To make this point more palpable, I will turn to a specific example. While undertaking this book, I found myself recalling a comic strip I had not seen in decades. In what follows, I write on this strip because of the work I am able to do with it: namely, the work of illustrating the process of rewriting and complicating the notion of misreading while touching upon other terms and concepts germane to discussions of textual analysis and literary interpretation.

THE RETURN OF THE MISREADER

In the late 1970s, an age before the Internet, my parents purchased *The World Book Encyclopedia* so my brothers and I could do research for school projects at home. Among the many beige-and-brown volumes spanning two shelves of a bookcase located in what our family called the TV room, a handful contained illustrations I would look at from time to time. Chief among these was a comic strip featured in the entry for "Cartoon" (Kurtzworth 195).

Below the heading "How to Draw a Comic Strip," the strip was shown in five stages of development, beginning with the initial drafting of matchstick figures and word balloons and concluding with this final ink rendering:

Did you respond to the strip with a laugh or a smile, an indifferent shrug, or a furrowed brow? I wonder what readers make of this cartoon because it has long perplexed me.

In elementary school I was classified as a "slow reader." I toiled to decipher sentences and felt overwhelmed by all the word-filled pages in the books I was instructed to read. Needless to say, I did not "read for pleasure"—not unless one counts the comic books and strips I regularly devoured. I struggled to comprehend what I read for school, but the two-panel *World Book* strip confused me on a different level. Being a daily reader of newspaper comics and a regular borrower of oversized library book collections of old strips, I felt myself to be a particularly competent reader in this regard. I was deeply familiar with the comic strip as a genre or category of cultural text marked by the use of particular storytelling methods and conventions, and yet I could not make sense of the *World Book* strip.

As a struggling student who felt overwhelmed by all I had to learn, I identified with the boy wearing a baseball cap in the strip. Indeed, his sentiment made basic sense to me: long ago, studying history in school must have been easier because there was so much less of it to learn, so many fewer names and dates to memorize—right? I might have taken this to be the strip's message had my awareness of comic-strip conventions not led me to expect a humorous punch line, and to see in the other boy's dazed response an indication of how I too should regard his friend's remark. Cartoonists call this type of sight gag, in which "a blast of absurdity has knocked the character on his ass, or caused him to lose consciousness altogether," a *plop* or *plop take* (Miller 379). I did not know the term but certainly knew the convention. Had I lacked familiarity with such conventions, I might have misread the strip without knowing it. Knowing the comic-strip genre, however, I reread the strip with the troubling sense that I was missing something. I knew I misread it because I did not get the joke.

Writing on the comic strip now, I see much that I did not observe then: that the one boy's ungrammatical speech ("wisht," "wouldn' of") marks him as a less literate, seemingly poorer student than his friend, whose comparative smarts are marked first by the schoolhouse that crowns him (echoing his crown-shaped cap) and then by the spiral signifying dazed disbelief in the face of his pal's simple-mindedness. The bad student's baseball cap is an emblem of sport (physical and social outdoor play), which is popularly opposed to book learning (mental and solitary—even antisocial—indoor labor). In the first panel, the good student leads with a book, the symbol of knowledge, in hand; the bad student, by contrast, has his schoolbooks slung over his back like a burden preferably avoided (out of sight, out of mind). In the second panel, the boy who knows better is literally taken aback; it's as if his friend's remark defeats all attempts to instill learning. The schoolhouse is spring-ejected from the panel (the sprung coil appearing in its place) and the book of knowledge falls to the ground.

The story I am writing (in rewriting the comic strip) might culminate in the triumphant return of the reader: transformed by a late-blooming love of reading and extensive schooling into an English professor and professional interpreter of texts, I now see all there is to observe in the comic strip—even more, I presume, than its author intended. This would be an exciting story to tell, but it would be untrue, and not only because no interpretation can exhaust how a text may be interpreted. The fact is that even now something of the misreader persists in my relation to this strip, for it still strikes me as a curious puzzle—as "funny peculiar" rather than "funny ha-ha." Rereading the cartoon now, I continue to feel that its humor eludes me. (Perhaps, I think, it is simply not funny.)

To be sure, I recognize the boy's wish to have been born 500 years ago—and thus to have lived an entirely different life and now be long dead—as a comically extreme response to having to learn history in school. But if therein lies the joke, I am still more interested in what I take to be the boy's misconception of history, an aspect of the strip that leads into thought-provoking territory at odds with simple appreciation of the gag. If nothing kills a joke more than explaining it, contemplating the mind-set of the joke's protagonist must run a close second. Still, this is what draws my interest. The boy in the baseball cap appears to believe that history was taught in school 500 years ago much as it is now, only with far less subject matter to cover. But in the fifteenth century, neither school nor history as a discipline—nor childhood, for that matter—existed as the boy knows them. Ironically, his profoundly ahistorical fantasy of escaping into the past in order to avoid learning about it suggests he has not *really* "had to learn so much history"—for if he had, he would know better than to make such a wish. Might this too be the joke?

Yet another possibility comes to mind when I locate the strip within the tradition of the *double act*, which has its roots in late nineteenth-century vaudeville theater, where a sensible and serious figure, the straight man, would be paired with the less intelligent, less cultured figure, the funny man. Typified by the 1930s Abbott and Costello skit "Who's on First?" (which restages an older vaudeville routine), the double act plays out in innumerable films, television shows, and cartoons to this day. While the funny man is the butt of the joke, audiences also laugh at the straight man as he loses his cool and is driven crazy by his witless partner. Interpreted within this tradition, the comic strip stages, for laughs, an exchange in which the "straight" student is dumbfounded by the "funny" student's reasoning. In a comic reversal, the good student can provide no response to his friend's explanation, not because he has been outsmarted, but because he has been completely out*dumbed*.

THE TEXT AND THE WORK

Why should I be so fond of the *World Book* comic strip when I do not share, much less grasp, its humor? The strip has long fascinated me as a kind of conundrum, its mystery playfully at odds with the simplicity expected of a two-panel gag cartoon. While I may not get the joke, I like what I am able to make of it. A cartoonist drew the strip, including the school and the swirl, but I have animated it by telling a story in which the school is a crown that is spring-ejected from the panel. In writing this story, I have rewritten the strip by adapting it not only to my own medium (writing rather than cartooning) but also to my own sensibility.

I had reread the strip countless times in an attempt to understand its meaning, but only in the process of rewriting it did I come to see the school not as a building in the distance but as an icon hovering over the one boy's head in the foreground. This entailed coming to see the simply drawn schoolhouse, literally labeled "school," not only in literal terms that serve to identify the characters and set the scene (here are two schoolboys walking home from school) but also in figurative terms: the schoolhouse is a symbol of the one boy's school smarts, signifying his greater knowledge attained through learning. I find that much of the pleasure of analyzing texts lies in such moments of discovery, when something one has overlooked or long seen in the same entrenched way appears anew, suggesting a compelling alternative meaning.

My affection for the comic strip speaks to a larger point: we like the texts that we like because of what we are able to make of them (even when, not knowing what to make of elusive, inscrutable texts, we make them into enigmas). You may be reminded of this if you lend a beloved novel to a friend, who, it turns out, neither likes the book nor understands what you see in it. Then you might wish that you could have lent your friend not the book so much as your experience of reading it—which is to say, what you made of the novel. Or, to employ terms from literary theory, you might wish you could have lent your friend not the *text* but the *work*. Whereas the words that make up the text can be read over and over again, the work we make of them varies with each reading. The comic strip I read as a child is the same text I read as an adult, the same text you have read in this book (although its context has changed considerably), but in each case it is a different work.

The text, then, is what we share in common, though at the same time it is something of which we never quite get hold; for in the very act of reading the text we ascribe it meaning, making the text into a work. For this reason, Peter Swirski remarks that "literary text" is a contradiction in terms, given that "one cannot appreciate literary attributes such as influence, genre, and originality without stepping outside the text to the work" (46). In other words, even to regard a text as a poem, a short story, or a novel is to ascribe it meaning that makes the text—what Swirski calls "the sequence of letters on the page" (47)—into something else: literature. His point is a good one to keep in mind, but I will still refer to literary texts (and, even worse, at times will use the terms *work* and *text* interchangeably), recognizing that a text remains open to being realized as any number of works even after it has been classified as literature.

In rereading a text, we never experience it in quite the same way; indeed, often we are struck by previously overlooked elements that lead us to see it differently—that is, to see a different work. But if one's own reading experience can never be repeated, not exactly, a story told about a text's significance or meaning may nevertheless harden into place, as when it is repeated by a teacher, published by a critic or scholar, or attributed to the text's author. Such a story may delimit how a text is read or—more likely, since reading is a difficult activity to control—what aspects of one's reading experience are deemed worthy of acknowledging and sharing with others through discussion and in writing. Thus while in theory a text is infinitely reinterpretable, in practice an authorized interpretation may easily impinge upon or displace a reader's own sense or understanding of a text.

And the same must be said of one's own written interpretation. While I experience a different work each time I reread a text, my rewriting of that text remains fixed once it takes the form of a completed piece of writing, and may limit my ability to engage and contemplate the text in new and different ways—particularly if I am invested in defending and reasserting my interpretation. While the need to move beyond a given interpretation or conception of the work is clear in the case of misreading, this book seeks to move readers and writers to take as hypotheses rather than facts even those interpretations they find most compelling or correct. It proposes that even our most persuasive and brilliant interpretations become impediments to understanding when they are treated as "the last word," the single right, correct, or best interpretation.

CREATIVE REWRITING

My interpretations of the comic strip provide an illustration of *the hermeneutic circle*, hermeneutics being the study of the methods and principles of interpretation. The hermeneutic circle designates the recursive process whereby we interpret a text by understanding its parts in terms of the whole and the whole in terms of its parts. In effect, neither whole nor part is read independently or objectively, as each is understood in terms of the other. For example, I understand the comic strip based on how I interpret its parts or details (the words "wisht" and "wouldn' of," the schoolbooks, the boys' caps, the schoolhouse, and the spiral), but I also select and interpret these details in accordance with my understanding of the strip.

Further complicating matters, the text as a whole is read as part of a still larger whole constituted by the associations readers bring to that text. This larger whole may be intertextual, relating the text to other texts, or contextual, situating the text within a genre, tradition, or cultural-historical moment. The relationship between context and intertextuality is also circular. Even without knowing how a text fits within or responds to a specific genre, a reader may, through his or her familiarity with similar texts, consciously or unconsciously identify it with certain rules or conventions (for instance, the use of sequential panels and word balloons in comic strips, or the comedic tradition of the double act).

Literary interpretation is a genre of academic writing in which claims may be made on the basis of textual, contextual, or intertextual evidence. As Sheridan Blau observes, every viable interpretation is "supported by evidence to warrant it. In other words, the discourse of interpretation proceeds according to the rules of evidentiary reasoning, and the adequacy and persuasiveness of such reasoning serves as the standard by which all interpretations are evaluated" (75). Without this evidentiary basis, the story one tells about what and how a text means may be pure invention, with no claim on that text or other readers. The stories I have told about the comic strip refer to textual elements or details that readers of the strip can see for themselves. Relating these details to genre conventions and traditions, I seek to influence readers to perceive these elements as I do, as textual evidence that supports my explication of what the strip means and how its parts work to allow for that meaning.

My analysis of the comic strip calls attention to its textuality, by which I mean its material or formal elements (the panels, drawings, and words). At the same time, it would have readers imagine the strip's characters, setting, and events in a certain way: beyond seeing the school as an icon and the swirl as a spring, they should imagine the storyworld depicted in the comic strip as one inhabited by a bright student and his dim-witted friend. Interpretations of narratives are essentially stories about stories that say to readers, "Imagine making sense of the text (and staging its storyworld) in this way." Wanting to make the stories I tell about the strip both convincing and compelling, I cite textual elements to support my interpretation and use them as the raw material to write my own stories.

This point can be put another way. According to James Phelan, readers of literary narrative "develop interests and responses of three broad kinds, each related to a particular component of the narrative: mimetic, thematic, and synthetic." The *mimetic* concerns "characters as possible people" existing in a narrative world like our own, or the reader's suspension of disbelief and immersion in the storyworld. The *thematic* concerns "the cultural, ideological, philosophical, or ethical issues being addressed by the narrative," and thus larger questions of meaning. And the *synthetic* concerns characters and storyworld as "artificial constructs" crafted through writing (*Living* 20). Phelan observes that certain genres give prominence to a particular component of the narrative:

> Realistic fiction seeks to create the illusion that everything is mimetic and nothing synthetic, or, in other words, that the characters act as they do by

their own choice rather than at the behest of the author; metafiction, on the other hand, foregrounds the synthetic component, making us aware of its own construction. (*Living* 20)

Regardless of genre, most readers, students among them, typically engage narratives on a mimetic level, as if responding to real people and actual events rather than to a writer's creations. Literary scholars and critics, by contrast, are apt to respond to a narrative's synthetic component, disrupting what Phelan calls "the mimetic illusion" by drawing attention to its construction in writing (*Living* 28). This is not to say that recognition of the synthetic is necessarily antithetical to mimetic concerns. Rather than destroying the illusion of an as-if-real world, scholarly analysis of a text's construction or design may involve reimagining that world and its characters in particular ways.

In rewriting the comic strip, for instance, my attention to synthetic elements led me to imagine the strip's characters as two types of "possible people." The schoolhouse and schoolbook became corroborating evidence of one character's identity as the good student, the sensible straight man to his clueless schoolmate's funny man. And yet, truth be told, nowhere in the two-panel strip is this boy explicitly identified as more studious or intelligent than his friend in the baseball cap. Perhaps if the boy with the crown-shaped beanie were to say something more than "Why?" he would speak with the same poor grammar as his friend. From this we may deduce that as much as my interpretation is based on close textual analysis of the strip, the story it tells is not so much verified as occasioned by details I have taken as textual cues and upon which I have imaginatively elaborated. Insofar as literary interpretation is the product of evidentiary reasoning intertwined with imaginative thinking, all rewriting is a form of creative writing.

INTERPRETIVE POSSIBILITIES

When does rewriting veer into misreading? How does one distinguish a valid interpretation of a literary text from a misinterpretation? Literary theorists and critics have proposed a variety of answers. Since a text has no determinate meaning, some have argued, there is no such thing as misreading; there are only variant readings. Others have taken the opposite position: because there is no single right interpretation, and because all interpretations are partial and necessarily differ from the texts they interpret, all readings are misreadings. But while such arguments are intriguing in theory, and are copiously attested to in literary scholarship published over the last fifty years, teachers and students of literature know very well that some literary interpretations are praised as perceptive and convincing while others are downgraded for being flawed or mistaken, just as literary scholars know that the textual interpretations offered in their published writings are often presented as correctives to other writers' flawed interpretations. At the very least, then, misreadings are *perceived* to exist, with significant real-world effects relating to how the work of students and scholars is evaluated. Given this, we might ask what attitude should be taken toward alleged misreaders and their misreadings.

Over eight decades ago, I. A. Richards sought to assess his students' skills at interpreting literature by having them "comment freely in writing" on a number of poems (*Practical* 3). Based on their writings, he diagnosed a "widespread inability to construe meaning" (294). He found that a "poor capacity to interpret complex and unfamiliar meanings" led his students to fall back on stock responses (295), "views and emotions already fully prepared in the reader's mind" that were unwarranted by the poems (14). His 1929 book *Practical Criticism: A Study of Literary Judgment*, which describes their critical difficulties in great detail, closes with the following word of caution:

> The wild interpretations of others must not be regarded as the antics of incompetents, but as dangers that we ourselves only narrowly escape, if, indeed, we do. We must see in the misreadings of others the actualisation of possibilities threatened in the early stages of our own readings. The only proper attitude is to look upon a successful interpretation, a correct understanding, as a triumph against odds. We must cease to regard a misinterpretation as a mere unlucky accident. We must treat it as the normal and probable event. (315)

Here Richards warns his fellow teachers and scholars of literature that their own interpretations are less unlike "the misreadings of others" (namely, their students) than they wish to believe. For the odds are against us, the opportunities to err so great, the possibilities for misinterpretation so many, that a literary text is more likely to be misread than correctly understood by *any* reader. We have met the misreader and he is us.

I find it instructive to juxtapose Richards's view of literary interpretation with one written forty-five years later by Wolfgang Iser. In his 1974 study *The Implied Reader*, Iser proposes that a literary text such as a novel is realized (or, as Richards has it, actualized) when a reader responds to what he calls "the 'unwritten' part of a text" (275). The reader actively makes connections and imagines a storyworld based on the sequence of letters on the page, effectively "filling in the gaps left by the text itself" (280). On this point Iser writes:

> These gaps ... may be filled in different ways. For this reason, one text is potentially capable of several different realizations, and no reading can ever exhaust the full potential, for each individual reader will fill in the gaps in his own way, thereby excluding the various other possibilities; as he reads, he will make his own decision as to how the gap is to be filled.... With "traditional" texts this process was more or less unconscious, but modern texts frequently exploit it quite deliberately. They are often so fragmentary that one's attention is almost exclusively occupied with the search for connections between the fragments ... With all literary texts, then, we may say that the reading process is selective, and the potential text is infinitely richer than any of its individual realizations. (*Implied* 280)

Our two theorists concern themselves with contrasting interpretive possibilities: Richards with those readers fail to reject, Iser with those readers fail to consider. The decision making that allows Richards's reader to avoid misreadings and arrive at a correct understanding of a literary text, as if through a process of elimination, is, for Iser, precisely what makes any such understanding partial and less meaningful than one that engages "the potential text" that contains multitudes, an unrealizable plethora of works. Indeed, for Iser understanding lies less in a specific, successful interpretation of a literary text than in an appreciation of that text's capacity to allow for ever more interpretations.

A tenet of this book is that misreadings, rather than leading us astray, can contribute meaningfully and powerfully to our understandings of literature—that they too are texts with potential. To realize their potential, we need to appreciate that the work of interpretation requires more than formulating "a successful interpretation, a correct understanding" of a text by eliminating other interpretive possibilities. Rather, it involves reading, misreading, rereading, and rewriting in collaboration with other readers and writers, exposing ourselves to a range of interpretive possibilities, both "wild" and "successful," for what they can reveal about the limits imposed by any single interpretation and allow us to glimpse of the potential text. The trick is to gain a perspective from which various rewritings of the text, including misreadings, can be analyzed alongside the text they rewrite. This perspective will not be gained so long as we are narrowly focused on arriving at a most correct interpretation.

Still, we might ask, is it enough to accumulate multiple interpretations of a literary text? Or does literary interpretation undertaken as an individual and collaborative activity involve something more discriminating than compiling an increasing number of ways in which readers have made sense of a text? Should we not, at the very least, assess these various interpretive possibilities—the various ways in which gaps have been filled and fragments connected—and compare their validity? That I refer to any of my students' responses to "The Man in the Well" as misreadings indicates that I do recognize a distinction akin to that which Richards draws between "wild" and "successful" interpretations. I hold that some interpretations are more credible than others, and that some are so untrue to the texts they would explicate that they can deservedly be called misreadings. But here too distinctions are necessary. While some misreadings may prove constructive, perhaps by introducing counterintuitive ways of thinking about a text, not all will. Some misreadings result from less instructive missteps or errors.

In short, to say that a text is "potentially capable of several different realizations" is not to say that all realizations are equally valid, compelling, or significant. Literary interpretations vary tremendously in terms of how persuasive, informed, thought-provoking, perceptive, adroitly written, and attentive to the text they may be. Our pursuit of the potential text entails drawing, not discounting, these distinctions.

THE OTHERNESS OF LITERATURE

College students today are no better and perhaps far worse at interpreting literature than those studied by Richards in the 1920s, or so suggests Robert Scholes in his 2002 essay "The Transition to College Reading." Scholes holds that teachers now face in their students "a reading problem of massive dimensions" (165), one that he seeks to describe with the help of a fellow teacher of literature:

> My colleague Tamar Katz, like many perceptive teachers, has caught a glimpse of the real problem, which she puts this way: "They want to read every text as saying something extremely familiar that they might agree with." The problem emerges as one of difference, or otherness—a difficulty in moving from the words of the text to some set of intentions that are different from one's own, some values or presuppositions different from

one's own and possibly opposed to them. This problem, as I see it, has two closely related parts. One is a failure to focus sharply on the language of the text. The other is a failure to imagine the otherness of the text's author. (166)

Let us set aside for the moment the first part of the problem, that involving the language of the text, as Scholes is principally concerned with the second, the failure of students to perceive and evaluate the author's intention.

Thirty-five years after Barthes announced the death of the author and the birth of the reader, Scholes proposes that the reader's dominance over the author has become a momentous problem. He writes that "if the words belong to the reader, they are likely to express the reader's thoughts" (166). In other words, readers are likely to take recourse in what Richards calls irrelevant associations and stock responses, reading the words of the text in familiarizing terms that fail to address how the text might complicate or refute those very terms. If students are to grasp and evaluate complex and unfamiliar meanings, Scholes argues, they must read "as if the words belonged to a person at some distance from [them]selves in thought or feeling" (166), for only then can they "imagine themselves in the place of another and understand views different from their own" (168). This other person is the author. While Scholes hardly believes that the words mean *only* what the author intended for them to mean, he maintains that reading for the author's intention must precede other ways of reading or responding to a text. "The author must live before the author can die," he declares. "We teachers must help our students bring the author to life" (166).

How is this to be done? Scholes recommends that students in literature courses read "more overtly persuasive or argumentative texts"—that is, fewer works of poetry and fiction and more articles and essays that make explicit arguments and take positions (170). He reasons that "critical texts, if properly chosen, will differ with one another, so that reading them will lead students to recognize difference itself as they situate their own readings in relation to those of the critics" (170). In other words, students will be more likely to recognize authors' views, and differentiate them from their own, if the texts they read are composed by writers who aim to make their own views known in a clear and convincing manner, often by opposing them to views held by others. Of course, this hardly addresses the challenge of reading works of literature that are not written to advance an argument or to persuade readers to adopt the author's position on a contested issue. Consequently, the turn to critical texts would not help students become better, more engaged interpreters of literary fiction, so much as spare them the work of contending with the ambiguity and indeterminacy that characterize so much of that fiction.

To this I would add that if our aim is to help readers imagine otherness, turning away from literary texts is an odd solution. After all, literature is valued precisely for granting readers imaginary access to other times and places, and to the inner lives of people quite different from themselves. "If trying on the perspectives of others is at the heart of reading, then the importance of providing access to different perspectives necessarily follows," writes Michael W. Smith in his discussion of teaching multicultural literature. He notes that this involves more than assigning works by non-white authors, for "if teachers select texts written by people of color because they are accessible to White audiences, much of their power will be lost." For Smith, providing access to different perspectives involves selecting literary texts that are not accessible to students on their own terms, but that "call for students to keep their distance and to question constantly whether the personal experiences, beliefs, and standards of interpretation that they are applying are the ones that they are called upon to employ" (Rabinowitz and Smith 128).

Scholes would have us conceive of otherness in the more restricted sense of the different positions taken by critics, making "the other" the author whose views on a familiar subject differ from those of the reader. While I invariably do assign critical texts and works of nonfiction in literature courses, I take issue with this too-limited conception of otherness, and with an approach that would have students "recognize difference itself" by situating "their own readings in relation to those of the critics" without also recognizing difference among themselves. A student can learn much by comparing his or her response to a literary text to those of classmates, noting divergences and similarities in their rewritings of it. Literature courses can usefully include, then, not only literary texts and critical texts but student texts as well.

Lest we overlook the first part of the reading problem, the "failure to focus sharply on the language of the text," we should attend to the otherness of literature, the difference posed by literary language and fictionality. Addressing the particularity of fiction, Phelan writes that while all narrative involves "somebody telling somebody else on some occasion and for some purpose(s) that something happened," in the case of narrative fiction "the rhetorical situation is doubled: the narrator tells the story to the narratee for her purposes, while the author communicates to her audience for her own purposes both that story and the narrator's telling of it" (*Living* 18). In short, readers of fiction are privy to a double act of communication.

Taking Mark Twain's *Adventures of Huckleberry Finn* as an example, Phelan and Peter J. Rabinowitz write that "Huck tells his story to his audience for his own purposes" shortly after the recounted events have occurred, "while at a much later historical moment, Twain communicates both Huck's story and Huck's telling of it to *his* audience for *his* own purposes" ("Narrative as Rhetoric" 4).

Huckleberry Finn provides a good example because the author/narrator distinction is particularly evident when stories are told by what Phelan terms *character narrators*, storytellers who "combin[e] in one figure (the 'I') the roles of both narrator and character" (*Living* 1). It is still more evident when these storytellers are unreliable narrators, characters who cannot be taken at their word. Huck is an unreliable character narrator because his naive assessments of his own thoughts and actions cannot be taken at their word. When he admits his sinfulness for helping Jim escape slavery, we understand that Twain is conveying Huck's virtuosity to readers. That there are at least two sets of purposes or intentions to negotiate in fictional narratives accounts in no small part for the difficulty readers face in "moving from the words of the text to some set of intentions that are different from [their] own." Yet Scholes repeatedly identifies the otherness that students fail to imagine with the author, never mentioning the narrator who tells the story or the characters who populate it.

The otherness of literary writing also lies in the emphases placed on form—concern for the sound, appearance, rhythm, and feel of written words, both apart from and in relation to their meaning—and on meaning that is figurative or metaphorical and not simply literal. As Jonathan Culler puts it, "Literature is language that 'foregrounds' language itself: makes it strange, thrusts it at you—'Look! I'm language!'—so you can't forget that you are dealing with language shaped in odd ways" (*Literary* 28). He writes that readers of literary texts will "struggle to interpret elements that flout principles of efficient communication" because they "assume that in literature complications of language ultimately have a communicative purpose" (*Literary* 27). But of course not all readers and not all students of literature will assume this or struggle to interpret language they find strange, odd, different, other. Instead, they may skim the text for more easily understood passages. One cannot simply fault students for this if, as Blau believes, "an intolerance for difficulty and an assumption that difficulty is a sign of one's own insufficiency are precisely what a good deal of conventional instruction in reading and literature conspires to teach our students" (30).

I have my doubts that reading persuasive or argumentative texts that follow principles of efficient communication will help students read literary texts that are frequently designed to flout such principles and confront readers with interpretive difficulty. I am more hopeful that, in struggling to interpret literary texts, students might become better readers of texts of all kinds, including more overtly persuasive and argumentative ones, if only because they will be more attentive to language and less apt to replace curiosity and recognition of ambiguity with unexamined certainty. Regardless of what we read, training in literary analysis can lead us to examine the words that make up a text, to construe less overt meanings, and to recognize narrators not as authors but as rhetorical devices. Culler writes that "many of the features of literature follow from the willingness of readers to pay attention, to explore uncertainties, and not immediately ask 'what do you mean by that?'" (*Literary* 27). We will have come some way to solving our reading problem if such a willingness to explore uncertain ground without grasping for the familiar informs our response to all sorts of texts.

INTERPRETIVE PROGRESS

When my students and I discuss a literary text, our goal is to progress toward greater understanding by sharing and discussing our various interpretive responses, as well as those of the critics we read, and by revisiting the text together. The object of our understanding is not limited to the specific text we are discussing, but concerns two wider areas of knowledge and practice: literature and textual analysis. Our ultimate goal is not to comprehend any one text, though that is important as the means to broader understanding. Rather, it is twofold: we aim, first, to develop our knowledge of literary language, forms, styles, conventions, genres, theories, and histories; and, second, to hone our skills at scrutinizing texts of all kinds.

Through rereading, writing, research, and dialogue, we work to improve our understanding of a text's language, design, meanings, and complexities. We want to grapple with the ideas and issues a text raises, and how it raises them, in ways that are increasingly informed, observant, and inquisitive. This involves being attentive to textual elements we previously overlooked, addressing those that confuse us, reconsidering those we have construed in certain limited ways, and contemplating the text as a whole from varied perspectives. We strive to develop more nuanced and fuller understandings of a text, but without expecting to arrive at a single correct interpretation. Indeed, although we are interested in points of interpretive agreement and disagreement, consensus is not the goal.

This bears repeating, given that consensus is often the goal of collaborative work. I recall a group of four students who, after discussing their written responses to "Grief," a short story by Anton Chekhov, cowrote a paper in which their diverse ways of construing the story were whittled down to a single, unlikely interpretation—improbably, the least sensible of their four written responses to the story. Worse still, they made no progress beyond their initial responses to the story. Hoping to present "the right answer," they did not address the difficulties they each experienced in making sense of the story, much less any questions raised by the differing ways they had rewritten the text.

"Questions are more relevant than answers," writes Stuart Firestein in *Ignorance: How It Drives Science*. "Questions are bigger than answers. One good question can give rise to several layers of answers, can inspire decades-long searches for solutions, can generate whole new fields of inquiry, and can prompt changes in entrenched thinking. Answers, on the other hand, often end the process" (11). Though Firestein, a biologist, is describing the scientific process, his remark applies to literary studies. Various literary theories, each established as a challenge to prevailing practices of literary study, can be identified by the different types of questions their practitioners ask of literary texts. Furthermore, the very work of literary interpretation involves moving beyond the answers provided by interpretations that would "end the process" or, in Barthes's words, "close the writing" ("Death" 147). It involves reckoning with questions that may have gone unasked because they are counterintuitive, lying outside entrenched ways of thinking, or that seem misguided and likely to incite misreading.

Though with this book I seek to show how misreadings can lead us to ask good questions, I would not praise the inexperience or inattentiveness that can lead to misreading. Firestein distinguishes "knowledgeable ignorance, perceptive ignorance, insightful ignorance" that "leads us to frame better questions, the first step to getting better answers," from the sort of ignorance that "shows itself as a stubborn devotion to uninformed opinions, ignoring (same root) contrary ideas, opinions, or data" (6–7). As Blau observes, some students misinterpret literature "not because they . . . don't have the necessary cultural knowledge or literary skills, but because they won't focus attentively on the story and do the necessary thoughtful work"—work that involves "thinking through the reasonableness of possible explanations or interpretations for the actions and events represented in a story" (116). Beyond cultural knowledge and literary skills, interpretive progress requires a willingness to read and contemplate what one has read in the sort of sustained, focused way I have heard some students describe as "thinking too much."

In *Becoming a Reader*, J. A. Appleyard describes this thoughtful work in terms of progressive stages of development. For children, he writes, reading involves identification with characters and immersion in plot situations; only as adolescents do readers take the step of reflecting on what they read. Initially these reflections involve judging literature in terms of its "truthfulness to life," as measured against readers' own experiences, as limited as those may be (108). Responding to a text as if everything is mimetic and nothing synthetic, adolescent readers are chiefly concerned with how characters' motives and feelings may resemble their own. A "more developed way of thinking about fiction shows up," Appleyard contends, only when they engage the thematic by talking about a story's meaning. This involves a "higher level of abstraction," as readers think beyond characters and events to formulate generalizations about "the significance of the story taken as a whole" (111).

At this stage, according to Appleyard, significance is conceived "as a given of the story, a single summary formula that the reader has to get out of it ('Did you get the meaning?')" (112). However, adolescents soon discover that "other readers find different things when they read the same text" (130). Faced with this "confusing relativism," they want there to be a single meaning, moral, or lesson—and "the author looks like the obvious source of stable meaning" (132). Appleyard writes: "They debate about interpretations, but the point at issue is which is the right one. The answer is assumed to be a fact of the text, put there by the author, known by expert literary authorities—among whom may be the teacher" (112). He adds that "many high school and college students do not get any further than this in their attitude toward the meaning of a story" (113).

What might getting further than this entail? Not disregarding the author, according to Appleyard, because readers "may simply transfer the need for a single factual answer from the author to the text and guess at any bit of concrete evidence that looks like it might possibly lead to the right answer" (134). Moreover, he contends, the concept of the author's intention helpfully "implies that a story has a design, which in turn implies that its meaning is a function of its design, which can be analyzed in an evidentiary way" by readers (113). Still, for Appleyard it is not enough to recognize that "the text is something constructed by an author whose intentions for it can be imagined and deciphered" (129); readers should also realize that "the text is constructed not only by the writer but also by the reader and by all the codes and cultural contexts they both depend on" (129–30).

These cultural contexts and codes, including genre conventions, are the shared language with which we communicate, and miscommunicate, with one another.

The various stages of literary response described by Appleyard are well represented by my students' written responses to "The Man in the Well." Interpretive progress occurs when individual students develop as readers (and, I would add, as writers) in much the way Appleyard describes, replacing approaches that ignore the synthetic and thematic dimensions of the short story, or that conceive of them in simplistic ways, with more complex understandings of how the text is constructed and literary meaning is made. This progress, the main concern of my teaching, is an outgrowth of our collaborative and cumulative effort to improve upon our original interpretations of the short story by formulating, through discussion and in writing, analyses that are more astute, comprehensive, and credible. Working together, we can see how responses that recognize the "cultural contexts and codes" involving the text and its reception have greater explanatory power and reach than those that assess the text largely in terms of a reader's own experiences and beliefs. As we develop a more productive framework for interpreting the text, we progress as a class toward a multifaceted understanding of "The Man in the Well" that is richer than any of the individual interpretations with which we began.

Does this mean that those analyzing the short story after us need to acquaint themselves with the understanding we have achieved if they are to progress any further in their analyses of Sher's story? Not necessarily. Scholars hope that their contributions will be cited by others and become, if only for a time, an essential part of the conversation (as in, "How can you possibly write on 'The Man in the Well' without having read Weissman?"). And, as Harris suggests, scholars writing on a literary text do typically research and respond to what scholars and critics before them have said about that text. At the same time, there is typically far more written on the (canonical) texts scholars are likely to analyze than one will ever have the time or inclination to read. More to the point, literary analysis is not an activity marked by linear progress, a forward march to full understanding.

The reality is far messier than that: writers address texts in different cultural contexts and at different historical moments, applying different theoretical frameworks, posing different questions, and pursuing different ends. While a particular question can be answered more thoroughly and effectively over time, a recently published analysis of James Joyce's "Araby" applying cognitive science is not inherently superior to a New Critical close reading of the short story published half a century ago. Progress takes the form of a mushrooming array of critical commentary rather than a singular interpretation continually refined over time.

WRITER-RESPONSE THEORY

This book is designed to involve you as a participant in the collaborative process of analyzing a single work of short fiction. This introduction is followed by the full text of "The Man in the Well." To fully participate in the occasion of this book, you should follow your reading of the short story by writing a short interpretive response explaining what you make of it. (I ask my students to type a one-page, single-spaced paper; some extend their responses to a second page.) In this way you can join the dialogue constituted by the many people who have written on, or rewritten, "The Man in the Well," relating your rewriting of the story to those articulated by other voices in the chapters that follow.

Casual readers may opt not to draft a response to the short story, figuring that, having read "The Man in the Well," they know well enough what they make of the story without "putting it in writing"—as if that "it" exists prior to being realized through the thought-provoking act of writing. Now why should any readers prefer *not* to formulate and record their thoughts on the short story in writing? The answer, as anyone who takes the time and effort to write a response might tell you, is that writing takes time and effort. As I have been arguing, it is one thing to interpret a text while reading it and then when musing over what one has read, and quite another to interpret it in writing. Writing can be a time-consuming, isolating, and stressful activity, particularly when we know that others will be reading and judging what we write. This book contends that literary interpretation is practiced less in the act of reading a text—scanning its words and working to comprehend the narrative line by line, passage by passage—than in the act of rewriting it by telling a story about its significance or meaning.

"Literature in the Reader," a 1970 essay by Stanley Fish, is a landmark work of reader-response theory, a branch of literary studies popular in the 1970s and early 1980s that focused on how readers experience and make meaning of literary texts. There Fish remarks, "No one would argue that the act of reading can take place in the absence of someone who reads . . . but curiously enough when it comes time to make analytical statements about the end product of reading (meaning or understanding), the reader is usually forgotten or ignored" (22). A decade later, Fish would observe in his essay "What Makes an Interpretation Acceptable?" that whereas "twenty years ago one of the things that literary critics didn't do was talk about the reader, at least in a way that made his experience the focus of the critical act," the reader had now become the central subject of conference panels, workshops, and scholarly books and essays (344). This would not be the case for long, however: in the mid-to-late 1980s, talk about how readers make meaning increasingly gave way to talk about the text and its ideological, unstable, and multiple meanings. Patricia Harkin offers an explanation for this development, claiming that at a time when "compositionists sought to use reader-response theory to teach students to read difficult texts," literary scholars, fearing that too much attention to reader-response would cause them to be perceived as teachers rather than researchers and scholars, turned to more esoteric "high theory" ("Reception" 419).

But if reader-response theory was too tied to teaching for literary scholars, Harkin adds, it also came to be seen as too tied to reading for compositionists. As composition studies came to define itself (and distinguish itself from literary studies) as a discipline based in "writing *as opposed to reading*," reader-response theory, with its emphasis on reading literature, was largely abandoned ("Reception" 420–21). As Harkin puts it, "a pedagogical or curricular decision *not* to teach literary texts in writing courses became or entailed a decision not to teach reading" ("Reception" 421). Now, as I write this, some composition scholars are hailing a "revival of interest in reading in English Studies" (Salvatori and Donahue 199), which is all for the good. Still, for decades in literary studies it has not been the reader so much as the writer who has been largely forgotten or ignored by theorists and critics.

This book recognizes "the writer" as both author and reader: the author as a writer of literary texts, and the reader as a writer of "analytical statements about the end product of reading" those texts (Fish 22). With this book, which I like to imagine as a proto-work of writer-response theory, I seek to address how both kinds of writers make literary texts meaningful. The first chapter, "Misreadings," draws on many of my students' written responses to "The Man in the Well," analyzing striking commonalities and differences that emerge when they are examined together. As its title indicates, this chapter will focus on those responses that I find misinterpret the short story. My aim in attending to them is to explore what misreadings might teach us about the texts they rewrite. The second chapter, "Authorities," turns to those student responses I find most credible and have used my authority as the teacher to validate. The chapter then turns to two other figures of authority, the scholar and the author. After presenting my own evolving interpretation of "The Man in the Well," I discuss what author Ira Sher has to say about his short story and its many interpretations.

The third chapter, "Genres," returns to Scholes's belief that reading for the author's intention should precede other ways of reading the text. It does so by considering Peter J. Rabinowitz's concept of *authorial reading* and his contention that misreading often results from a failure to recognize the genre within which the author expected his or her work to be read. This chapter revisits my students' responses, exploring how our unfamiliarity with certain genres and their conventions, and our deep familiarity with others, accounts for how we construe the story and rewrite it to fit genre expectations. The book then concludes with a dialogue between two writers, Ira Sher and me, in which we discuss "The Man in the Well" in light of the many ways in which it is rewritten and theorized in this book. Phelan writes that "one significant value of reading narrative is the opportunity it offers to encounter other minds—that of the author who has constructed the narrative and those of other readers also interested in shared readings" (*Living* 19). The afterword seeks to render this encounter visible in ways that will lead readers to extend the dialogue beyond these pages.

INDEBTEDNESS

In bringing together the voices of teacher, students, author, and readers of a shared literary text, I mean to model literary analysis as a collaborative process. That said, it would be disingenuous of me to suggest that all these "voices" appear in this book as equal participants. Aside from the collaboratively written afterword, this book presents the collaborative work of literary analysis from the privileged viewpoint of a single author: me. I have chosen which student responses to include and the contexts in which they are included. While I have sought to present a fair and accurate picture of what my students have made of "The Man in the Well," the inclusion of their responses is conditioned by my own aims in writing this book. In the interest of concision, I selectively quote from my students' responses and abridge those I present (nearly) in full, under the titles students have given them, by cutting (and marking with ellipses) material I consider redundant or tangential to the lines of thought I wish to emphasize. Also, whereas my students' commentaries are each limited to a single-spaced page or two (and, in some cases, an equally short follow-up response), I discuss "The Man in the Well" at length in the chapters that follow, presenting interpretations I have developed over a considerable span of time (literally years) and with the aid of what my students and Ira Sher have written about the story.

Like scholarly work in general, my analysis is both individual and collaborative in nature. The form taken by most scholarly work—single-authored books and essays—creates the impression that scholarship is produced by solitary thinkers working in isolation. To be sure, scholarly work bears "the visible traces of other texts" in the form of notes, citations, bibliographies, and discussion of those texts, and it joins debates on particular subjects (Harris 2). Nevertheless, it is easy to forget Harris's point that academic writing is rooted in the work of other writers. But then, this holds for literary writing as well. "The writing process is never a pure monologue," notes Barbara Tomlinson in her study *Authors on Writing*. "Authors enter a dialogue already in progress, 'answering' other writers, and producing messages that provoke answers of their own" (99). She observes that for writers of fiction, nonfiction, poetry, and plays, writing is "both an individual activity and a collective practice," as "the words we write always echo, answer, amplify, and occlude words written by others" (1). In one way or another, or in a great many ways, our writing is indebted to what others have written.

My own indebtedness is indicated by the use I make of my students' work and the scholarly and critical writings cited in these pages. This book utilizes writings by literary scholars working in a number of fields, including but not limited to reader-response theory (Fish, Harkin, Iser), narrative theory (Abbott, Booth), rhetorical narrative theory (Phelan, Rabinowitz), and cognitive literary studies (Troscianko, Zunshine). It also draws on work by seminal figures associated with psychoanalytic theory (Freud, Lacan) and poststructuralist theory (Barthes, Foucault), although scholars in the aforementioned fields have often seen themselves as working outside of, if not against, the tradition of "high theory" represented by these big-name figures. This book draws as well on work done in the fields of composition studies (Corbett, Devitt, Harris, Murray, Newkirk, Qualley), creative writing studies (Boswell, Burroway, Carlson, Gardner), and education (Blau, Lee, Smith). While my approach is interdisciplinary insofar as it draws on other disciplines, such as psychology (Baron-Cohen, Gilligan, Janis, Kohlberg, Lerner) and philosophy (Levinson), it is more markedly *intra*disciplinary in its attempt to work across and integrate various areas of English studies.

This book implicitly argues for an approach to literary interpretation, and textual analysis more broadly, that is informed and enriched by work done in the fields of creative writing and composition and rhetoric. These fields' contributions to literary study are particularly valuable, indeed necessary, because considerations of writing and pedagogy have largely fallen outside the purview of "serious" literary scholarship, so great is the divide in literary studies between teaching (pedagogy) and scholarship (theory). Readers of literary theory and criticism may easily forget that the authors of that work are not only theorists and critics but also teachers—indeed, teachers of the very subjects and texts about which they write—so infrequently are pedagogical concerns explicitly addressed in their work. Scholarship in composition and creative writing, by contrast, reflects the degree to which those fields are principally concerned with matters pertaining to the practice and teaching of writing. The pertinence of this scholarship for rethinking the methods and goals of literary analysis becomes clear when the interpretation of literature is recognized as a writing-based practice.

That said, work by a good number of literary scholars does address how authors write works of literature and how students read and write about that literature. In addition to notable literary theorists (such as Culler and Scholes) who have long addressed pedagogical concerns, some theoretical schools stand apart from the dominant tradition in literary studies, which, from the advent of New Criticism to the heyday of poststructuralism and beyond, has privileged the text in ways that discourage significant consideration of how authors and readers make meaning. Work done in rhetorical narrative theory has proven most relevant for this study, as it both emphasizes the author's role in the production of narrative meaning and theorizes literary interpretation as an activity that is learned, taught, and practiced by readers with varying degrees of success.

I hope you will find in reading and discussing this book that it is not how we finally come to interpret a work of literature—if ever we do reach such finality—that determines the value and meaningfulness of a given text. Rather, a literary text is valuable and meaningful insofar as it affords us the playful and profound experience of thinking in depth by testing our habits of mind and exercising our ingenuity, creativity, reasoning, and understanding. Richards prefaced his 1928 study *Principles of Literary Criticism* with the famous words, "A book is a machine to think with" (vii). I trust you will find Ira Sher's short story "The Man in the Well" to be an exquisitely captivating little machine in this regard, one that offers keen challenges and pleasures, and that here affords us an opportunity to rethink the theory and practice of literary interpretation.

THE MAN IN THE WELL

Ira Sher

I was nine when I discovered the man in the well in an abandoned farm-lot near my home. I was with a group of friends, playing hide and go seek or something when I found the well, and then I heard the voice of the man in the well calling out for help.

I think it's important that we decided not to help him. Everyone, like myself, was probably on the verge of fetching a rope, or asking where we could find a ladder, but then we looked around at each other and it was decided. I don't remember if we told ourselves a reason why we couldn't help him, but we had decided then. Because of this, I never went very close to the lip of the well, or I only came up on my hands and knees, so that he couldn't see me; and just as we wouldn't allow him to see us, I know that none of us ever saw the man in the well—the well was too dark for that, too deep, even when the sun was high up, angling light down the stone sides like golden hair.

I remember that we were still full of games and laughter when we called down to him. He had heard us shouting while we were playing, and he had been hollering for us to come; he was so relieved at that moment.

"God, get me out. I've been here for days." He must have known we were children, because he immediately instructed us to "go get a ladder, get help."

At first afraid to disobey the voice from the man in the well, we turned around and actually began to walk toward the nearest house, which was Arthur's. But along the way we slowed down, and then we stopped, and after waiting what seemed like a good while, we quietly came back to the well.

We stood or lay around the lip, listening for maybe half an hour, and then Arthur, after some hesitation, called down, "What's your name?" This, after all, seemed like the most natural question.

The man answered back immediately, "Do you have the ladder?"

We all looked at Arthur, and he called back down, "No, we couldn't find one."

Now that we had established some sort of a dialogue, everyone had questions he or she wanted to ask the man in the well, but the man wouldn't stop speaking:

"Go tell your parents there's someone in this well. If they have a rope or a ladder..." he trailed off. His voice was raw and sometimes he would cough. "Just tell your parents."

We were quiet, but this time no one stood up or moved. Someone, I think little Jason, called down, "Hello. Is it dark?" and then, after a moment, "Can you see the sky?"

He didn't answer but instead told us to go again.

When we were quiet for a bit, he called to see if we had gone.

After a pause, Wendy crawled right to the edge so that her hair lifted slightly in the updraft. "Is there any water down there?"

"Have they gone for help?" he asked.

She looked around at us, and then she called down, "Yes, they're all gone now. Isn't there any water down there?" I don't think anyone smiled at how easy it was to deceive him—this was too important. "Isn't there?" she said again.

"No," he said. "It's very dry." He cleared his throat. "Do you think it will rain?"

She stood up and took in the whole sky with her blue eyes, making sure. "No, I don't think so." We heard him coughing in the well, and we waited for a while, thinking about him waiting in the well.

Resting on the grass and cement by the well, I tried to picture him. I tried to imagine the gesture of his hand reaching to cover his mouth, each time he coughed. Or perhaps he was too tired to make that gesture, each time. After an hour, he began calling again, but for some reason we didn't want to answer. We got up and began running, filling up with panic as we moved, until we were racing across the ruts of the old field. I kept turning, stumbling as I looked behind. Perhaps he had heard us getting up and running away from the well. Only Wendy stayed by the well for a while, watching us run as his calling grew louder and wilder, until finally she ran, too, and then we were all far away.

The next morning we came back, most of us carrying bread or fruit or something to eat in our pockets. Arthur brought a canvas bag from his house and a plastic jug of water.

When we got to the well we stood around quietly for a moment listening for him.

"Maybe he's asleep," Wendy said.

We sat down around the mouth of the well on the old concrete slab, warming in the sun and coursing with ants and tiny insects. Aaron called down then, when everyone was comfortable, and the man answered right away, as if he had been listening to us the whole time.

"Did your parents get help?"

Arthur kneeled at the edge of the well and called "Watch out," and then he let the bag fall after holding it out for a moment, maybe for the man to see. It hit the ground more quickly than I had expected; that, combined with a feeling that he could hear everything we said, made him suddenly closer, as if he might be able to see us. I wanted to be very quiet, so that if he heard or saw anyone, he would not notice me. The man in the well started coughing, and Arthur volunteered, "There's some water in the bag. We all brought something."

We could hear him moving around down there. After a few minutes he asked us, "When are they coming? What did your parents say?"

We all looked at each other, aware that he couldn't address anyone in particular. He must have understood this, because he called out in his thin, groping voice, "What are your names?"

No one answered until Aaron, who was the oldest, said, "My father said he's coming, with the police. And he knows what to do." We admired Aaron very much for coming up with this, on the spot.

"Are they on their way?" the man in the well asked. We could hear that he was eating.

"My father said don't worry, because he's coming with the police."

Little Jason came up next to Aaron, and asked, "What's your name?" because we still didn't know what to call him. When we talked among ourselves, he had simply become "the man."

He didn't answer, so Jason asked him how old he was, and then Grace came up too and asked him something, I don't remember. We all asked such stupid questions, and he wouldn't answer anyone. Finally, we all stopped talking, and we lay down on the cement.

It was a hot day, so after a while, Grace got up, and then little Jason and another young boy, Robert I think, and went to town to sit in the cool movie theater. That was what we did most afternoons back then. After an hour everyone had left except Wendy and myself, and I was beginning to think I would go, too.

He called up to us all of a sudden. "Are they coming now?"

"Yes," Wendy said, looking at me, and I nodded my head. She sounded certain: "I think they're almost here. Aaron said his dad is almost here."

As soon as she said it she was sorry, because she'd broken one of the rules. I could see it on her face, eyes filling with space as she moved back from the well. Now he had one of our names. She said "They're going to come" to cover up the mistake, but there it was, and there was nothing to do about it.

The man in the well didn't say anything for a few minutes. Then he surprised us again by asking, "Is it going to rain?"

Wendy stood up and turned around like she had done the other day, but the sky was clear. "No," she said.

Then he asked again, "They're coming, you said. Aaron's dad," and he shouted, "Right?" so that we jumped, and stood up, and began running away, just as we had the day before. We could hear him shouting for a while, and we were afraid someone might hear. I thought that toward the end maybe he had said he was sorry. But I never asked Wendy what she thought he'd said.

Everyone was there again on the following morning. It was all I could think about during supper the night before, and then the anticipation in the morning over breakfast. My mother was very upset with something at the time. I could hear her weeping at night in her room downstairs, and the stubborn murmur of my father. There was a feeling to those days, months actually, that I can't describe without resorting to the man in the well, as if through a great whispering, like a gathering of clouds, or the long sound, the turbulent wreck of the ocean.

At the well we put together the things to eat we had smuggled out, but we hadn't even gotten them all in the bag when the voice of the man in the well soared out sharply, "They're on their way, now?"

We stood very still, so that he couldn't hear us, but I knew what was coming and I couldn't do anything to soften or blur the words of the voice.

"Aaron," he pronounced, and I had imagined him practicing that voice all night long, and holding it in his mouth so that he wouldn't let it slip away in his sleep. Aaron lost all the color in his face, and he looked at us with suspicion, as if we had somehow taken on a part of the man in the well. I didn't even glance at Wendy. We were both too embarrassed—neither of us said anything; we were all quiet then.

Arthur finished assembling the bag, and we could see his hands shaking as he dropped it into the well. We heard the man in the well moving around.

After ten minutes or so, Grace called down to him, "What's your name?" but someone pulled her back from the well, and we became silent again. Today the question humiliated us with its simplicity.

There was no sound for a while from the well, except for the cloth noises and the scraping the man in the well made as he moved around. Then he called out, in a pleasant voice, "Aaron, what do you think my name is?"

Aaron, who had been very still this whole time, looked around at all of us again. We knew he was afraid; his fingers were pulling with a separate life at the collar of his shirt, and maybe because she felt badly for him, Wendy answered instead: "Is your name Charles?" It sounded inane, but the man in the well answered.

"No," the man said.

She thought for a moment. "Edgar."

"No, no."

Little Jason called out, "David?"

"No," the man in the well said.

Then Aaron, who had been absolutely quiet, said "Arthur" in a small, clear voice, and we all started. I could see Arthur was furious, but Aaron was older and bigger than he was, and nothing could be said or done without giving himself, his name, away; we knew the man in the well was listening for the changes in our breath, anything. Aaron didn't look at Arthur, or anyone, and then he began giving all of our names, one at a time. We all watched him, trembling, our faces the faces I had seen pasted on the spectators in the freak tent when the circus had come to town. We were watching such a deformity take place before our eyes; and I remember the spasm of anger when he said my name, and felt the man in the well soak it up—because the man in the well understood. The man in the well didn't say anything, now.

When Aaron was done, we all waited for the man in the well to speak up. I stood on one leg, then the other, and eventually I sat down. We had to wait for an hour, and today no one wanted to leave to lie in the shade or hide in the velvet movie seats.

At last, the man in the well said, "All right, then. Arthur. What do you think I look like?" We heard him cough a couple of times, and then a sound like the smacking of lips. Arthur, who was sitting on the ground with his chin propped on his fists, didn't say anything. How could he—I knew I couldn't answer, myself, if the man in the well called me by name. He called a few of us, and I watched the shudder move from face to face.

Then he was quiet for a while. It was afternoon now, and the light was changing, withdrawing from the well. It was as if the well was filling up with earth. The man in the well moved around a bit, and then he called Jason. He asked, "How old do you think I am, Jason?" He didn't seem to care that no one would answer, or he seemed to expect that no one would. He said, "Wendy. Are they coming now? Is Aaron's dad coming now?" He walked around a bit, we heard him rummage in the bag of food, and he said, "All right. What's my name?" He used everyone's name; he asked everyone. When he said my name, I felt the water clouding my eyes, and I wanted to throw stones, dirt down the well to crush out his voice. But we couldn't do anything, none of us did—because then he would know.

In the evening we could tell he was getting tired. He wasn't saying much, and seemed to have lost interest in us. Before we left that day, as we were rising quietly and looking at the dark shadows of the trees we had to move through to reach our homes, he said, "Why didn't you tell anyone?" He coughed. "Didn't you want to tell anyone?" Perhaps he heard the hesitation in our breaths, but he wasn't going to help us now. It was almost night then, and we were spared the detail of having to see and read each other's faces.

That night it rained, and I listened to the rain on the roof and my mother sobbing, downstairs, until I fell asleep. After that we didn't play by the well anymore; even when we were much older, we didn't go back. I will never go back.

CHAPTER 1

MISREADINGS

CLOUDED BY GAPS

While all literary texts challenge readers to evoke a coherent and meaningful storyworld, Ira Sher's "The Man in the Well," composed of just a few sparsely written pages, is particularly demanding in this regard. Riddled with omissions and indeterminacy, the short story is, as Iser might put it, in large part "unwritten." My students have described it as vague, incomplete, and "clouded by gaps." They have expressed uncertainty over whether they are looking too deeply or not deeply enough into the story, perhaps because its language seems flatly literal while at the same time suggesting an underlying symbolic, even archetypal resonance. The rare appearances of explicitly figurative language (the description of sunlight "angling" down the stone lining of the well shaft "like golden hair"; the children's faces likened to those "pasted on the spectators in the freak tent" at the circus; and the sudden welter of images in the narrator's evocation of "a great whispering, like a gathering of clouds, or the long sound, the turbulent wreck of the ocean," stand out against the unadorned, minimalist writing that is otherwise characteristic of the short story.

"The Man in the Well" is what Umberto Eco would call an *open text*, for in leaving out much of the descriptive and narrative information that more closed texts provide readers, it requires readers to take a more active role in constructing the story and construing its meaning. Closed texts, according to Eco, "aim at pulling the reader along a predetermined path, carefully displaying their effects so as to arouse pity or fear, excitement or depression at the due place and at the right moment. Every step of the 'story' elicits just the expectation that its further course will satisfy" (8). Much like Barthes's distinction between writerly and readerly texts, Eco's is ultimately a distinction between two acts of reading: one passive and prescribed, the other active and free. Readers of open texts, guided by fewer recognizable cues, need to make their own way, drawing causal connections between events, discerning relationships between characters, and responding in fittingly affective and ethical ways to the story. In the absence of narrative closure or an ending that satisfies expectations, frequently by resolving conflict and restoring order, readers are left to reach their own conclusions regarding what has occurred in the story, what might happen or have happened next, what it all means, and how they feel about it.

Readers of Sher's story are not told why the children decided not to help the man get out of the well, just that "it was decided." But this is only the most obvious gap in a short story that leaves so much unsaid that readers might make a game of listing all that remains open-ended, obscure, and indeterminate. Here I will identify a few of these gaps, to which you may add many more. We are given few clues as to when and where the story of an incident from the narrator's childhood is set, and at what distance in time from its occurrence the character narrator recounts it. Nor do we know what has occasioned this recounting, or (even as we play the part of the listener) to whom the story is being recounted. We do not know how many children were playing with the nine-year-old narrator at the farm-lot or how old these other children were. We are given the names of six children—Arthur, Wendy, Aaron, little Jason, Grace, and Robert (or perhaps seven, if little Jason is not the same boy twice referred to as Jason)—but we never learn the name of the man in the well, nor that of the character narrator. Indeed, we do not know whether the character narrator is male or female—though we also may not know that we lack this knowledge, so ready are most readers to assume a male narrator for this story.

This may be because readers, raised in a culture that universalizes male personhood and treats being female as a special case, tend to assume a male narrator unless informed otherwise (much as they will assume a white narrator), or because readers, presuming that the literary imagination is limited by biology, will expect a male author to create a male narrator. A handful of my students have assumed that the character narrator is author Ira Sher, writing, in one instance, that "in the end of the story the children, including

Sher, all stopped going to the well." Another student remarks, "I initially assumed that the author was telling his story. It never occurred to me to think otherwise. So, when we began to discuss that the character could possibly have been a girl, I was stunned." Readers who make this assumption mistake the text's genre, reading "The Man in the Well" as nonfiction rather than fiction, as a personal essay rather than a short story.

I assume a male narrator when reading "The Man in the Well," and while the aforementioned factors may play a part, there is a more immediate reason. I first encountered the story when listening to the public radio program *This American Life*, and there it is told by a composed male voice. (In fact, the short story is read aloud by Sher and followed by host Ira Glass's statement to listeners: "Just in case there's any ambiguity about it, it's a work of fiction.") Having come to the story through its oral performance, I cannot experience a "pure" first reading of it. On the radio program, the narration is accompanied by haunting choral singing, an ethereal chant that winds its way through the narrative, building and falling away. This droning refrain (performed by the Bulgarian State National Radio and Television Female Vocal Chorus) haunts my readings of the short story, intensifying my sense that this tale emerges from a subterranean region of darkness and mystery, as well as my unease in sharing in the dark and mysterious ritual of its telling. In the same way, I presume a male character narrator because I recall the voice that recites the story on *This American Life* when I read the text. Still, nothing in the text as written necessitates or justifies my filling this gap in this way. I can no more ascertain with certainty whether the character narrator is male or female than I can know whether the text is a story told aloud by the character narrator to one or more listeners or a story she or he has committed to paper, with or without a reader in mind.

MINDBLINDED BY FICTION

The rhetoric of gaps and gap-filling provides one way of addressing how readers interpret literature in the face of textual indeterminacy. Drawing on Iser's work, Patricia Harkin contends that to read a text as literature is to find gaps and fill them "by *imagining* connections among the bits of information that the text does provide" (*Acts* 55). She explains: "The more we imagine connections, and the more connections we imagine, the more we read 'literally.' What makes a text literary is the kind of reading a reader gives to it, a consciousness of reading for gaps" (*Acts* 56). Still, other ways of thinking about literary reading are available, including those that draw on recent work in cognitive psychology to expound upon the reader's act of imagining. A number of scholars taking a cognitive approach to literary studies, most notably Lisa Zunshine, have addressed the act of reading fiction in terms of *mind reading*. Here mind reading refers not to magical acts of telepathy but to what Zunshine calls "the evolved cognitive adaptation that prompts us to explain observable behavior"—such as facial expressions, gestures, vocal intonations, and actions—"as caused by unobservable mental states, such as thoughts, feelings, and intentions" (Savarese and Zunshine 21). People mind read whenever they imagine, based on body language and other cues, what others may be thinking, feeling, believing, desiring.

Zunshine draws our attention to how much literary gap-filling involves mind reading, writing,

> The very process of making sense of what we read appears to be grounded in our ability to invest the flimsy verbal constructions that we generously call "characters" with a potential for a variety of thoughts, feelings, and desires and then to look for the "cues" that would allow us to guess at their feelings and thus predict their actions. (*Why* 10)

She proposes that the same cognitive mechanisms that evolved to help human beings survive in the real world are triggered when we read fiction, causing readers to attribute mental lives to fictional characters although "on some level" they know that these characters are not real people (*Why* 10). Fiction works, in short, because people are incessant mind readers. We mind read constantly, in large part unconsciously, and very often incorrectly.

"Given how many of our attributions and interpretations of thoughts and feelings are wrong or only approximately correct," writes Zunshine, "[psychologists] might as well call it mind misreading. But since evolution doesn't deal in perfection, we have to fumble through by 'reading minds' as best we can" (*Getting* 2). Literature allows for such fumbling in more controlled circumstances, through cleverly constructed and artfully crafted narratives. Much of the pleasure we take in reading fiction may be located in the direct access readers are given to characters' inner thoughts and feelings, to fictional minds that may be known with certainty. Yet in *Why We Read Fiction,* Zunshine focuses on literature's capacity to "play with our mind-reading adaptations by keeping them off-balance" (*Getting* 24). We read fiction, she proposes, to experience "the mind-reading *uncertainty* that the manipulation of mental states induces in us: the characters manipulate mental states of each other, the narrator manipulates mental states of the reader, and so forth" (*Getting* 24). Fiction provides "a pleasurable and intensive workout" when, far from offering fictive certainty, it "engages, teases, and pushes to its tentative limits our mind-reading capacity" (*Why* 4, 164).

Zunshine's understanding of mind reading draws from the work of psychologist Simon Baron-Cohen, who in his 1995 book *Mindblindness* asks readers to contemplate being unaware that bodies are animated by minds: "Imagine what your world would be like if you were . . . blind to the existence of mental things. I mean, of course, blind to things like thoughts, beliefs, knowledge, desires, and intentions, which for most of us self-evidently underlie behavior" (1). Tragically, he writes, this is "not an idle thought experiment or a piece of science fiction" but a reality for "children and adults with the biological condition of autism [who] suffer, to varying degrees, from mindblindness" (5). Describing such mindblindness, Zunshine writes that whereas the average mind reader might mistake "her friend's tears of joy as tears of grief," an autistic person might "not even kno[w] that the water coursing down her friend's face is supposed to be somehow indicative of his feelings at that moment" (*Why* 13–14).

Inspired by the work of Ralph James Savarese, a scholar in the field of disability studies, Zunshine has since renounced the equation between autism and mindblindness. Savarese attributes popular and scientific misperceptions of autism to scientists who seldom listen to autistics and who, drawing mistaken conclusions from observing their behavior, believe that autistic subjects do not experience empathy when it is rather the case that they do not display empathy in normative ways (Savarese and Zunshine 18–19). On this point Zunshine notes a "profound irony": autistics have been labeled "mindblind" by observers who are mindblind when it comes to reading the minds of persons exhibiting unconventional behavior (Savarese and Zunshine 22). And yet, Savarese notes,

> we must recognize that autism is heterogeneous and that some autistics . . . buy into mindblindness. Think of Temple Grandin, for example. But even here we need to be cautious. For one thing, we have extrapolated too much from Grandin: not all, maybe not even a majority of, so-called high-functioning autistics . . . believe that they have difficulty reading other minds. For another, Grandin explicitly states that she has gotten better at this activity, which suggests that such a deficit is anything but strictly innate or hardwired. (25)

Whereas Savarese appears troubled that Grandin, an autism activist and professor of animal science, might consider herself "mindblind," Zunshine posits that the concept has value when used not as an "actual descriptor of autism" but as a metaphor to describe specific instances of "communication failure" or interpretive frustration (Savarese and Zunshine 24, 25).

In relation to literature, mindblindness may describe the mind-reading uncertainty experienced by readers who find themselves unable to determine characters' states of mind. The degree to which fiction challenges readers' mind-reading capabilities will vary from text to text. Zunshine observes that while "all fictional texts rely on and thus experiment with their readers' ability to keep track of *who* thought, wanted, and felt *what* and under what circumstances, some authors clearly invest more of their energy into exploiting this ability than others" (*Why* 75). Without presuming that Sher wrote "The Man in the Well" with this end in mind, I would propose that his short story tests readers by having them experience mindblindness of a sort. It does so through a preponderance of gaps in the narrative that bear on the thoughts and feelings of the character narrator, the children, and the man in the well.

Our effort "to read behavior in terms of mental states" (Baron-Cohen 5) is challenged from the story's second paragraph, where we read:

> I think it's important that we decided not to help him. Everyone, like myself, was probably on the verge of fetching a rope, or asking where we could find a ladder, but then we looked around at each other and it was decided. I don't remember if we told ourselves a reason why we couldn't help him, but we had decided then.

"... we decided ... it was decided ... we had decided then." The narrator emphasizes that theirs was a conscious decision not to help the man, but it is precisely this consciousness—what the children were thinking and feeling—that his narration obfuscates. For what reason did the children decide not to help the man? In stating that his friends were, like him, probably about to fetch a rope or ask about a ladder, the narrator does not engage in mind reading; instead, he applies the recollection of his own intentions to "everyone." He remembers being "on the verge" of getting a rope or ladder, but nothing relating to why he decided not to. That decision is attributed to a "we," a group mind whose reasoning the narrator is either unable or unwilling to convey. That readers cannot tell which indicates a difficulty in mind reading not only the children but also the narrator.

As if teasing the reader with the redacted moment of decision making, Sher returns to it in the story's fifth paragraph, where a move from acquiescence to defiance is again described, though differently. We read:

At first afraid to disobey the voice from the man in the well, we turned around and actually began to walk toward the nearest house, which was Arthur's. But along the way we slowed down, and then we stopped, and after waiting what seemed like a good while, we quietly came back to the well.

By telling what the children felt initially (they were "afraid to disobey"), this recounting brings us closer to their state of mind; at the same time, it takes us further away, as the narrator's description of the children's walk includes no mention of their having *decided* anything. Their movements away from and back to the well signify a change of mind without indicating what was thought or felt, how or why the children came to disobey the man's instruction to "go get a ladder, get help."

I was reminded of my attempts to ascertain what these children were thinking when reading a passage by Oliver Sacks that Zunshine cites in *Why We Read Fiction*. The passage, from Sacks's book *An Anthropologist on Mars*, concerns the aforementioned Temple Grandin. It describes how, as a girl, Grandin encountered her schoolmates: "Something was going on between the other kids, something swift, subtle, constantly changing—an exchange of meanings, a negotiation, a swiftness of understanding so remarkable that sometimes she wondered if they were all telepathic" (qtd. in Zunshine, *Why* 9). In Sher's story, the children's decision not to help the man in the well appears to have been made with this very swiftness of understanding. They looked at each other as they stood around the well, or they stopped en route to Arthur's house, "and it was decided." Given this seemingly unspoken decision making, readers may be excused for wondering if these children were not all telepathic.

Unable to perceive whatever exchange of meanings accompanied the children's decision, I feel mindblinded as a reader. Seeking to connect the children's mental states to their behavior, I follow the narrator into the mindblinding fog that envelops both the story he tells and the circumstances of its telling.

THE READER IN THE WELL

I began teaching "The Man in the Well" by asking students to write a short paper responding to a question that called on their mind-reading capabilities. I phrased it as follows: "Why do the children act as they do in the story?" In a way, this question places readers in a position not unlike that of the man in the well. While first-time readers of the short story are told from its third sentence that the children decided not to help the man, like the man they must wait to learn whether or not the children will come to his aid in the end. And, like the man in the well, readers who know how the story ends are left to wonder why the children left him where they found him, alone in the darkness of the well on the abandoned farm-lot. Indeed, the question I posed to my students echoes those the man asked the children at the story's conclusion—"Why didn't you tell anyone?" and "Didn't you want to tell anyone?"—questions that indicate the limits of the man's mind-reading ability.

Perhaps, then, "The Man in the Well" has the effect of placing its readers in "the well," immersing them in the condition of unknowing. There one searches for cues to gain a foothold, to orient oneself in a particular story-world by imagining its characters, events, and settings based on what may be learned and inferred from the text. Much as the man was at the mercy of the children, so the reader depends upon the text to provide a kind of rope or ladder with which he or she can escape unknowingness and reach a meaningful understanding of the story. By its conclusion, the man appeared to understand his situation: he knew the names of the children, as well as something of their character, and that they had neither searched for a ladder nor told their parents of his existence, but had deceived him on both counts. He also came to know and, it seems, accept his fate, realizing that the children would not be saving him. In short, over the course of three days the man's understanding has caught up with that of the story's readers. But because this is an understanding of *what* happened in the story and not of *why* it happened, readers, like the man in the well, may feel left in the dark at its conclusion.

This uncertainty will disturb most readers, especially those who find the children's actions troublingly inexplicable and those who expect the story to provide closure by ending on a more decisive note, if not one that provides a moral by reestablishing the ethical standards the children have defied. "I found this story to be somewhat disturbing," writes one of my students who gives explicit expression to her discomfort. "The children knowingly sentenced the man in the well to death and they didn't show much remorse in doing so.... I am having a hard time interpreting what this story might mean and I find this frustrating because I would like an explanation of why the children would do such a thing." Students who provide such explanations in their response papers may be credited for exceeding her in their efforts to find answers; then again, this student may be credited for resisting the urge to write her way out of the well, out of the difficult place of uncertainty in which she finds the story has left her.

Another student writes that the story is "very bothersome to read because the reader can see and feel the distress of the man and how he is trapped, both by the well and the children's refusal to help." She adds that "the reader is as helpless as the man" because she cannot alter the children's actions and because the narrator, who has "complete control" in telling the story, was one of the children who refused to help. This student's identification with the man, braced by her description of how the reader and the man are both at the mercy of the children, makes her response unusual. More often my students rewrite the story in ways that allow them to join the children who gathered on the grass and cement around the lip of the well, at a safe distance from the man trapped in its darkness.

Interpreting the "The Man in the Well" generally involves creating what H. Porter Abbott calls *interpretive closure* by rewriting the open text as a closed text (*Cambridge* 88). "Probably the most difficult thing about reading narratives is to remain in a state of uncertainty," writes Abbott. "If a narrative won't close by itself, one often tries to close it, even if it means shutting one's eyes to some of the details and imagining others that aren't there" (*Cambridge* 89). Like the closed texts described by Eco, one's literary interpretations might "aim at pulling the reader along a predetermined path" while neglecting expanses of less familiar textual ground (Eco 8). In presenting exculpatory explanations of the children's actions, my students' responses would attain interpretive closure by taking the reader along a path that circumvents the well.

"The Man in the Well" may be regarded not only as an open or writerly text but also as what Abbott calls a *resistant text*. Resistant texts are those that "lead us not simply to acknowledge that we don't know but to feel the insistent presence of this condition" (*Real* 9). Their readers are "made not only to know that they don't know, which is a matter of understanding, but also to be immersed in the condition of unknowing, which is a matter of experience" (*Real* 3). I understand that there is much I do not know about Sher's story, as my description of its many gaps illustrates. Still, in elaborating upon these gaps I discuss the story with a knowingness that belies the uncertainty and uneasiness I experience when rereading it—the feeling of encountering a voice and a world that remain in some part troublingly, hauntingly unknowable. Abbott remarks that this experience "need not forestall efforts to interpret" a resistant text, but "if an interpretation does aspire to account for the work as a whole, it must find a place for this special experience" by addressing how the narrative resists the reader's interpretive efforts and arouses uncertainty (*Real* 12).

If, as Abbott claims, it is difficult when reading a narrative to remain in a state of uncertainty, this is all the more true when writing on one, and it is truer still when the writer is a student assigned the task of interpreting a literary narrative. Students understandably assume they should come up with the right answer, and so they struggle with and against the literary text to attain certainty regarding its meaning. The resulting interpretations are arguably less expressive of their authors' experiences of reading "The Man in the Well"—which include immersion in "the condition of unknowing"—than of their attempts, as Abbott puts it, "to restore normality, to settle a text's disturbing quality and bring it into line," rewriting its narrative to attain closure (*Cambridge* 87). In considering some of these rewritings that strike me as notable misreadings, I want to suggest that instead of resisting the resistant text and seeking to escape the uncertainty of the well, we can learn more by remaining in its depths, feeling our way by listening attentively to the different voices we hear.

THREE STUDENTS WRITING

Betty's Response: "Kids Will Be Kids"

The children act the way they do in the story because of what they are . . . children. An online dictionary states that a child is "one who is childish and immature." They play games and do not do the right thing due to their immaturity and childish ways. It is almost as if they do not know any better. The thrill and excitement that the children experience as they continued to go back to the well made the whole experience worthwhile. Their natural nature was the reason that they cared about the man at all. Overall, the main reason why Arthur, Wendy, Aaron, Grace, and Jason behaved in such a manner was simply due to their innocence. . . .

Their innocent and fresh minds have a lot to learn still, so we pardon them. Even though the children in the story do the "wrong" thing, they would still be pardoned. They might get yelled at, or be punished, but in the big picture they still have a good enough excuse for not helping the man out of the well. . . . They didn't want their excitement to end, so getting him out of the hole was not the answer. . . . Their nature wanted to keep the man alive, so they did just that. . . . They brought necessities for the man to survive, and worked together to do so.

The children played games with the man in the well. This was fun and exciting to them. They knew they had control, so they played around with it. . . . The man played games right back with them. This kept them on their toes, and was something more exciting compared to everyday life stuff. They lied to "the man" and told him that help was on the way. They wanted to play with the man's head and thoughts to have control. They ignored his cries, and made rules to their game. . . . Only an immature, childish mind would play such games with a man whose life was at stake.

Games are supposed to be fun. The children's innocence and immaturity desires the excitement of games and fun, so why wouldn't they play one?

Langston's Response: "The Perils of Obedience"

I think the kids in the story reacted they way they did because they were all following the lead of the oldest one, Aaron. It is fairly obvious that when a group of kids are friends, the oldest usually tends to be the leader, the decision maker, and the one emulated. I think Aaron is a troubled kid based on his actions and therefore a bad example for the younger kids to follow. He seems like the kind of kid who was maybe abused by his parents or mistreated in some way so that all he can be is cruel as a product of his environment and how he was raised. I think Aaron convinced the six younger impressionable kids to abandon their natural reaction to help someone in need. Aaron could have easily convinced the younger ones to go along with his plans by saying it was just a game or by convincing them that they would get in trouble for telling an adult. This way he could see how far he could take the situation while living out a perverse fantasy. . . .

I felt that Aaron's actions proved he was a troubled kid, had power over the younger kids, and was the manipulator of the entire situation. This is evident in the text when it said that Aaron was admired by the younger kids for creating an inventive lie to the man in the well that help was coming. This proved they looked up to him. Also when Wendy accidentally leaked his name to the man in the well, Aaron exacted revenge by naming all of them. They all felt powerless to stop him since he was the oldest and the text referenced them being afraid of him since he was bigger in age and most likely size.

Aaron was the influence that resulted in the children's bizarre reaction not to help the man in the well. . . . Since their conscience was nagging away at them because they knew what they were doing was wrong, they had to in some way justify it to themselves. I think they justified their actions . . . by dehumanizing the man in the well as just a faceless stranger, a voice from the dark. This is evident by the fact that the kids were horrified when the man knew their names because this not only meant they could get in trouble but most importantly, it made him closer to them as a real person. Paradoxically, the same human nature that wanted to suppress the man in the well as not real was also naturally curious of who he was, which resulted in treating him somewhat humanely. I think this was evident by the fact that they desperately wanted to learn his name . . . and they fed him for two days. . . .

The fact that the kids all felt remorse at the end says to me that they were consciously aware that they did something wrong. . . . I think it ties back into my main point that an outside factor, which I believe to be Aaron, changed their natural inclination to help someone in trouble. . . . After all, being so young it was probably easier and safer to conform to the will of the oldest rather than risk defying him. Not to mention, he could have been their only role model and older person in their lives to pay attention to them since the narrator's parents seemed distracted, uninterested, or neglectful to their kid.

It is common knowledge that kids are impressionable; they are open to be molded into whatever kind of person you want to teach them to be. If they have good socializing agents such as good parents, education, and positive friends, they will most like turn out fine but if they have bad role models, they will inevitably be bad themselves with the exception of a few.

Melanie's Response: "A Well of Problems"

In "The Man in the Well" there are many aspects of the children's actions that confuse me but in general they seem to be acting like regular children. . . . My initial reaction, also the one that seems most logical, is that the children do not tell anyone about the man because they found him while they were playing somewhere they were not permitted to be. This reason alone leaves too many gaps open and too many aspects of the story unanswered, such as the reason for the mother in the story . . . I thought a lot harder and then came up with something a little more concrete.

. . . I generated the idea that the children were abused in some way by this man in the well in the past. This seems to be a strong possibility because the children seem afraid to let the man know their names, as if they are trying to keep their anonymity. . . . This would also explain them not seeming to feel remorse or guilt for letting a man die.

The role of the mother in the story seems to play a very large role in the explanation of events that take place, although her presence seems small. At first she is weeping while the father murmurs stubbornly, and then she sobs the night it rains. We are led to wonder, "Why is the father stubborn? Why is she crying? Why is she in the story at all?" Because she seems like such a small part in such a vague piece, the only thing I can assume is that she is some clue to the story and that *her sobbing relates somehow to the children and the man in the well. This is what makes me feel more strongly that the man had abused the children in some way.*

The mother is sobbing because she knows that a man abused her child and/or other children. The father is stubborn because he thinks it should be kept quiet and she wants him to do something about it. This opens up a lot of other questions such as, "Do they know he is in the well? Did they put him there?" . . . The children taunt him because they are angry and upset about how he treated them.

Something else I had considered, because of dwelling on the mother and father's roles in the story, is that the mother is sobbing because the father is the one doing the abusing. The narrator retreats to the man in the well in his mind to escape the feelings he has towards his father for abusing him. This would mean the man in the well represents the child feeling trapped and the tears from his mother drowning him as he tries to ignore his problems.

This story was very well written so that it leaves a number of meanings open to the reader. The man in the well can represent a literal existence, a metaphor for feeling trapped, or a combination of the two.

WE PARDON THE CHILDREN

While the responses written by Betty, Langston, and Melanie take a variety of twists and turns in the course of presenting their differing interpretations of "The Man in the Well," here I will address what they share in common. The three responses are illustrative of what I have found most striking about my students' interpretations of the short story: how many of them, really most of them, seek to excuse the children who decided not to help the desperate man by justifying their actions or absolving them of responsibility. These are children who answered the man's cries for help by choosing neither to fetch a rope or a ladder nor to get their parents, but to keep him confined, and who, after three days, left the man to perish from dehydration and starvation, alone at the bottom of a deep, dark hole. What might absolve them? I have found that a great many students exonerate the children by inventing character traits, backstories, and mitigating circumstances that relocate, diminish, or altogether negate blame and responsibility. Insofar as their responses deny the children's moral agency or justify their behavior through recourse to factors and beliefs that have little basis in the text, I regard them as misreadings.

Take, for instance, the initial explanation offered by Melanie in "A Well of Problems": the children did not inform any adults that a man was trapped in a well because they could not do so without revealing that they had been playing at the farm-lot, where their parents had forbidden them to go. In remarking that "this reason alone leaves too many gaps open and too many aspects of the story answered" to suffice, Melanie demonstrates an awareness that interpretive claims should find significant support in the text, yet she offers no indication as to why, in the absence of such support, the forbidden farm-lot explanation still "seems most logical." Its hypothetical basis is expressed by another student who writes, "The man in the well could have been the least of their worries if they were in an area they were not supposed to be in the first place." As nothing in the text indicates that the children were instructed by their parents to stay away from the old farm-lot, students argue the likelihood of this scenario by making an appeal to simple logic or plain sense. In this vein, one remarks: "A sensible person knows wells are a dangerous playground. Someone could fall down the well, get hurt, trapped. I made a logical assumption that the children acted as they did because they didn't want to get in trouble for being somewhere they were told not to be." This assumption explains the children's perplexing actions in the most familiar terms: children are afraid of getting in trouble for defying their parents. This stereotype, rather than reasoning from textual evidence, accounts for the prevalence of such explanations.

Because assumptions that strike us as only sensible are those we are less likely to check against the text, we should be mindful that this is no assurance of their validity. And indeed, in the text I see no indication that the children or their parents even knew of the well before the nine-year-old protagonist, while "playing hide and go seek or something," happened upon it. For that matter, only in rereading the words "I found the well, and then I heard the voice of the man in the well calling out for help," do I realize that my own sensible-enough assumption—that the protagonist heard the man's calls for help and, in following them, discovered the well—contradicts what is stated clearly enough in the text: only after finding the well did the protagonist hear the man's voice.

In another response relating to parental prohibitions, a student writes that she finds it "only sensible to suggest" that the man was made "to suffer and never escape" because the children had been taught not to talk to strangers. She supports this claim not with textual evidence—after all, the children do talk to the man—but with reference to her own experience, writing, "I was taught never to speak, or let alone tell my name to someone I don't know. This led me to believe that although the children spoke to the stranger from above the well, their faces were never seen by the stranger and perhaps [they] thought they weren't really disobeying their parents." In other words, the children hid themselves from the man and left him in the well because they were obeying the spirit, if not the law, of their parents' teachings. As odd as this reasoning may be, it is echoed by another student who writes, "Many times I was told as a child to never talk to strangers. Although the children talked to the man many times, the fact that they would not let the man see their faces or know their names led me to believe that . . . they had been raised correctly and told not to talk to strangers."

Beyond the question of its textual basis, the claim that the children did not tell their parents about the man trapped in the well because they feared being punished raises an important question concerning the children's moral understanding. Simply put, did these youngsters have the capacity to understand that the trouble they might get into for playing at the farm-lot or talking to a stranger was nothing compared to the wrong they would be committing by refusing to help someone in a life-threatening situation? Not according to a great number of my students whose written responses evoke the familiar trope of childhood innocence. "I believe the kids acted as they did basically because they didn't know any better and really felt as if they were doing nothing wrong," writes one student. "It's not as if the kids were possessed or actually trying to kill this man; these kids were just being kids and doing what it is kids do." Similar claims made by other students include the following: "These children were just naive and taught not to go near or even speak to strangers"; "They do not have the mature morals to appreciate why adults would know that they ought to save the man's life"; "Children at this age have not fully developed their minds. They are incapable to make moral decisions on their own"; and "They were only children anyway. Were they really expected to save a man's life?" My students repeatedly claim that the children did not understand the seriousness, the severity, or the magnitude of the situation in which they found themselves when they found the man. Though they may have acted selfishly and deceitfully, they did so only because they were not yet mature; "their intent," in the words of one student, "was not malicious at all."

I had expected the flipside of a belief in childhood innocence, uncorrupted by adulthood, to make an appearance in many of my students' papers. But the belief that children are naturally savage and, freed from parental or adult supervision, will engage in violent, antisocial behavior does not appear to inform their responses. With the possible exception of one of my students, who believes "the author was trying to imply humans are inherently selfish, but are kept in check by authority," none offer *Lord of the Flies*–themed interpretations of the short story. Instead, children appear as naïfs. In a great many student papers, the children's treatment of the man is attributed to their natural curiosity, their delight in playing games, or their boredom. Thus a student writes that "they were not aware of the seriousness of the situation and saw it more like a game," an extension of the play they had been engaged in prior to discovering the man. Another comments that for children who had little to do during their "childhood afternoons" other than go to the movies, "finding a man stranded in the local well for days on end would be a very exciting change of pace." Another concludes, "All in all, these children don't intentionally mean to harm this man in the well. They were just trying to amuse themselves, by keeping this 'pet' alive. These children, I believe, were just being children."

The comparison of the man in the well to a pet—a creature like a bug, a mouse, or a lizard, captured by a child and kept secretly because "your parents would never let you keep it"—recurs in several student papers. A student named Victor recalls catching toads in his yard, keeping them as pets in a box filled with sticks and leaves, and making them "complete little obstacle courses" until they died from mistreatment. The "unintended cruelty" of his childhood pet-keeping serves as his key to understanding the children in the short story, who are said to share the same "innocent desire" to keep and care for "another life form" that drove him to capture toads. Victor believes that the children "tried to maintain [the man] like they would any other creature, without truly realizing the severity of their actions." In his rewriting of the story, only when the man knew their names did the children realize that they were not caring for a pet but keeping a human being captive—at which point "the situation became far too adult for the children to understand, and so they ignored it, hoping it would go away." Like many other students, Victor concludes that while the children did act cruelly, they did so unwittingly, being too young and immature to know better.

So far I have considered students' written responses that absolve the children of responsibility for wrongdoing by denying them the capacity to comprehend sufficiently the harmful consequences or the immorality of their actions. In her response "Kids Will Be Kids," Betty takes the very threat posed by the children's actions as evidence of such innocence, writing that "only an immature, childish mind" would play a game that puts a man's life at stake. She identifies the children's "natural nature" with their desire to care for the man and feed him, while attributing their interest in exerting power and control over him to nothing more sinister than a childlike desire to play games. "Their innocent and fresh minds have a lot to learn still, so we pardon them," she writes. "Even though the children in the story do the 'wrong' thing, they would still be pardoned." Yet, not all students find the children to be so innocent, so unaware that they were harming the man by deceiving him and refusing to free him from the well. For many of them, pardoning the children involves not denying their capacity to act immorally but locating responsibility and blame for their actions elsewhere.

MITIGATING FACTORS

The work of minimizing blame by relegating responsibility to a few bad apples is well illustrated by Langston's response, "The Perils of Obedience," which states that while the children were "consciously aware that they did something wrong," this wrongdoing was due to an anomalous "outside factor" that corrupted them, countermanding their "natural inclination to help someone in trouble." This factor is Aaron, whom Langston characterizes as a miscreant who led his younger, impressionable playmates to behave in a manner contrary to their own nature. This rewriting of the story indicates that had Aaron not been there at the farm-lot, the children surely would have helped the man get out of the well; that they did not is attributed solely to a troubled child's role as "the manipulator of the entire situation." Langston speculates that "Aaron could have easily convinced the younger ones to go along with his plans by saying it was just a game or by convincing them that they would get in trouble for telling an adult." Actions that other students attribute to the children's naivety are here attributed to Aaron's trickery.

Langston's speculations are necessary because the story includes no description of Aaron manipulating the other children. Indeed, Aaron bears no mention whatsoever in the first section of the story, which recounts events that occurred the day the children discovered the man in the well. Rather, the narrator refers to the children's seemingly unanimous decision, though in the most elusive terms: "I don't remember if we told ourselves a reason why we couldn't help him, but we had decided then." If any child took on more of a leadership role, I imagine it was not Aaron but Arthur, the first character named in the story. It was Arthur who first spoke to the man, "establish[ing] some sort of a dialogue," and who first lied to him by implying that he and the other children had looked for a ladder. Moreover, Arthur appears to have led the effort to provide the man with food and water, because it was he who brought, assembled, and dropped the bag into the well.

Perhaps the active role Arthur assumed accounts for why, on the third day, when Aaron told the man the names of the other children, he began by naming Arthur. The narrator recounts, "I could see Arthur was furious, but Aaron was older and bigger than he was, *and nothing could be said or done without giving himself, his name, away; we knew the man in the well was listening for the changes in our breath, anything."* Langston disregards the part of this sentence that I have italicized, and thus the children's curious fear that the man in the well might identify them, or their voices, by name. He notes only that the children "all felt powerless" to stop Aaron because "he was bigger in age and most likely size." In short, the children in his rewriting of the story feared not the man in the well but Aaron. Why, of all the children, should Aaron alone have lacked a "natural" inclination to help those in need? The answer lies not in the story but in the stock character Langston makes of Aaron: he is the neighborhood bully who coerces younger and weaker children into following his lead. Playing off the stock belief that victims of child abuse grow up to be abusers, Langston pictures Aaron as "the kind of kid who was maybe abused by his parents or mistreated in some way so that all he can be is cruel."

With this remark, Langston introduces another "outside factor" that might account for the children's unnatural refusal to help the man: bad parenting. In addition to proposing that Aaron's parents might be blamed for his cruelty, he proposes that the narrator's parents and, by extension, those of the other children might be blamed for having neglected their sons and daughters, leaving them to see Aaron—perhaps the only "older person in their lives to pay attention to them"—as a role model. Several students attribute the children's actions to parental neglect, including one who offers this explanation of the narrator's willingness to join his friends in not helping the man: "Children have their parents as role models, and if the parents are always hostile towards one another, the children will learn to be hostile towards other people." Many students presume that "the majority of kids have problems at home," as one puts it. A classmate claims that the children spent "most afternoons back then" sitting in the cool movie theater because they lacked adult supervision at home. "As a result," she writes, "no one was there to teach them good morals and values." Another similarly contends that "these children's parents must not have been very involved in their lives," since the children "were not taught at home how to deal with certain situations. They were not taught how to help others in time of need." Again, in the absence of textual support, students turn to what makes "plain sense": because bad parenting is a culturally familiar, stock explanation for children's misconduct, the children's misconduct in the story is taken as evidence of bad parenting.

These students' responses attribute the children's actions to the negative influence of immoral others, contending that these others (the troubled kid, bad parents), and not the children who decided not to help the man, are guilty of cruelty or neglect. For still more students, the immoral other is the man in the well himself. I recall Melanie's response, "A Well of Problems," where she posits the "strong possibility" that "the children were abused in some way by this man in the well in the past." Although no such previous encounter is suggested by the narrator, this rewriting of the story serves to explain why the children felt no "remorse or guilt for letting a man die": they were "angry and upset" by what he had done to them. Melanie's interpretation, like Langston's, suggests the currency of child abuse as an explanatory factor, a ready diagnosis for disturbing behavior; but whereas Langston situates blame within the group of children by relegating responsibility and intent to just one of them, Melanie locates blame outside the group, essentially reversing the roles of victim and victimizer. That is, by introducing a backstory to the story told by the narrator, she portrays the man not as the innocent victim of the children who refused him aid but as their former abuser receiving his comeuppance.

This may seem a surprising move, but Melanie is far from alone in finding the man to be a suspicious character and blaming him for his predicament. "For all [the children] knew, he could be a killer or an escaped convict (what was he doing on an abandoned farm anyway?), and they were in part protecting themselves by neglecting to help the man," remarks one student; another similarly speculates, "Maybe the man in the hole is on the run from authorities and . . . picked one less than perfect place to hide; perhaps that is what the children are thinking." If not a child abuser or wanted criminal, the man was at the very least a frightening figure, a stranger whom the children were right to fear. "For all they know, he could have been the boogieman," a student remarks. "They realized that by keeping him in the well, they were protecting themselves." Another comments: "Having a stranger know your name makes you feel like they know you. Knowing your name could lead to finding out where you live, where you go to school, or any other information about you. And that is truly a scary thing." Remarks such as these might explain the children's hesitancy to bring the man a rope or a ladder, but not their resistance to telling their parents that a strange man was trapped in a well on the old farm-lot. Indeed, one might think these children would be more likely to alert their parents the more they perceived the man to be a threat to their safety.

Some students go further in attributing the children's refusal to help the man to failings on his part, including one who faults him for his "strange behavior" of taunting the children with questions that made them uneasy, scaring them away "indefinitely." She concludes, "Although not sure why they decided not to help him at the time, the narrator must realize later that the choice to not help the man might have been a smarter choice in the end. The children realize the possible danger of the situation after the man reveals his true, devious personality later in the story." Another student, Cheryl, writes,

> As the story goes on, numerous times the children tried to get to know the man but he was too concerned about getting out of the well.... Even after one girl deceivingly told the man that the other kids went to get help, the man did not try to connect with her. He didn't even ask her name; he simply answered her question about the existence of water in the well and focused on himself again: "'No,' he said, 'it is very dry'... 'Do you think it will rain?'" So, after waiting a while, the children left the man there, in the well, because he was too preoccupied with himself and too demanding, and he was just a man in the well without a name and a face. The children lost interest in him because he was not interested in the kids.

Here the man is faulted not for scaring the children but for boring them by being overly concerned with his own needs—never mind the gravity of his situation. Unlike many of her peers, Cheryl does not assert that the children were innocents but remarks, instead, that "humans have a dark side" that leads them to do "bad things to others." Still, she assumes a basic goodness on their part, writing, "I believe if the man in the well had been friendly and kind towards the children, they would eventually have helped him." And so it seems that the man was responsible for his fate: instead of acting in a way that would invite the children's assistance, he dug himself in deeper.

TWO STUDENTS WRITING

Allison's Response: "The Empty Well"

Ira Sher's "The Man in the Well" depicts a few days in the lives of pre-teenage children ... Decades ago, before ... cell phones, electronic games, DVD players and even computers, children had limited entertainment resources. Hopscotch and hide and go seek were main sources of fun. No modern technology is mentioned throughout the story which can lead the reader to another conclusion: Imagination flourishes with boredom. These children seem to have a need for unique amusement, and pretending a man is trapped in a well for a few days provides that.

Two instances within the story directly lead to the determination that the man in the well was a fabrication. First, the narrator is careful to initially point out that they never actually saw the man.... There is also no description of the man's voice or accent. The narrator simply refers to the voice as being scratchy, a description most reasonable people would assume to be true of someone trapped in a well without food or water.

Second, the decision not to help the man in the well is made early and never discussed. Had there actually been a real man trapped in that well, there would have been controversy in the group over telling a parent or police officer. During the conversation the children had with the man in the well, Aaron tells him, "My father said he's coming, with the police. And he knows what to do." This statement leaves no room to question whether the children knew right from wrong. The oldest child knew that a dangerous situation, like the man stuck at the bottom of the well, would need adult attention. The other children admire Aaron for coming up with a believable response which proves they knew it was the right thing to do as well.

The reason the children choose to leave the man in the well is obvious. Had they agreed to help him, their imagined adventure would have been over.

Jordan's Response: "The Man Not in the Well"

After reading "The Man in the Well" for a second time, the story made me feel the children were very creative when it came to using their imaginations. It is possible that the man inside the well was a fictional character and did not truly exist....

Children have the ability to use their imaginations in order to create scenarios that are completely fictional in order to keep themselves entertained. The narrator states, "I think it's important that we decided not to help him," referring to the man inside the well. Generally, most children are in favor of helping an individual that is in need of help.... Instead the children decide to leave the man in the well. In fact they leave him there multiple days with not a single child to mention anything to their parents at the end of the day when they left the well.

... Another example that suggests that the man in the well is an imaginative character is where the children decide to put food down the well for the man to eat. If the children were that concerned about the man that they deemed it was necessary to feed him because they felt like he might be starving, one would most likely think they would have rescued him from the well in the first place.

Most children were not put on earth to see people suffer and if the man were real, and truly in trouble, he most likely would have been rescued immediately. Instead, the evidence suggests the man in the well may be just a game. The narrator states in the last line that they never played by the well anymore, even when they were much older, suggesting that maybe their game was just not fun anymore and that they were moving on to better things.

EMPTYING THE WELL

Allison's and Jordan's responses illustrate a fourth way to absolve the children of guilt and responsibility: rather than assert their inability to act maliciously or immorally, attribute their actions to corrupting outside factors, or blame the man for his predicament, they posit that there was no man in the well. If the man was nothing more than the children's invention, an imagined component in a game of pretend the children played by the well over the course of three days, then no one was harmed by their actions and no wrong was committed. Several students reach this conclusion, essentially contending that there could not have been a man trapped in the well because, if there had been, the children certainly would have saved him. As one student puts it: "I believe this short story is an example of these children's imaginations because of the fact that they did not decide to help him. Morally children would be the first to want to be a hero and help this man." Another writes, "The whole story did not make sense to me because why wouldn't the kids help the man if he were real. Why wouldn't anyone help someone in need, it is just something that one does." She concludes that "maybe he was not real and that the kids imagined him and were playing around and that is why they did not tell anyone. Kids around the age of nine still play games and pretend so it could be very possible that they were imagining him."

In "The Empty Well," Allison likewise reasons that the man is a fabrication because the children "knew right from wrong"; that the group of children might have knowingly done wrong seems an impossibility. Whereas Aaron, in his role as the oldest child, appears in Langston's interpretation as a manipulative troublemaker who led the other children to act immorally, in Allison's response he appears as the most mature member of the group, the one who "knew that a dangerous situation, like the man stuck at the bottom of the well, would need adult attention." Had there been an actual man trapped at the bottom of the well, she suggests, at least Aaron would have argued for doing "the right thing," and "there would have been controversy in the group over telling a parent or police officer" rather than unified agreement not to get help. The lack of any such controversy is taken to indicate that the children only pretended a man was in the well in order to satisfy their need for "unique amusement."

The presumption informing these responses is not simply that the children were morally incapable of refusing the man's appeals for help, as is the case with those who argue the innate innocence of children. More striking, it is that the idea of children refusing to help someone in dire need is so difficult to imagine that one would not find it depicted even in an imaginative work of fiction. Or perhaps it would be more accurate to say that children capable of acting so callously can *only* be imagined, and therefore must be regarded as good children playacting at being bad, creating what Jordan calls "scenarios that are completely fictional in order to keep themselves entertained." Immoral children, it seems, are so "completely fictional" that they cannot belong to a storyworld that readers, in suspending disbelief, take to be real.

Appleyard observes that many students come to college reading literature in a manner so focused on story and so inattentive to writing that "they do not see the text." He explains:

> Of course they read the words on the page, but they do not focus any attention to them as the place where a problem of interpretation is to be encountered. Instead they look through them, at the characters and at the actions the characters are engaged in, at the world depicted in the story. (127)

He contends that although these students, like all readers, "actively construct the story and its characters out of the material offered by a text as they read," they do so without being aware of this process, much less reflecting upon it; instead, they identify with characters and become involved in plot situations. "For them," he writes, "the story is a given, and the text is simply the invisible medium of its transmission" (129).

Because they see the text as if looking through a window at the real world outside, or overlook the synthetic as they focus intently on the mimetic, these readers do not engage literature as *writing*. Consequently, they neglect to consider the nonliteral or metaphorical character of literary language—envisioning, for instance, the well in Sher's short story as a physical part of the setting without considering its figurative or symbolic meaning. Another consequence, as Appleyard notes, is that readers will discuss fictional characters, settings, and events not as artificial constructs but "as though they really exist or have happened" (128). My students offer such mimetically focused responses when their explanations of why the children act as they do in the story lead them to expand upon the "real" world of the story rather than comb the words of the text for clues.

This is notably the case with students making the empty-well argument, given that they resolve the problem posed by the children's refusal to help the man by reimagining what "really" happened in the world of the story without addressing the text, the words with which the story is narrated and written. For example, in a response titled "Just a Figment of Your Imagination," Jill writes, "I absolutely fail to believe that not one child out of the bunch wouldn't have either told his or her parents outright or had a slip of the tongue and accidentally 'told' on the group." She might have faulted the author for portraying the children unrealistically, or she might have doubted the reliability of the narrator, claiming that he must be misremembering or misreporting the story, in whole or part. But Jill neither faults the author nor mistrusts the narrator. Instead, she rewrites the story to account for the otherwise unbelievable element, thereby maintaining belief in the world inhabited by the children. "No one told because there was nothing to tell," she concludes. "They all knew that they would be going back the next day to start the story up again and continue on with their fun. Bringing food and water in small sacks was all a part of the story. It was a way to make it more real." Jill's response is similarly interested in making what is fictional seem more real.

A response that draws attention to the narrative's synthetic component—to how the story is narrated or written—breaks the mimetic illusion of a real world. The responses of these students, by contrast, serve, in Phelan's words, "to preserve the mimetic component of the story" (*Living* 25) by denying the reality of that part of the story they find troubling and retaining the rest. By emptying the well, my students explain away elements that pose a challenge to their beliefs regarding the morality of children, and so allow themselves to maintain their belief—or suspend their disbelief—in the world of the children playing at the abandoned farm-lot. Yet in doing so, they introduce an element of make-believe that may spread to incorporate other aspects of the story. If there was no man in well, perhaps too there was no group of friends playing by the well. Perhaps the character narrator, having discovered the well while playing alone at the old farm-lot, played a game of make-believe in which he invented not just the man but also the other children. But why stop there? Perhaps there was no well and no abandoned farm-lot near his home, but only the nine-year-old character narrator alone in his room, imagining all of this: children playing at the farm-lot, finding the well, hearing the voice of the man calling out for help, deciding not to help him, and so on. Or perhaps there is only the adult character narrator telling an entirely made-up story.

Is this line of thought not moving us closer to the truth of the story, its point of origin at the scene of writing? All we need do is take one step further and posit that the character narrator is himself a fabrication, an invention of the author, and we have replaced the fictional storyworld with the past reality of Ira Sher sitting in a room, composing "The Man in the Well"—a short story that invites its readers to imagine a world in which a group of children playing on an abandoned farm-lot discovered a man trapped in a well and chose not to save him.

UNDERREADING AND OVERREADING

The student responses discussed in this chapter provide a sampling of those I have deemed misreadings. This is not to say that I graded them poorly, but that I judged them to be flawed interpretations of "The Man in the Well." In what ways are they flawed? I might say that my students err in trying to deny the guilt of the children in a story that is about these children's very effort—and the narrator's ongoing effort—to hide from their own guilty feelings. Yet, I am uncomfortable with this answer because it suggests that I regard as misreadings those responses to the short story that do not accord with my own sense of what the story is about. Seeking to justify my response to these students' interpretations in less self-interested terms, I turn to the text.

In *Literature as Exploration,* one of the earliest works to examine how student readers interpret poetry and fiction, Louise M. Rosenblatt observes that "very complex and thorny problems concerning the criteria of soundness to be applied to any interpretation" arise from the fact that there is no "single correct reading of a literary text" (267). But, she writes, even if we are unable "to arrive at a unanimous agreement concerning the best interpretation . . . we can arrive at some consensus about interpretations that are to be rejected as ignoring large elements in the work or as introducing irrelevant or exaggerated responses" (267–68). To reach a shared understanding of when misreading has occurred, writes Rosenblatt, "we can always move from our personal responses and interpretations back to the text. What in the text justifies our response? This is what scientists would call our control, the means of avoiding arbitrary and irrelevant interpretations" (268). Any student who has been instructed to support her or his claims with textual evidence is acquainted with this long-established method for arguing an interpretation's validity.

Abbott provides useful terms for the two acts of misreading that, for Rosenblatt, characterize "interpretations that are to be rejected." In reading literary texts, he writes, "almost invariably, we overlook things that are there and put in things that are not there. We *underread* and we *overread*" (*Cambridge* 86). We underread and overread to some degree as a matter of course, due to the nature of literary narrative. On the one hand, even apart from an inclination to skim over unfamiliar words, odd phrases, and passages that are not readily comprehensible, it is difficult if not impossible for readers to attend to every element in a text of any significant length—and so we underread. On the other, reading literature involves utilizing one's imagination, knowledge, memory, and experience to fill in gaps, adding to what is left unspecified or only suggested by the text. Literary reading involves envisioning a storyworld that is not "there" in the words of the text but constructed from them—and so we overread by necessity.

"Even if we come as close as we humanly can to avoid underreading and overreading," writes Abbott, "we still have to fill things in if we are to make sense of the narratives we read or see" (*Cambridge* 90). Indeed, for Iser the reading process in large part involves "filling in the gaps left by the text itself" (*Implied* 280). Still, overreading seems less an essential component of literary reading than an error to be avoided when Abbott writes that defending an interpretation of a short story "against the charge of overreading" requires finding evidence in the text to support it (*Cambridge* 95). That under- and overreading may be regarded as both unavoidable aspects of reading and avoidable forms of misreading suggests that while all readers underread and overread, we are charged with doing so only when the things we overlook or add to a text exceed some limit of acceptability—when, for instance, what we "put in" the text cannot be adequately justified by what is already there, or when what we overlook proves to be significant. But exactly where on the continuum of under- and overreading these lines may be drawn, demarcating a range of "just right" reading, is difficult to say.

Rosenblatt claims that the question of validity in interpretation is "much more difficult to settle in theory than to face in practical interpretation of particular texts" (267), and I do find that I can readily identify where underreading and overreading occur in my students' writings on "The Man in the Well." Most evident are instances of overreading in which students explain the children's behavior by adding to the text such invented narrative elements as the parents' prohibition against playing by the well, Aaron's troubled childhood and manipulation of the other children, and the man's having abused the children sometime in the past. I see underreading at work in those responses that assert the children's inability to know what they were doing was wrong or immoral, and those that refer only to the fun and excitement these children experienced in making a game of the man's plight. Both neglect many passages in the text that bear on the children's more complicated emotional responses to the man and the situation in which they put themselves by deciding not to help him—defensive responses of fear, anger, and shame that will be discussed in the next chapter.

And what of those responses that contend the man in the well was a made-up figure in a game of make-believe? I believe that they present a creative and clever response to the story at the cost of excessive overreading—adding to the text the children's collaborative effort to playact or perform as if there were a man in the well—and underreading. The latter is illustrated by the brevity with which students making the empty-well argument address the story's conclusion, if they address it at all. Allison writes that the children left the man in the well so that their "imagined adventure" would not end, but she offers no explanation as to how or why it did end, while Jordan writes only that "maybe their game was just not fun anymore" and so they "mov[ed] on to better things." Jill offers this fuller explanation:

> Children can be quite imaginative but they can also tire quickly with situations that are monotonous. I think that by the end of day two going into day three that it's possible that some of the children had had enough and were ready to move on to the next venture. I'm sure that it wasn't planned that Wendy gave up a name to "the man" but it happened. Still playing along with the story, the other children may have seen this as a weakness that was able to end it. Even though the man had absolutely no clue who the children were or where they lived (he was, remember, just in their imagination), this one slip managed to expose each and every one of them and make them vulnerable to him which ended the fun altogether.

Here, as with her suggestion that the children brought food and water to the well in order to make "the story" seem more real, Jill exceeds her peers in trying to account for what transpires in the tale told by the narrator. Given this, her response illustrates the difficulty of rewriting the narrative to account for how the three-day game of make believe came to an end if there was no man in the well to address each child by name. Are we to imagine that Aaron or Arthur called out in the voice of the man in the well? Or did each child voice the man in turn? Though Jill begins by stating that monotony brought the story they were playacting to an end, she then states that it ended when the children came to feel exposed and vulnerable to the man—that is, threatened rather than bored. We are left to wonder how Wendy, in speaking Aaron's name, "managed to expose each and every one" of the children and "make them vulnerable" to the man if he did not exist.

Moreover, we are left to wonder what this construal of the story means in terms of its telling. If the man in the well was, in the words of one student, "something of a group hallucination or simply a child's game of pretend," why has the narrator chosen to recount the story as if the man were real? Why is the man given dialogue, and why does the narrator refer to the sounds of the man coughing, smacking his lips, and moving around in the well? And why has author Ira Sher, in writing the short story, not made it clear that there was no man in the well, that he was only a made-up figure in the children's game of pretend? That these questions go unasked in student responses is not surprising, given the proclivity of readers to overlook the text. To answer them is to turn one's attention from the story one makes for oneself to the text composed by the author and shared by all readers of "The Man in the Well."

FAULTY REASONING

In describing some of my students' responses as misreadings, I do not mean to suggest that these reveal errors in how students have *read* the short story. Rather, I attribute their misreadings to errors they make as *writers* presenting claims to support particular understandings of the story—errors that may include a failure to reread the text while writing on it. Rereading is our best guard against excess under- and overreading, which give rise to misreading only to the extent that they result in interpretative claims based in faulty reasoning.

In *Classical Rhetoric for the Modern Student,* Edward P. J. Corbett explains that fallacies of reasoning occur when "conclusions or generalizations . . . 'do not follow' from the premises. A logical fallacy is, at bottom, an instance of incoherence—the chain of reasoning does not link together" (73). To illustrate such an instance, I will return to Langston's response, "The Perils of Obedience," where he makes the following argument:

> Children have a natural inclination to help others in need.
> The children did not help the man in the well.
> Therefore, the oldest child made the other children act against their nature.

This argument begins with a faulty premise, a proposition lacking evidence, and ends with a non sequitur, a conclusion that does not follow from the premises. Moreover, this premise requires Langston to explain why, if children have a natural inclination to help others in need, the oldest child should prove an exception. His answer, that Aaron is cruel because of "how he was raised," leads Langston to stray from his opening proposition to the notion that children's moral behavior owes less to "natural inclination" than to socialization. Kids, he writes, are "open to be molded into whatever kind of person you want to teach them to be."

For another example, let us turn to "A Well of Problems," where Melanie argues:

> The children are afraid to let the man know their names.
> The children feel no remorse or guilt for letting the man die.
> Therefore, the children were abused by the man in the past.

That the premises in this causal chain do not "link together" with the conclusion is most apparent when a paragraph from Melanie's response is rewritten as a logical argument. Using Corbett's terms, I can describe her argument (and Langston's as well) as a faulty causal generalization, given that it "fail[s] to establish that a potential cause of an effect could and did operate in a particular situation" (77), though this seems a belabored way of stating that she invents a cause for the children's actions that has no basis in the text.

Rewriting our interpretations of "The Man in the Well" as a series of logical arguments can be a worthwhile exercise, as it helps us recognize and evaluate our claims and the bases on which we make them. Moreover, it emphasizes something about the genre of literary analysis that teachers take for granted but students may not realize fully: namely, that writing an interpretation involves using evidentiary reasoning to construct cogent arguments, that these arguments concern how and what a text means, and that the free play of the reader's imagination becomes an obstruction when it finds expression in claims of cause-and-effect that defy reason. That said, examining a literary interpretation as a series of logical arguments takes us only so far, because, in reflecting on our own and others' interpretations of "The Man in the Well," we need to do more than note where a writer's reasoning fails. If we want our understanding of a literary text to exceed the reach of our own well-reasoned arguments, if we want to probe aspects of the text that continue to confuse or escape us, we need to explore what seemingly *un*reasonable responses might indicate about the short story.

I invariably encounter such responses when discussing "The Man in the Well" with students and, in one case, with colleagues, professors in other departments at my university who suggested that there was no man in the well, that perhaps the man was dangerous, and that the children might have been too young to realize that what they were doing was wrong. Nearly three decades ago, Peter J. Rabinowitz observed that persistent misreadings, ones that are "widespread rather than idiosyncratic," usually originate "not in the readers as individuals, but in the culture that has taught them to read" (*Before* 193). This being the case, it is not enough to note ways in which interpretations of "The Man in the Well" are undermined by faulty reasoning. The fact that so many readers of the short story misconstrue it in particular, recurring ways suggests some kind of cultural logic at work.

RISK-AVERSE READING

In focusing on Langston's treatment of Aaron in his rewriting of "The Man in the Well," I have neglected a noteworthy aspect of his response that shows him addressing the children's behavior in more astute terms. Even as he blames Aaron for the children's actions, Langston recognizes that the children "knew what they were doing was wrong" and "had to in some way justify it to themselves," making their wrongdoing feel right. This they did, he writes, by "dehumanizing" the man in the well, making him seem "not real." Now, as we have seen, not only the children in the story took up this strategy; many of its readers have likewise dehumanized or derealized the man in their written responses. Why should Langston, having observed the children's efforts to mitigate their guilt, choose to join them in this effort? Why should so many students work to make the immorality of the children's actions seem "not real," to the point of proposing that the man was a bogey or that there was no man in the well?

An answer is suggested by a student whose response, unlike most, describes what she experienced while reading the short story. Morgan writes:

> "The Man in the Well" is very different from stories I have read before. Within the first paragraph I assumed the story was going to be about children rescuing a man who had fallen in the well and the story would be predictable. But the next sentence states, "I think it's important that we decided not to help him." I was thrown completely off guard; there was no supporting evidence in the beginning as to why they wouldn't help the man, only that they were not going to help him. . . .
>
> I consider these kids to be mean and rude to leave this man stranded, thinking that help is on the way. It made me angry thinking why they were lying to him; it seemed like they wanted to have full control over him and his fate.

Faced with these mean and rude children, Morgan found the short story "very confusing to read because it challenged what is right and morally correct." Faced with the children's abandonment of the man at the story's close, she questioned whether they were even capable of such behavior. "It made me wonder whether or not he even existed or if he was just their imagination," she writes. In a follow-up paper, Melanie comments, "A small part of me believed that he was real and I was just in shock [as] to how these children treated him. It was repulsive to think that they would rather have him die than help him live." Her reflections suggest that readers may tell themselves that the man was a figment of the children's imaginations in order to quell such unsettling feelings.

This will work, however, only if one overlooks questions posed by the children's game of make-believe. "Looking back," writes Morgan, "I can't justify the imaginary man theory that I had; why would these children be so corrupt [as] to make such a game?" The supposition that the man in the well was a made-up figure raises the question of why the children should want to play a game in which they refuse to help a stranger in dire need of their assistance, just as the supposition that Aaron led the children to misbehave raises the question of why, if not all the children, this one boy should want to deny the man help. That these questions are not asked, or are answered rather unconvincingly through hasty generalizations, suggests some avoidance on the part of those interpreting the short story.

My point, in short, is that many instances of misreading may result from efforts to avoid what Donna Qualley calls *risky reading*: an engagement with texts that occurs when readers question "the kinds of preunderstandings they bring to a text" and "ope[n] themselves to the multiple and contrasting perspectives of others" (*Turns* 65, 62). When one engages in risky reading, she writes, "one's own beliefs and assumptions are disclosed, and may themselves become the object of interpretation, critique, and even metamorphosis. It is this *risk* of alteration to one's views of the world that makes this kind of reading dangerous, but also valuable" (*Turns* 61). For Qualley, this risk is valuable because, for learning to occur, we need to modify or move beyond "what's in our head" to attain "a more complicated understanding" (*Turns* 62). Though the sorts of texts she has in mind are essays, works of fiction also present readers with ideas and scenarios that are foreign to their thinking, ideas such as that ordinary children may commit immoral acts.

Prior to reading my students' responses, I believed that because "The Man in the Well" challenges readers' conventional assumptions, an earnest response to it would necessarily result in risky reading. I found instead that many of my students engage in risk-averse reading, responding to the short story in ways that deny what makes it, in Morgan's apt words, "confusing to read"—namely, the story's refusal to distinguish "what is right and morally correct."

As Qualley notes, risky reading may involve examining one's "uncritical acceptance of the culture's ready-made beliefs" (*Turns* 62). One ready-made belief that readers may bring to Sher's story is *the belief in a just world*. Melvin J. Lerner defines this widely held belief as an orientation to one's environment based in the assumption that events, even tragic ones, "occur for good, understandable reasons" (vii). Because a just world is one in which "people get what they deserve," Lerner remarks, "people not only populate their world with good and bad characters, they also become emotionally invested in the scenarios, to the point where they need to see the good prevail and only the bad suffer" (14–15). He notes that this applies to fictional events no less than real ones, such that audiences want the fates of fictional characters to be just or deserved. "People are not upset, in fact they may feel quite good, if the villain, someone who deserves to suffer, is punished," he writes. "But if an innocent person suffers, then the 'sense of injustice' is aroused" (15).

Lerner writes that people faced with the suffering of an innocent person may employ mechanisms to reduce "the distress associated with witnessing an injustice," mechanisms that involve acts of interpretation (20). These include reinterpreting the outcome so that "the victim's fate is seen as rather desirable" (20); reinterpreting the cause so as to "attribute the victim's fate to something he did or failed to do" (21); and reinterpreting the character of the victim "either to eliminate our awareness of his suffering, or to persuade ourselves that he is not really suffering at all, or that he is the kind of person who brings suffering upon himself, or that he is somewhat less than human" (6). I observe these mechanisms at work in student responses that interpret the man in the well as a child abuser or a criminal, that fault him for how he interacts with the children, and that remove him from the scenario by positing that he did not exist, not really. I believe that these interpretations are occasioned by risk-averse reading, just as I believe "The Man in the Well" is a short story that disrupts the belief in a just world.

RISKY WRITING

Though I presume that risk-averse reading underlies those student responses I take to be misreadings, in looking more closely at these texts I find a countervailing element that complicates these writers' aversion to risky reading—a quality that can be described in terms of risky writing. David Bartholomae remarks of student writers, "It is very hard for them to take on the role—the voice, the persona—of an authority whose authority is rooted in scholarship, analysis, or research" (62). Doing so requires them to "dare to speak [a specialized language] or to carry off the bluff, since speaking and writing will most certainly be required long before the skill is 'learned'" (61). Students engage in risky writing by daring to perform as literary scholars, adopting the language of literary analysis as best they can. And it occurs as well when students, who may well assume that speaking as a literary scholar involves arguing a single "thesis" concerning a text's meaning, risk their perceived authority by allowing themselves to voice their uncertainty and posit or gesture toward other interpretive possibilities.

In addressing my students' responses in this chapter, I have rewritten them in ways that are simplifying, drawing from each a story the student writer tells about "The Man in the Well." In some cases, I have done so at the cost of recognizing moments in student texts that complicate or run counter to these stories that, in one way or another, excuse the children's actions. For example, I have discussed how Langston's response, "The Perils of Obedience," shifts all blame for the children's actions onto Aaron, but this is not true of an interesting passage in which he writes that the children, knowing they were doing wrong, sought to justify their actions:

> I think they justified their actions ... by dehumanizing the man in the well as just a faceless stranger, a voice from the dark. This is [made] evident by the fact that the kids were horrified when the man knew their names because ... it made him closer to them as a real person. Paradoxically, the same human nature that wanted to suppress the man in the well as not real was also naturally curious of who he was, which resulted in treating him somewhat humanely.

This intriguing passage readily brings to mind Lerner's writings on the mechanisms people use to reduce the distress they feel as witnesses to another's suffering. It marks a moment in the text where the writer enters into riskier territory than that marked by the more familiar theme of the troubled kid who leads his otherwise good-natured friends to participate in wrongful behavior—a moment that deserves to be developed through further writing. Thus while "The Perils of Obedience" falls short if it is taken to represent the sum total of Langston's reading and thinking about "The Man in the Well," it holds substantial promise if taken as the first draft of this writer's engagement with the story.

The hint of another such moment appears in Betty's response, "Kids Will Be Kids," where she writes of the children: "They wanted to play with the man's head and thoughts to have control." This sentence identifies a motive for the children's treatment of the man that is otherwise not addressed, given the emphasis placed on the children's innocence and immaturity and their desire for excitement and fun. Betty might have truly engaged in risky writing had I pressed her to develop this aspect of her response touching on the children's desire to exert control over an adult figure.

Perhaps the most notable instance of risky writing occurs in Melanie's response, "A Well of Problems," as it is here that a student writer's effort to come to an understanding of the short story by writing about it is most apparent. The paper presents a line of thinking that developed only after Melanie completed her first reading of "The Man in the Well," in response to her "initial reaction" to the short story. As the verb tense switches from past ("I generated the idea") to present ("the only thing I can assume is"), Melanie appears to switch from recounting how she interpreted the short story to working out an interpretation in the course of writing about it. She concludes by mentioning "something else [she] had considered," an interpretive possibility that could not be foreseen at the start her paper: namely, that "the narrator retreats to the man in the well in his mind to escape the feelings he has towards his father for abusing him."

One can argue that Melanie is overreading—for what in the text indicates that, as a child, the narrator was abused by his father?—and leave it at that. But in doing so, one would miss her important insight that all we know of the man in the well and the children who discovered him is conveyed to us by the narrator—and we need not take the story he tells literally. Melanie's insight that "the man in the well can represent a literal existence, a metaphor for feeling trapped, or a combination of the two" goes still further in recognizing the metaphorical character of literary writing. In the course of composing her thoughts on "The Man in the Well," Melanie concludes not with a single coherent interpretation of the short story, but with the realization that the man does not need to be a make-believe figure in order to serve as a metaphor for what the narrator experienced at home in his family. By leading readers to see that the man can exist both as an as-if-real character and as a symbol for some meaning, her response opens up new interpretive possibilities.

Much as Richards refers to "wild interpretations" as dangers to be avoided (*Practical* 315), so Rosenblatt writes of "interpretations that are to be rejected" for their inadequacies (268). Certainly some interpretive claims are simply misinformed; I think, for instance, of a student who writes,

"The story is written in the first person, and therefore the reader is expected to assume that the one talking is the author, Ira Sher." I do reject this move of equating a first-person narrator with the author of a work of fiction, and no doubt there are many other interpretive moves I would regard as missteps to be avoided. But this is not to say that all such missteps are without merit or interest. Indeed, we can learn more by studying many of the interpretations we take to be misreadings than by dismissing them as failed attempts at reading literature. Like Rosenblatt, I refer to the text when formulating my own interpretations and assessing those of other writers; but, unlike her, I do not regard it as an objective measuring instrument. As Alison Lee observes, although some interpretations "appear to be 'better' than others because they legitimate themselves through close reference to evidence 'in' the text," what constitutes "the text" is not a given: "References to textual evidence to justify a reading are always made within a particular context, which allows a foregrounding of some elements of the text and a suppressing or overlooking of other elements" (101). In other words, what is cited and recognized as "the text" necessarily involves some measure of overreading and underreading.

Reversing Rosenblatt's statement that the text is our means of avoiding arbitrary and irrelevant interpretations, I want to suggest that seemingly arbitrary and irrelevant interpretations can draw our attention from commonly foregrounded elements to repeatedly overlooked ones. Misreadings, in other words, can promote risky reading. This is not to say that an interpretation that challenges commonly held beliefs is more compelling than a competing interpretation on that basis alone. Moreover, even the riskiest of readings, when embraced as a successful interpretation of a text, risks becoming a ready-made conclusion, a preunderstanding brought to bear on the text, a set of beliefs and assumptions no longer subject to "interpretation, critique, and . . . metamorphosis" (Qualley, *Turns* 61). Misreadings can serve to disrupt such interpretive stasis.

In teaching "The Man in the Well," I have worried that my interpretation has become a kind of preunderstanding that I bring to my readings of the short story as well as my students' papers. Aware that teachers as well as students may read in risk-averse ways, Qualley writes that she periodically rereads student papers that evoke strong, sometimes negative responses in her. "Because I am consciously seeking to identify and examine my own preconceptions and prejudices," she writes, "I am more likely to remain open to [such] papers" (*Turns* 92). I have similarly sought to reflect critically on my reading and teaching practices by being more attentive to student responses that strike me as misreadings. Before turning to my own interpretation of Sher's short story in the next chapter, I will close this chapter by discussing the student response that I have long regarded as an exemplary misreading of Sher's story, and my belated exchange with its author.

ONE STUDENT WRITING

Krista's Response: "The Great Depression"

I feel the children's actions can be directly related to the time period. Based on clues obtained from the story, I believe the time it took place was during the Great Depression.

The narrator begins the story by telling us "I was nine when I discovered the man in the well in an abandoned farm-lot near my home." This is the first clue that tells us that this could be taking place in a poor era, or a poor neighborhood. . . . Why isn't [the farm-lot] used for farming anymore? I believe it . . . was abandoned when either the farmer ran out of money, or the land was part of the Dust Bowl during the Great Depression, therefore incapable of being farmed. Another clue that points to the story being set in the Dust Bowl is the way the man in the well continues to ask if it is going to rain. . . . The man in the well also coughs a lot which can be the result of being in the Dust Bowl. The theater is also a clue to the time period. . . . Going to the movies was a common activity during the time of the Great Depression because it was the only place in town with air conditioning.

I also believe that the state of the mother proves that this story took place during the Great Depression. The child tells us, "My mother was very upset with something at the time." The mother is very likely upset about the financial state of the family or the country as a whole. Directly after he tells us that his mother is upset, he goes on to say, "There was a feeling to those days, months actually, that I can't describe without resorting to the man in the well, as if through a great whispering, like a gathering of clouds, or the long sound, the turbulent wreck of the ocean." This implies the feelings that may have been felt during this time. The author refers to the "gathering clouds" which can mean a darker period, or a sad time. Also the "turbulent wreck of the ocean" may refer to the stock market crash, or the chaos and panic developed from the Great Depression. . . .

I also believe the previous quote explains how the Great Depression shaped the children's actions. He tells us that he cannot explain the emotion of the time without referring to the man in the well. The man was desperate, as were people living during that time. The children themselves may have been so desperate that they did not feel the need to rescue him. They may have been concerned with their own well-being and did not want to worry about another person. They did have some heart and provided him with little food but they did not want to take on the full responsibility of saving and taking care of him when they knew their own families were struggling.

The children were cruel to the man in the well because they lived during a cruel period. The anger and stress that was derived from the struggle of their families was taken out on the man in the well. It was not an intentional cruelty but one that was derived from the negative feelings and emotions associated with the Great Depression.

AN EXEMPLARY MISREADING

While working on this book, I would sometimes discuss it with colleagues who questioned whether any literary interpretation can truly be wrong—a misreading rather than a variant reading. Krista's response paper on "The Man in the Well" was invariably the one I would offer as a clear case of misreading. It was among the first I received when I began teaching the short story, and I remember feeling bewildered by it. On what possible basis could a student contend that this story is set in the drought and dust storm–ravaged Great Plains of the 1930s? Another student writes, "I do wish there was some sort of time reference. Was this a contemporary story? Or set in the 1800s? Because at first I thought maybe the man was a black man, and that's why they weren't helping him. Then I realized they never really do see what he looks like." Whereas this student rejects her initial thought, Krista does not question her notion that the story is set in the Dust Bowl although nothing in the text affirms it. There is no mention of the dust storms that devastated farmsteads and homes, ruining crops and displacing thousands of farm families, nor is there mention of economic hardship of any kind. Thus I contend that the "The Great Depression" is an unequivocal, clear case of misreading due to overreading.

Rereading Krista's paper now, I see that she evokes the Dust Bowl in response to two words that appear in the story's first sentence: "abandoned farm-lot." I imagine most readers will not dwell on these words, although, when one thinks of it, much can be made of them. For instance, one may infer that the children were at play outdoors in a relatively large rural space that, being uninhabited, left them unsupervised. Further, one might imagine that the extremely minimal description of the story's main setting establishes it as a site of abandonment, and so foreshadows the children's forsaking of the man and moral responsibility. Read symbolically another way, the loss of once-fertile farmland might suggest the lost power or virility of the man trapped in the barren well. The two-word descriptor also describes a place that, once part of the adult world, now existed within the secret world of children's play.

While the words "abandoned farm-lot" are rich in potential meaning, they also withhold meaning. For Krista, the words constitute a substantial gap that requires filling. Why was the farm-lot abandoned and no longer used for farming? To my mind, this is a inessential question, no more answerable in certain terms than it is relevant to the story's meaning. But the question loomed large for Krista, and I assume for this reason: she believed the answer could provide her with a key to understanding the children's actions. She considers two possible answers: either "the farmer ran out of money" and had to leave his farm, or "the land was part of the Dust Bowl," and the farmer numbered among the thousands of migrants who moved west in a desperate search for work during the Great Depression, leaving behind millions of acres of barren farmland. Certainly there are a great many reasons why farmland might be abandoned, but even the one alternative Krista offers to the Dust Bowl explanation is no sooner mentioned than set aside.

Though Krista turns to textual details to support her interpretation, such as the children's theater-going and the mother's weeping, these details are not, as she would have it, clues that point to the Dust Bowl setting, but rather material that can be made to fit that prescriptive reading. For instance, she attributes the man's frequent coughing to Dust Bowl conditions rather than to his being trapped in the well for days without water, although none of the children cough and there is no reference to the dry, windblown soil—to the presence of "dusters"—that marked such conditions. Overreading a few details and underreading others (such as that "the sky was clear"), Krista's rewriting of the short story presents her belief that it is set in "the Dust Bowl during the Great Depression" without questioning the basis of that belief and her investment in adhering to it to the exclusion of other ways of experiencing and interpreting the text.

Unfortunately, I did not ask Krista to engage in such questioning when she was my student. As her written response to "The Man in the Well" became my go-to example of misreading, however, I increasingly wondered how she had come to situate the short story in the Dust Bowl until one day, four years after receiving her paper, I decided to ask her. I found Krista, who had since graduated college, on Facebook, and wrote her to ask if she remembered her response to Sher's short story. If so, could she explain how she had concluded that the story of the children finding the man in the well was set in the Dust Bowl? At first I received no reply and assumed that my former student's interest in returning to her past work and reflecting on it was negligible. Not long after, however, I received a detailed reply that was so intelligent, thoughtfully written, and generously offered that I felt humbled for having regarded her Dust Bowl interpretation with some derision.

RETURN TO THE DUST BOWL

Krista's explanation begins not with the short story, but with an account of how she reads fiction: "I've always had an active imagination which has caused me to draw elaborate conclusions from the smallest pieces of information." She explains that on the basis of "a few words, a sentence, or a tone," her mind will "create the entire visual world in which the story takes place" and maintain it unless something in the text directly opposes the world she has imagined. "My job is to visualize things," states Krista, who recently started her own graphic design studio. "And because I have been a visual person all my life, and have refined my skills to do it as an adult profession, my mind can create a visual environment, I suspect, faster and more elaborately than the average person, who may not visualize information on such a regular and detailed basis." She proposes that her visual nature may lead her to picture a storyworld too hastily, rushing to conclusions on the basis of what she encounters in a text's opening sentences. "And," she adds, "if I am not told or shown otherwise by the author, my mind will continue to elaborate on this vision, whether it is accurate or not."

Reflecting on her response to the short story led Krista to recall that although she was "typically an average or above average student" in elementary school, she routinely performed poorly on reading comprehension exercises. "Was it because I would draw elaborate conclusions about the stories we read even at that age?" she asks. "Was it because my mind was off creating its own worlds, instead of creating the world the author was trying to communicate?" In describing how she has long read fiction, Krista identifies a practice of visualization that receives no mention in the response paper she wrote on "The Man in the Well," despite its centrality to how she experiences literature. Why? Academic conventions concerning literary interpretations or "readings" very rarely acknowledge this aspect of the reading process or treat imagining as having a significant bearing on how readers make meaning of literary texts. In an essay on the mental pictures formed by readers, Ellen J. Esrock explains why this is so: the most influential literary theories in the latter half of the twentieth century "posited an exclusively linguistically oriented reader," a reader who "functions only as an interpreter of linguistic meaning" and not as a creator of mental imagery (153). The reason for this, she writes, is that "literary scholars from the time of I. A. Richards onward" have been influenced by a linguistic turn in Western philosophy, a movement away from privileging the visual and toward "valoriz[ing] language as the medium of thought and the means by which we construct our worlds" (153).

Put simply, a belief in seeing as the primary means of knowing was superseded by the idea that we know not by seeing but by having language with which to comprehend what we see. Writing may be the clearest example of this, as you need to know the language in which I am writing in order to see the markings you are now reading as meaningful words forming an intelligible sentence. Or, if seeing is knowing, it is only language that enables us to see (as in, "I see what you mean"). And because language is a human creation, the meaning of what we see is something we construct rather than an essential attribute of things seen. Applied to literary reading, this idea suggests that meaning does not reside in what we see with our eyes—the written marks that constitute the text—but in what we make by giving them meaning as words, sentences, stories. No doubt, my own thinking belongs to the tradition identified by Esrock. Yet, influenced by Krista, I am also interested in recovering what this tradition obscures by recognizing the part mental imagery plays in interpretive reading. Recognizing this dimension of reading takes effort, as it is counterintuitive for literary scholars and students working within a linguicentric tradition to reflect on the mental images they form as readers.

Moreover, mental imagery is more complicated than Esrock's consideration of "the reader's creation of visual imagery" might suggest (153). Writing fifteen years after Esrock, and informed by the "imagery debate" among philosophers and psychologists over the nature and substance of mental images, Emily T. Troscianko contends that we misrepresent imaginative experience when we describe it in terms of seeing, visualizing, or picturing. In her 2013 essay "Reading Imaginatively," she remarks that "although individual differences in people's imaginative capacities mean that some people may imagine in what feels like pictorial detail" (186), this feeling is deceptive: if asked to specify details, a reader will realize how very little she or he has truly "pictured." Troscianko holds that our mental images are what philosophers call *inexplicitly noncommittal,* meaning that they lack both pictorial detail and any indication that this detail is missing.

Taking an example from Troscianko, let us imagine we have read about a black cat. Were its paws black or white? If the cat's paws were not described or otherwise made relevant by the text, then "there will never be a fact of the matter about whether [our] 'image' contained white paws or not; they neither were nor weren't white (or any other colour)" (Troscianko 186). Nor were they conspicuously absent (we did not imagine a cat with stumps instead of paws); rather, this aspect of the cat remains indeterminate. Now, given that one would expect a picture of a cat to show its paws, whereas "a linguistic description of a cat has complete freedom not to specify the colour of the paws" or depict them in any way (Troscianko 187), we may conclude that the imagined cat is less visual than linguistic after all. "Language shares with the imagination this capacity to be inexplicitly noncommittal," writes Troscianko (187). I want to propose that, like our image of the cat, our realization of a literary text remains inexplicitly noncommittal to a significant degree, and that, in its indeterminacy, the story we imagine or "picture in our head" is more like the text than a film adaptation of it.

This is why, as Iser remarks in his 1978 study *The Act of Reading*, "the spontaneous reaction is one of disappointment" when we watch the film version of a literary text we have read: "the film is optical and presents a given object, whereas the imagination remains unfettered. Objects, unlike imaginings, are highly determinate, and it is this determinacy which makes us feel disappointed" (138). Iser provides this example:

> If, for instance, I see the film of *Tom Jones,* and try to summon up my past images of the character, they will seem strangely diffuse, but this impression will not necessarily make me prefer the optical picture. If I ask whether my imaginary Tom Jones was big or small, blue-eyed or dark-haired, the optical poverty of my image will become all too evident, but it is precisely this openness that will make me resent the determinacy of the film version. Our mental images do not serve to make the characters physically visible; their optical poverty is an indication of the fact that they illuminate the character, not as an object, but as a bearer of meaning. (*Act* 138)

Troscianko restates this last, important point thirty-five years after Iser as follows: "Mental imagery, as opposed to pictures, seems to contain its interpretation within it" (184). To wit, Iser's image of Tom Jones is not descriptive of his appearance but interpretive of his character. Still, Iser's main problem with the film is not that it interprets *Tom Jones* differently than he does, but that it all too determinant, too definitive in its rewriting of the novel. The same may be said of any so-called single right interpretation of a literary text. The more it advances a particular "reading," the less likely it is to acknowledge the text's indeterminacy, the degree to which the narrative is explicitly and inexplicitly noncommittal.

Returning to Krista, I wonder if she forms particularly vivid mental images as a reader or if, being a highly visual person, she is more apt to describe her mental images in pictorially vivid terms. In either case, she found "The Man in the Well" to be too indeterminate. Feeling that Sher's short story did not provide her with "the descriptions needed to build the world based on the author's vision," Krista drew upon what she calls "previously created imagery" to imagine its storyworld, recalling two works of fiction that are commonly assigned to young students: Harper Lee's *To Kill a Mockingbird* and Karen Hesse's *Out of the Dust*. Why these two books, which are set, respectively, in Alabama during the Great Depression and in the Oklahoma Dust Bowl? "Maybe it was the voice or tone that somehow made that connection for me," she writes. "I am really unsure about this.... I do not know why my mind landed on the image of the Great Depression in the Dust Bowl instead of any other pre-created world stored in my mind." Here as elsewhere in telling the story of how she arrived at her Dust Bowl interpretation, Krista expresses uncertainty. Being self-aware of what one's mind is doing while one reads a work of literature is difficult enough; writing an account of how one interpreted a story read days, months, or years ago necessarily involves as much supposition as recollection.

The process by which one arrived at a certain literary interpretation is difficult if not impossible to retrace; moreover, one may continue to revise one's conception of a work, on an unconscious level, long after reading and writing on it. For instance, Krista writes, "When thinking back on 'The Man in the Well' the main character in my head is a girl." Why is this, given that the narrator-protagonist's sex is unspecified in the text? Krista proposes that here too her reading was influenced by *To Kill a Mockingbird* and *Out of the Dust*, as the character narrator in both novels is a girl. This struck me as a likely explanation, until I reread Krista's response paper and found that there she refers to the main character as "the child," "the author," and "he." It would appear that Krista imagined the character narrator as a girl only after writing her response paper and discussing "The Man in the Well" with other students in class.

Notably, Krista identifies Lee's and Hesse's novels, both of which she read for school, as books that she "relatively enjoyed" despite her disinterest in reading at the time she encountered them. She recalls the particular effort she put into visualizing the Dust Bowl when reading *Out of the Dust*, commenting that perhaps her effort "made this particular environment stand out more" than others she had created as a reader of literature. And yet, in looking at Hesse's book, a verse novel in the form of diary-like poems written by Billie Jo, a fourteen-year-old girl, I find descriptions of an environment bearing little resemblance to that of Sher's story. In one instance, Billie Jo writes of an abandoned farm: "Everywhere I looked were dunes of rippled dust. / The wind roared like fire. / The door to the house hung open and there was / dust inside / several feet deep" (64). A world of difference lies between this landscape and the old farm-lot where a group of children were at play. Had the story of the man in the well been set in the Dust Bowl, I imagine that the man would have feared above all drowning in several feet of dust.

Reading literature involves filling gaps through overreading in ways that consciously and unconsciously make use of a reader's familiarity with other texts. That Krista supplemented the story of the man in the well with "previously created imagery" related to the Great Depression is not in itself problematic; the problem arises when, claiming that "the Great Depression shaped the children's actions," she treats this borrowed imagery as a plot element or bearer of meaning. Krista misreads due to faulty reasoning that allows her to consider imagery created through intertextual association as a causal factor. Granting what she has imaginatively added to the story the status of textual evidence, she cites economic and environmental conditions to explain character motivation. While finding that they acted cruelly and mistreated the man, Krista excuses the children by portraying them as victims of "a cruel period" who never intended to act in callous and hurtful ways but were driven to do so by the harsh conditions in which they lived. In effect, it was not the children who acted cruelly, but the Great Depression that acted cruelly through them.

The implication is that under normal conditions the children would not have treated the man so mercilessly, but surely would have saved him. However, this is arguably the very opposite of what the short story suggests; for Krista can only make her case that extreme circumstances determined the children's behavior by adding to the text the very circumstances she treats as decisive. In this way, she overreads the short story as many students do, "filling in" factors to make the case that the children were acting against character, if not against their very nature as young innocents. In reflecting years later on her response to the short story, Krista is perceptive in addressing how mental imagery based in intertextual associations appears to have shaped it, but without considering the possibility that these associations may have been motivated by a wish to provide a context that would explain away the most troubling implications of the children's behavior. When I suggested as much in a follow-up email, she replied, "I have worked with a lot with children on a volunteer basis, and I have to believe that children are inherently good. I was likely searching for an excuse for the children."

If on the one hand my belated dialogue with Krista confirms my evaluation of her interpretation as a misreading, on the other it makes evident how much of her reading and thinking process I did not and could not consider when evaluating what she had written, although I regarded her response paper as a sufficient-enough indicator of both. When teachers of literature reflect on how much rereading, revising, research, and teaching shapes the literary interpretations they present in their scholarship and to students in class, it should hardly surprise them that many students' interpretations of a challenging literary text—typically written after a single reading of that text—appear to be misreadings. Indeed, teachers might recognize the folly of expecting students to produce perceptive interpretations on a first reading. Some more experienced and advanced students will, but they too need to learn how to interpret literary texts in ways that test and develop beyond what they find on an initial reading. For students, such learning involves revisiting not only the text but also their response to the text and the responses of their classmates. For teachers, it involves taking an approach to literature that treats a first interpretation of a text like the first draft of a paper, as material to be read alongside the interpreted text, discussed or workshopped in collaboration with other writers, and developed through revision. Misreadings read in this way are not impediments to understanding but the material out of which understanding develops.

CHAPTER 2
AUTHORITIES

GO GET A LADDER, GET HELP

In the previous chapter, I drew an analogy between the man in the well and the reader of "The Man in the Well" who hopes to acquire a rope or ladder with which to rise out of unknowingness and gain the firm ground of meaningful understanding. As no such rope or ladder is freely given, the reader may opt to escape the too-dark, too-deep well by joining the children assembled above it. Still, this escape is partial at best: the children offered no answer when asked, "Why didn't you tell anyone?" and, in the growing darkness of the third day, took refuge in not having to "read each other's faces" and see their own culpability writ there. Like the children gathered around the well at nightfall, readers may feel left in the dark at the story's conclusion, uncertain as to why the children refused to "go get a ladder, get help." But whereas the children never followed the man's instruction to go tell their parents someone was in the well, perplexed readers may look to an authority figure for help, someone who "knows what to do" with this unsettling short story.

For many students, the author and the teacher are such authorities. That students equate a story's meaning with "what the author is 'trying to say'" is "natural enough," according to Appleyard: "A story after all is self-evidently the product of a writer who on the face of it would seem to be the proprietor of its meaning, especially if meaning is taken to be what a person intends to say when he or she utters or writes down words" (132). Even so, the teacher, being physically present and charged with evaluating and grading student work, has an authority in the classroom that the author lacks. Moreover, while middle school and high school teachers may claim to speak for the authors whose works they assign, teachers of college literature courses typically instruct students to look to the text rather than the author for literary meaning. That said, students know to look not only to the text but also to the teacher who will grade what they write about the text.

Thus far I have discussed my students' written responses to "The Man in the Well" that I have found to be misreadings. What, then, of those that have struck me as valid interpretations of the short story? On what basis have I, in my authority as the teacher, found that certain students' rewritings of the short story present substantially more credible explanations of the children's behavior? For an answer I will turn to the student paper that struck me as most successful when I first taught Sher's short story, the one I describe in the introduction as notably astute and closest to my own. I follow it with one written by a classmate whose quite different response to the text now strikes me as an equally impressive and thought-provoking response to the short story.

TWO STUDENTS WRITING

Isaac's Response: "Power > Compassion"

Ira Sher's short story "The Man in the Well" describes a group of children who happen upon a man trapped in a well. They are fascinated by the man and, though they are given the opportunity to save him, they decide not to. This type of behavior seems antithetical to general human values of compassion, benevolence, and hospitality, however multiple examples can be given which show that humans often do not live up to these ideals. . . .

Stanley Milgram's psychology experiments in the 1960s revealed that under certain conditions, human beings are perfectly willing to subject other individuals to high amounts of suffering without feeling remorse or sympathy. Similarly, the Stanford prison experiments of the 1970s demonstrated that human beings, once placed in a position of power and authority, were generally willing to subject individuals to adverse and humiliating conditions. Christopher Browning, in his 1993 book Ordinary Men, *argues that the German SS units which shot thousands of innocent civilians during WWII were not governed by ideology, but rather were acting under extraordinary circumstances of the variety explored in the aforementioned psychological experiments. The general trend exhibited by these studies is that human beings tend to exploit existing power dynamics to ensure personal well-being, even at the cost of another's life.*

Children generally have little personal autonomy and are dependent upon others for survival. Once the man in the well was discovered, these children found themselves with a great deal of power, namely over the fate of the unfortunate man. It is not surprising that this tremendous amount of power and responsibility would be at once perplexing and fascinating to this group of naive youngsters. Although everything else in their lives is more or less governed by their parents, the man in the well was theirs. It was their secret and as soon as they told authorities it would be taken away from them. It was a power dynamic that they, for once, could exploit.

As long as anonymity was preserved between the man and the children, so too could guilt be obfuscated. It is for this reason that the children make a point to keep their identities secret and why they suddenly felt a burden of guilt when Wendy accidentally reveals Aaron's name. As days progressed it became less and less explainable why they left the man down in the well and with their names attached to the incident they surely faced responsibility. It is much easier to walk away than carry the burden of responsibility. After all, they never returned to the well.

Robin's Response: "Interpretation is Everything"

No matter how many times I read "The Man in the Well," I always reached the end thinking, "What is going on in this (literary) world?" I could not understand why children would act in this manner, or why someone in such dire need of help would not reveal his name immediately. I reread the story looking for any kind of symbolic clues to give insight to the moral downfall of these children but found only references to the "wrecked ocean" or a carnival freak show. Both such powerful images, but I found it impossible to relate them to the story. And then I wondered, is that the point? Are these children displaying their lack of morals so that I may analyze my own? This seemed to be the only conclusion I could come to.

There was not even a hint of an answer in the story for why the children chose their course of action. They had so much nonverbal communication that they only talked to the man in the well and never among themselves, or anyone else for that matter. The only other characters that are even introduced are the parents of the main character: a crying mother and stubborn father. They seemed to parallel the man and the children, respectively, but I still found myself asking why. Why are these two parents of one of the children in the group so important to the story? On the surface they seem to leave the story unaffected, but if this is the case why are they mentioned at all? What do they bring to the story? It is obvious that the author would like the audience to think that the protagonist has a troubled home life by referencing the parents. Simply placing the lack of morality in the story on the parents seems much too simple for this story. The parents are part of a much greater symbolic meaning, and who knows what that could be. . . .

I found it very interesting that the reader is unable to tell if the protagonist is male or female, or how many other children he/she is playing with. . . . It seems like the author kept so much from the reader that simply getting the reader to fill in the details and ultimately think about their own values is the point of the story. It seems irrelevant to the author why the children acted the way they did. It is only important that they made this decision and carried out these actions so that the reader may contemplate what he/she would have done in the same situation and why. . . .

I think that trying to imagine these characters as actual children in the real world would be foolish and simply frustrating. They do not behave in ways that make any sense to me. . . .

INTERPRETIVE CERTAINTY AND UNCERTAINTY

These two students' writings represent contrasting responses to "The Man in the Well" in a number of ways. Whereas Robin addresses what the story does not tell and what the reader does not know by identifying the text's many gaps and declining to fill them, Isaac offers a particularly *knowing* response by explaining the children's actions with reference to psychological studies of human behavior. Whereas he turns to real-world analogues to explain the children's actions, Robin denies that these characters' actions would make sense "in the real world." She responds to the opaqueness of the written text; he responds to the storyworld he imagines as a reader of that text. Her response is rhetorical in the sense that it acknowledges what Phelan calls "the reader's share in the production of meaning" as well as "the textual signals" the author provides to guide the reader ("Narrative" 297), even if she finds these signals quite difficult to follow. Isaac's response, by contrast, includes no mention of the reader (the word "I," which appears so often in Robin's response, is not used by Isaac). Nor does he mention the author: ignoring the synthetic component of the narrative, he focuses exclusively on the mimetic, treating "the characters as possible people and their world as like our own" (Phelan, "Narrative" 308) and the thematic, devoting one of his paper's four paragraphs to other cases that treat the same theme. Robin emphasizes the short story's textuality, identifying symbols, images, and characters while noting the absence of an explanation for the children's actions; Isaac makes the intertextuality of his interpretation explicit, naming the book he draws upon to explain those actions. She writes of her great uncertainty; he writes with great certainty.

Though Robin poses questions whereas Isaac presents an answer, she too offers a conclusion, positing that the author does not account for the children's actions for a reason: he wants readers to ponder what they would have done if they were among the children who found the man in the well, and thus "think about their own values." In her view, readers' reflections, and not fictional characters' motives, are "the point of the story." For Isaac, the point of the story is that human beings, even children, will "exploit existing power dynamics" for selfish gain, "even at the cost of another's life." Given their contrary responses, it may come as no surprise that Isaac took issue with Robin's evaluation of the story. In an effort to promote more self-reflective and collaborative reading, I asked my students to respond to a few of their classmates' analyses on a discussion board—only to discover they were less apt to build upon each others' interpretations than to treat literary interpretation as a competition.

Objecting to Robin's assessment of what is meaningful in the story, Isaac writes that "the author did not mention much about the gender of the narrator because it is pretty irrelevant to the story," whereas the children's decision to not save the man is highly relevant. "That decision obviously carried a great deal of significance upon their life, and this was made apparent by the gravity with which the children handled the situation," he explains, equating what is significant for the characters in the story with what has significance for the reader. Isaac concludes by telling Robin that what she wrote "says more about your frustration with grasping the meaning of the story than it says anything about the story. People do, in fact, act as the children do in real life (see Stanley Milgram's psychological experiments, or the Stanford prison experiments for such examples)."

In reply, Robin writes that while she finds the two experiments interesting and disturbing, she cannot agree that they are "valid instances of people acting as the children do." She points out that whereas Milgram tested his subjects' obedience to authority by instructing them to administer electric shocks to an individual they could hear but not see, and the subjects in Philip Zimbardo's Stanford prison experiments were assigned their roles as prisoners and guards, the children in Sher's story were not "placed into the situation by someone else" but "put themselves in a position of power," disobeying rather than complying with a figure of authority. Her point is bolstered by recent findings that Milgram's and Zimbardo's subjects sensed how the experimenter wanted them to behave and acted accordingly, some playing their part in a drama they saw through (Perry 132–40; Ronson 102–8).

Both Robin and Isaac make salient points: Robin's interpretation is limited by her resistance to imagining that children could act as the children do in the story, while Isaac's is limited by his inattentiveness to how the situation of the children in the story is unlike that of the subjects participating in the two experiments. Unfortunately, they use these points to dismiss rather than explore and develop their classmate's consideration of the short story in ways that might broaden their own. Isaac would not consider how the text might be written to create uncertainty in readers, while Robin would not consider what might be gained by relating what social psychologists say about human behavior to the short story. Because they treat their responses as irreconcilable interpretations, only one of which can be correct or valid, they do not move beyond the limits of their present understandings toward a richer conception of the potential text.

Some three decades ago, Thomas Newkirk noted that literature students are taught that the purpose of critical writing is "to demonstrate a coherent reading, not to explore the possibilities of the incoherencies in a reading. The tone frequently is that of a lawyer, not a reader" (757). Whereas Isaac's response skillfully captures this tone, Robin's counters it by conveying her uncertainties as a reader and, to some extent, her thought process. Newkirk contends that literature is typically taught in a way that "obscure[s] the process of forming an interpretation" (756), because "students never see instructors confused, never see them puzzled by a particular passage, never see how an interpretation is revised in subsequent readings" (757). More recently, Sheridan Blau has commented that

> readers who have never seen anything but finished readings from their teachers and whose teachers either avoid or stigmatize textual difficulties are likely to conceive of reading much the way inexperienced writers think of writing: as something that competent students or adults do in a single pass, in one effortless draft, without struggle and without frustration.... (31)

If the teacher's authority is identified with the seeming ease and certainty with which textual meaning is determined, students are likely to reproduce this certainty in their own writing, misrepresenting their actual reading experiences by excluding mention of what confuses or frustrates them. Or, if they admit to uncertainty, they are likely to blame the puzzling text for their confusion or fault themselves for being incapable readers. In either case, uncertainty is not recognized as a valuable response in its own right, although, as Blau succinctly points out, "the student who is confused is frequently the one who understands enough to see a problem, a problem that less perceptive students have not yet noticed or arrived at" (21). Readers may be less perceptive precisely because they are beholden to interpretations that keep them from considering other possibilities, other ways of thinking about the literature we read and respond to in writing.

Newkirk and Blau advocate that teachers make the process of literary interpretation visible in the classroom by working with students to interpret a challenging text that they themselves have not already read. The point of this exercise is not to arrive, together, at a most persuasive or authoritative interpretation of the text, but rather to experience what Newkirk refers to as "the muddling that occurs when readers confront difficult texts for the first time" (757). While I cannot recall just how I experienced and made sense of "The Man in the Well" upon first hearing and then reading it several years ago, in turning now to my own interpretation of this short story I will explore how muddling persists well beyond a first-time encounter with a literary text. Indeed, muddling and confusion recur throughout the process of rereading and rewriting a text, so that the act of interpretation can rightfully be understood as an ongoing give-and-take between conjectured certainty and recurring uncertainty.

A REVERSAL CROWD

My own interpretation of "The Man in the Well" bears some resemblance to that offered by Isaac as well as several other students who discuss the short story in terms of adult-child power relations. Much as Isaac refers to how the children found the power they held "over the fate of the unfortunate man . . . at once perplexing and fascinating," another writes that although the children were afraid to disobey an "adult figure," they were intrigued by "the thought that they overpowered him and he needed their help to survive." She adds, "It is a very cruel way of thinking but the children were tired of always listening to adults, [and] they seemed to like the fact they were in charge." Another student notes the pleasure the children took in holding power over the man, writing:

> When an adult tells you to do something, you tend to obey. However, for this very reason the children decide not to find someone to help the man.

> For the first time in their young lives, the children find themselves in a rare position of power and decide to postpone finding help. Rather than obeying the voice, the children unanimously decide to take advantage of their unusual situation and have fun with the stranger before finding help.

Yet another student similarly remarks: "The children seemed to hold the power and that gave them an upper hand as well as confidence in the relationship. This is not often the case in a child's life because most things are ruled and decided by parents, teachers or other adults."

My interpretation differs from these responses in at least one significant respect: I contend that the children's actions—lying to the man, bringing him food and water, asking him "such stupid questions"—were less a confident expression *of* power than an uneasy negotiation *with* power. Little in the text suggests to me that the children exhibited much confidence or had much fun; for the most part they stood or sat on the grass or the concrete slab under the hot summer sun, gathered around the mouth of the well in silence. When they failed in their efforts to elicit answers from the man on the second day, most of the children left "to sit in the cool movie theater" in town, though all were drawn back to the well the following morning. To be sure, the children exercised power in refusing to help the man out of the well. Once they had done so, however, they were no longer comfortably in control but caught in a drama that, played out over three days, chiefly involved the children's efforts to manage their fear.

This fear accounts for the children's initial response: "At first *afraid to disobey the voice* from the man in the well, we turned around and actually began to walk toward the nearest house" (my emphasis). This statement indicates that, at least according to the narrator, the children's initial response—setting off to get help—was based neither in an ethic of justice nor in an ethic of care. In other words, they went to get help neither because moral principles dictated that this was the right course of action, nor because fellow feeling or concern for a person in need compelled them to do so. Rather, they immediately set off to "go get a ladder, get help," as instructed for fear of what might happen if they disobeyed. In subsequently deciding to disobey his instruction and not help the man, the children reacted against this fear without dispelling it. A stranger who had been trapped in a well for days called out to them for help, but it was "the voice" they feared. Their fear of disobeying this voice was based not in a reasoned consideration of the trouble they might get into should the man somehow escape the well and make it known that they had refused to help him, but in something more immediate and deep-seated: namely, a fear of defying the voice of authority.

That the disembodied "voice from the man in the well" is a voice of authority is made clear when the narrator states: "He must have known we were children, because he immediately instructed us to 'go get a ladder, get help.'" With this statement the narrator engages in a retrospective act of mind reading, construing that because the man did not appeal to his potential rescuers but rather instructed them to get help, much as a parent or teacher might instruct a child, he undoubtedly presumed they were youngsters who would do as they were told. It follows that, in deciding not to help the man, the children were reacting against being treated like children in the belittling sense of being ordered about.

Whereas Isaac, in reflecting on "The Man in the Well," recalled the book *Ordinary Men,* with its discussion of Milgram's and Zimbardo's experiments, I found myself recalling another book: Elias Canetti's 1960 study of crowd behavior, *Crowds and Power.* I thought, in particular, of this passage:

> Every command leaves behind a painful *sting* in the person who is forced to carry it out. . . . People who are habitually ordered about are full of them, and feel a strong urge to get rid of them. They can free themselves in two different ways. They can pass on to others the orders which they have received from above; but, for them to be able to do this, there must be others below them who are ready to accept their orders. Or they can try to pay back their superiors themselves what they have suffered and stored up from them. One man alone, weak and helpless as he is, will only rarely be fortunate enough to find an opportunity for this, but, if many men find themselves together in a crowd, they may jointly succeed in what was denied them singly: together they can turn on those who, till now, have given them orders. (58)

Canetti calls the group that forms to gain "collective deliverance from the stings of command" a *reversal crowd*; his examples include "revolts of slaves against their masters, of soldiers against their officers, of coloured people against the whites who have settled in their midst" (59). I thought of Canetti when contemplating Sher's story because I recognized the group of children who defy the man as another reversal crowd.

In discovering the man in the well, these children found a rare opportunity to "pay back their superiors," though they were slow to realize this: used to being "habitually ordered about," they obediently walked off toward Arthur's house when told to "go get a ladder, get help." Only along the way did it occur to them that the voice giving orders "from above" was in no position to enforce them, coming as it did from "below them." In short, for the children it was not enough that they found themselves together in a crowd; their opportunity to revolt against adult authority arose only when they jointly discovered one of their superiors "alone, weak and helpless," in the well. In defying the man, the children effectively made him a scapegoat for the parents, teachers, and other adults who habitually ordered them about.

Several of my students have explained the children's actions by referring to the opportunity that joining together provided them, though in terms that differ significantly from Canetti's reversal crowd. A student named Eugene refers to "groupthink decision-making," noting that "none of the children question the decision to neglect the man. At first we are led to believe that the children understand and acknowledge society's expectations for them to help someone in need . . . as they go for help. It is as a group that they begin to ignore this ethical standard." As originally defined by Irving Janis, *groupthink* names a mode of thinking that occurs when a highly cohesive group of people engage in faulty decision making because a desire for "concurrence-thinking" or consensus inhibits the "critical thinking" that a realistic appraisal of alternative courses of action would require (9). Given that groupthink often involves "irrational and dehumanizing actions" directed at those outside the group (13), the application of this concept to the short story is promising, but Eugene does little with groupthink beyond use it as a ready-made term to label immoral acts in which a number of otherwise moral-minded individuals take part.

Some students apply the term *peer pressure* in the same way. One writes that the children acted out of "fear of going against what your friends are doing as a group, also known as peer pressure. . . . Since the narrator said that the kids 'were on the verge of fetching a rope or finding a ladder' it shows that they did in fact think about helping the man, but did not want to go against their friends' wishes." One might argue that pressure to conform to group norms is what caused the children to start off in search of a rope or ladder, except that peer pressure seems to concern only socially unacceptable or immoral acts. At the same time, it distances the children from the immorality of these acts by suggesting that each child would have helped the man if not "pressured" to do otherwise. Yet if this was the case, who were the peers exerting pressure? Through recourse to psychological terms (groupthink, peer pressure), these students locate the desire to disobey in a phenomenon rather than in the children themselves.

A student named Ruth offers perhaps the most sophisticated version of this response. In "Victim of an Unlikely Mob," she discusses "The Man in the Well" in terms of mob mentality, contending that the story explores "how, in a group setting, individuals with typically good morals can act immoral" by showing that "even a group of average children are not immune to participating in the inhumane actions of a mob." As for what initially motivated these children to refuse the man help, Ruth provides two answers: first, they were looking for a "diversion" during the tedious days of summer, and, second, the stress the narrator was experiencing at home created in him "a need for control" that he exercised over the man. Although the children were increasingly ashamed of their decision, she writes, "an important truth about mob mentality" is that "once all members of a group decide on a course of action, rarely will an individual member have the courage to suggest it was a mistake." Because the children's "morals or even relative innocence" could not deter them from acting as a mob, "a group of individuals who are each incapable of killing a man got together and did." The value of Sher's short story, for Ruth, is its message that anyone may commit immoral acts when caught in a group dynamic.

One is left to think that any action taken by a group will be unethical—that when individuals act as a collective, moral judgment is voided. Canetti's "reversal crowd" provides an alternative conception, for here the group—whether made up on citizens turning on a king, slaves turning on a master, or children turning on an adult—acts with moral purpose. This is not to approve of the actions taken by a reversal crowd, much less those taken by the children in Sher's story, whose resentment toward adult authority could hardly justify their actions. Rather, it is to recognize that the children's actions were not determined by an absence of thought or morality. Although Ruth may be correct in stating that persons in a group, having less sense of individual responsibility, are more "more likely to act out of character," this does not mean that those in a group act without moral purpose or motivation, or that their actions are not revealing of normally suppressed aspects of character. While I would join my students in recognizing the importance of attending to the group dynamic in "The Man in the Well," I would push readers to move beyond treating the group as what, in itself, accounts for the children's interactions with the man in the well.

THE OVERSEER IN THE WELL

Much as the group of children reminded me of Canetti's reversal crowd, so the image of the man in the well led me to recall Michel Foucault's oft-cited discussion of the Panopticon in his 1975 book *Discipline and Punish*. The Panopticon, a "model" prison designed and promoted by philosopher and social reformer Jeremy Bentham in the late eighteenth century, consists of a ring-shaped building with a tower standing at its center. From the central tower an overseer can see all of the inmates, who are isolated in rows of cells ringing the tower. As each inmate is "securely confined to a cell," separated by side walls that "prevent him from coming into contact with his companions," inmates cannot see each other; and neither can they see the overseer through the central tower's veiled windows (200). Consequently, writes Foucault, "in the peripheric ring one, one is totally seen, without ever seeing; in the central tower, one sees everything without ever being seen" (202). Explicating Bentham's principles, he observes that, for maximum control, power must be visible in the form of the central tower but, given the invisibility of the overseer, unverifiable: "the inmate must never know whether he is being looked at any one moment; but he must be sure that he may always be so" (201).

For Foucault the Panopticon "reverses the principle of the dungeon" by heightening the visibility of its inmates instead of hiding them away in darkness (200). It likewise reverses the principle of modern-day overcrowded prisons, wherein inmates are not isolated but brought together. Whereas Canetti addresses how weak and helpless individuals may revolt against power when they "find themselves together in a crowd," Foucault describes how the Panopticon's design serves power precisely by disassembling the crowd and making certain its inmates never have the opportunity to join together. "The crowd, a compact mass, a locus of multiple exchanges, individualities merging together, a collective effect, is abolished and replaced by a collection of separated individualities," he writes (201). Placed in a backlit cell, each inmate is "alone, perfectly individualized and constantly visible" to the overseer, who may or may not be observing him from the central tower (200). Foucault concludes that "the major effect of the Panopticon" is "to induce in the inmate a state of conscious and permanent visibility that assures the automatic functioning of power" (201). Knowing that he may be subject to surveillance at any moment, each inmate internalizes the overseer's watchful eye, monitoring his own behavior in a way that makes the presence of an actual overseer unnecessary. The inmate disciplines himself.

Returning to "The Man in the Well," I imagine the well in the abandoned farm-lot as an inverted Panopticon: a prison in which the inmates were free to gather as a crowd and the overseer was trapped in a cell. This prison had at its center not a tall central tower that made power visible, but a well that, like the dungeon Foucault opposes to the Panopticon, functioned "to enclose, to deprive of light and to hide" (200). And yet, despite the man's imprisonment in this cell, the children regarded him as an overseer and feared him as such. Like the overseer in the central tower, the man in the well could not be seen, whereas, like the inmates in the peripheric ring, the children—even as they hid themselves in the crowd—felt constantly at risk of being seen or observed. The narrator recalls feeling that the man in the well could hear "everything" the children said, adding, "I wanted to be very quiet, so that if he heard or saw anyone, he would not notice me." Anyone but me: to be noticed by the man was to be "individualized," observed apart from the crowd; moreover, it was to see oneself through the eye of the overseer, as one guilty of disobedience and deserving of punishment.

Discovering the man in the well afforded the children an opportunity not only to come together as a reversal crowd and turn against the voice of authority but also to keep the internalized eye of the overseer at bay. So long as their "separated individualities" remained hidden from the man in the well, the children could deny their guilt. In learning their names, the man effectively abolished the crowd, replacing it with a "collection of separated" children who saw themselves and each other as they imagined their parents would see them if they knew of their misdeeds. "It was almost night then," says the narrator, "and we were spared the detail of having to see and read each other's faces." The children's decision to finalize their escape from this prison and never return to the well suggests that they never faced this "detail." The narrator's refusal to identify himself (or herself) by name or sex indicates that he (she?) is still in hiding. Even as he states, "I will never go back," the telling of this story suggests a narrator who is still running from the voice of the man in the well, still stumbling while looking back, because the call of that voice has never left him.

In sum, "The Man in the Well" presents readers with the story of a group of children who came together as a reversal crowd, turning on the man when his command left behind a painful sting that these children were not going to suffer willingly. Still, their rebellion proved to be both misdirected and ineffective because they could not triumph over an authority they had already internalized. But can we say the man was successful in countering their rebellion? He was, after all, left by the children to perish in the well. If the man succeeded, it was not in getting the children to act morally and save him, but in getting them to feel a sense of guilt. Yet if the narrator's account—which conceals as much as it reveals of this event from childhood—is any indication, even this guilt has not been adequately faced.

As such, the story challenges readers with the idea that ethical behavior is rooted not in human nature, nor in principles of justice and respect for the dignity of others, nor in caring or fellow feeling, but in fear of a punishing authority. Moreover, this fear provides a treacherous foundation for moral development because it fosters resentment. And therein lies what my rewriting of "The Man in the Well" takes to be its point: challenging the received notion of childhood innocence as well as the presumption that morality is an unqualified force for good, Sher's short story indicates that morality can be experienced as a repressive and oppressive force that provokes us to rebel, to pursue freedom through transgressive, even unethical acts—and to punish ourselves for doing so.

This interpretation closely follows what I wrote about "The Man in the Well" in an essay on teaching the short story that appeared in an academic journal in 2010. Because readers of that piece would not have the short story at hand, I provided a plot summary before turning to Canetti's conception of reversal crowds and Foucault's theorization of the Panopticon to discuss how the children, empowered as a crowd, turned on adult authority. At the time, I thought I would simplify matters by omitting from that summary an aspect of the narrative that was inessential to my analysis; consequently, my retelling of the short story included no mention of the narrator's home life. I recall a comment from Melanie's paper: "The role of the mother in the story seems to play a very large role in the explanation of events that take place, although her presence seems small." I agree, and yet I felt capable of offering an interpretation of the children's actions that wrote the character narrator's parents out of the story.

Now this strikes me as a curious decision to have made. In the essay, I remark that my interpretation of the short story is just one "reading" or realization of the text's meaning, one indebted to my readings of other texts, most clearly *Crowds and Power* and *Discipline and Punish.* I note too that my written analysis, like most scholarly analyses of literary texts, is not indicative of how I have experienced the text when reading it. Instead, it reflects how I have come to think and write about it when not reading the short story, based on having reread it, in whole and part, countless times, over a span not of weeks, nor of months, but of years. My thinking about the short story is informed as well by all I have learned from my students in the course of teaching it. Despite this, my interpretation presented in the essay and the preceding two sections of this book offers no suggestion of its composite or collaborative nature. I observe, for instance, that the unnamed narrator is not identified by sex without revealing that I overlooked this gap in the text until students drew my attention to it.

In the essay, I follow my analysis of "The Man in the Well" with the admission that "my understanding of *what* the text means and of *how* the text means is a work in progress, undergoing revision whenever I return to the short story, write on it, reflect on earlier readings" (Weissman 45). I knew this in theory but am nevertheless surprised by how greatly this point has been borne out in practice—as will be shown in the next sections, where I examine that part of the story I previously omitted, rewriting "The Man in the Well" in a way that foregrounds rather than suppresses the place of the character narrator's mother and father in the narrative.

A PECULIAR PARAGRAPH

"The Man in the Well" is organized into three sections that correspond to the three days the children gathered at the well. The events of those three days are told in the past tense by the unnamed character narrator, who was nine years old when they took place. The distanced manner in which the adult narrator recounts what he and his friends did "back then" indicates a significant amount of time has passed between those events and their narration in the present. The world in which he and his friends passed hot summer days playing outside and cooling off in the movie theater in town seems to belong to a "simpler time." While he speaks of it in a largely dispassionate manner, the story the narrator tells has an elegiac quality that reflects the loss of this simpler time, and with it the loss of childhood.

The short story's third section, in which the narrator tells of the last day he and his friends were ever to return to the well, opens with what is arguably the most peculiar paragraph in this strange and intriguing text, for in addition to breaking radically with the chronological presentation of events that has structured the narrative progression up to this point, it introduces an abrupt change of setting and two new characters. Here is the paragraph in its entirety:

> Everyone was there again on the following morning. It was all I could think about during supper the night before, and then the anticipation in the morning over breakfast. My mother was very upset with something at the time. I could hear her weeping at night in her room downstairs, and the stubborn murmur of my father. There was a feeling to those days, months actually, that I can't describe without resorting to the man in the well, as if through a great whispering, like a gathering of clouds, or the long sound, the turbulent wreck of the ocean.

Up to this point, the setting for all narrated events has been "the abandoned farm-lot," an indistinctly rendered place that exists in my imagination as a well surrounded by an expanse of rough field scarred with ruts that attest to the rows of crops it once yielded. Somewhere beyond its periphery lie houses, and with this paragraph readers are suddenly, unexpectedly, taken inside one of them, the character narrator's childhood home. This shift to the home reminds readers that the three days recounted by the narrator alternate with nights at home, even if these nights go unmentioned or are described in the most minimal terms, an elusive sentence or two.

The shift in setting also marks a shift in time: we are taken back to the night and the morning before the children were "there again" at the well. A still greater temporal shift follows when the narrator refers to "those days, months actually," unexpectedly introducing a larger period of time in which the three days recounted by the narrator may be situated. This treatment of time is quite tricky. For years when reading that "mother was very upset with something at the time," I understood that time to be the night before and the morning of the third day. I assumed that the narrator heard his mother's weeping and his father's stubborn murmur the night before he and his friends made their last trip to the well. Only in the course of writing on this paragraph has it occurred to me that "the time" mother was very upset was not limited to that night or to those three days but lasted "months actually," during which time the narrator, then a nine-year-old child, repeatedly heard his mother sobbing and his father murmuring at night. This long period of unrest at home provides the context for understanding the narrator's discovery of the man in the well.

The narrator's remark that he cannot describe the "feeling" of those months (that is, how he felt at the time) without "resorting to the man in the well" suggests that he tells the story of the man in order to describe circumstances at home that as a child he must have found frightening and confusing, and as an adult still cannot address directly. At the same time, it suggests that the fear and confusion he felt at home *then* provides the context for understanding the story he tells *now* about the man in the well. Still, just how the elusively told story of the man in the well may be understood in terms of the untold story of "those days, months actually," and vice versa, remains unclear, and the pileup of imagery that concludes the paragraph, like much of what the narrator says, serves to occlude rather than clarify matters. A great whispering, a gathering of clouds, the long sound, the wreck of the ocean: these are images to get lost in, not signs by which readers might find their bearings.

Still, much can be made of the single sentence that describes, in more palpable terms, a recurring moment from the narrator's home life: "I could hear [my mother] weeping at night in her room downstairs, and the stubborn murmur of my father." When reading the story in the past, I have envisioned the following scene: a child is awakened in the night by the muffled, disconcerting sounds that come from his parents' bedroom below: his mother's crying and his father's stern, unyielding voice. Lying in bed in the gloomy stillness, he feels he is secretly, illicitly discovering something about his mother and father that is sad and cruel, that disrupts what he had believed about them and his place in the world. Now in rereading Sher's sentence and rewriting it to render this scene, I am startled to realize how much is my own invention, my own dramatic staging—for the sentence offers no description of where the character narrator was (other than upstairs) or what he was doing or feeling when he heard his mother weeping and his father's stubborn murmur. Setting my overreading aside, I return to the words of the sentence.

While what badly upset the mother remains unsaid, the father appears implicated, and while he may not be the cause of the mother's weeping, a "stubborn murmur" hardly seems a kind or loving response. Mention of "her room," rather than *their* room, the parental bedroom, implies the parents' separation and the father's intrusion. The sentence presents not a scene but an image: the child above, listening to sounds that come from a room below, sounds that include a man's voice. This image resonates with, in some sense repeats, that of this child situated on the ground above the unseen man in the well, silently listening to sounds from below: coughing, scraping, the voice of the man calling out. This similarity signals a correspondence between the mother's room and the well, and between the father's stubborn murmur and the voice of the man.

Whereas I identify the man in the well with the character narrator's father, Robin draws a different analogy, writing in her response that the character narrator's "crying mother and stubborn father . . . seemed to parallel the man and the children, respectively." In her compelling view, the man trapped in the well, crying out for help, is like the weeping mother, while the children, steadfast in their refusal to free him, are like the stubborn father. Stopping short of identifying the man with the mother, I have imagined him as a castrated father and the well as the mother's room downstairs, but with a difference. The mother may have been trapped in her room by and with the father, but the well (dry in the absence of her tears, barren in the absence of the maternal) held the father alone. To conceive of the well in these terms is imaginatively to free the mother and punish the father. Just who is punishing the father in this way—the character narrator, by recounting past events in terms that conflate the man in the well and his father; or author Ira Sher, by writing the father into the story's subtext; or me, by overreading the place of the father in this short story—I cannot say with certainty, but I imagine we are all implicated.

A FRATERNAL CLAN

At this point, I will relate another story of children who defy an adult figure of authority, this one told by Sigmund Freud, the father of psychoanalysis, in his 1913 book *Totem and Taboo*. Freud posits that the earliest human society took the form of a horde ruled over by the primal father, a violent and jealous patriarch who kept all the females for himself and cast out his sons when they outgrew childhood. One day the expelled brothers joined together as a fraternal clan, the earliest human manifestation of what Canetti calls a reversal crowd. "United," writes Freud, "they had the courage to do and succeeded in doing what would have been impossible for them individually": they "killed and devoured their father and so made an end of the patriarchal horde" (500). The sons had hated their father for denying them power, frustrating their desires, and expelling them from the horde, but they also loved him; and overcome by guilt and remorse, they reestablished his authority by prohibiting what he had forbidden. They did so, most notably, by instituting the incest taboo, which forbid the sons from having sexual relations with the females in their horde. "The dead father became stronger than the living one had been," writes Freud, for the reason that the primal father's rules became only more entrenched once his children internalized them, enforcing his law upon themselves "out of their filial sense of guilt" (501). Like the Panopticon's overseer, the father was more powerful when his actual presence was replaced by his imagined omnipresence.

With this story, Freud roots in prehistory his Oedipal theory of parent-child relations and moral development, according to which every male child has "a wish to get rid of his father in order to take his place with his mother" (640). Overcome with fear that he will be punished with castration for desiring his mother, the male child identifies with and internalizes his father, developing a conscience or *superego*—an internalized overseer—that exercises "moral censorship" over his desires (643). A female child, by contrast, has no such fear, for she assumes she has already been castrated. Consequently, she does not internalize the authority of the father and develop a moral conscience to the extent that males do. For Freud, this explains why "critics of every epoch" have found that women "show less sense of justice than men" (677), while for Freud's critics, this shows that Oedipal theory is rooted not in prehistory but in the sexism of Freud's time.

Freud's account of the primal horde is an archetypal story that has been told and retold innumerable times. "The Man in the Well" is one such retelling, a variation in which the children play the part of the rebellious sons and the man in the well is the primal father, the dead father calling out from the grave. In his 1930 book *Civilization and Its Discontents*, Freud writes that children, as well as many adults, "habitually allow themselves to do any bad thing which promises them enjoyment, so long as they are sure that authority will not know anything about it or cannot blame them for it; they are afraid only of being found out." That is the case, at least, until "authority is internalized through the establishment of a super-ego," at which point a "great change" occurs: "the fear of being found out comes to an end; the distinction, moreover, between doing something bad and wishing to do it disappears entirely, since nothing can be hidden from the super-ego, not even thoughts" (757). The children in Sher's story were fearful precisely because while they initially regarded the unseen man as an external authority whom, given his captivity, they could defy with little to no risk of punishment, he threatened to become an internal authority from which nothing could be hidden.

The children initially obeyed the man because they heard the authority of the father in his voice, and, in returning to the well after deciding not to help him, they still had to reckon with that patriarchal authority. This authority was undercut by the man's entrapment in the womb-like space of the well, an image that connotes disempowerment as much as the phallic central tower of the Panopticon symbolizes power. But if the man was held there, his voice could not be so easily confined, and not only because his shouting made the children "afraid someone might hear." His voice threatened to become a voice in their heads they could not control. The narrator describes how the children sought to engage the man in dialogue but were unable to restrain his voice: "everyone had questions he or she wanted to ask the man in the well, but the man wouldn't stop speaking." Ignoring their questions, he repeatedly instructed them to go for help. The voice of the man in the well, like the father's murmur, was chiefly characterized by stubbornness.

Rather than follow his instructions, the children lay around the lip of the well. The narrator recounts:

> When we were quiet for a bit, he called to see if we were gone.
> After a pause, Wendy crawled right to the edge so that her hair lifted slightly in the updraft. "Is there any water down there?"
> "Have they gone for help?" he asked.
> She looked around at us, and then she called down, "Yes, they're all gone now. Isn't there any water down there?" I don't think anyone smiled at how easy it was to deceive him—this was too important.

The children might have smiled had they regarded the man as a pet or mere plaything, but they were more startled than amused to discover the ease with which patriarchal authority could be fooled. Rather than embolden them, this revelation made the children uneasy, and when the man "began calling again" they lost their nerve:

> We got up and began running, filling up with panic as we moved, until we were racing across the ruts of the old field. I kept turning, stumbling as I looked behind. Perhaps he had heard us getting up and running away from the well. Only Wendy stayed by the well for a while, watching us run as his calling grew louder and wilder, until she finally ran too, and then we were all far away.

What did the nine-year-old child imagine he might see? His need to keep looking back suggests a frantic fear that the dead father, upon hearing them flee, might rise from the grave to punish his disobedient children. In returning the next morning to drop "bread or fruit or something to eat" and a jug of water into the well, the children effectively offered a sacrifice to mollify the voice that had frightened them away.

Why did Wendy remain at the well while the other children ran off? She alone appears to have lacked the fear that caused them to run away. The narrator speaks of having never gone "very close" to the lip of the well lest the man see him, and suggests that his friends were equally careful in this regard. Wendy, however, "crawled right to the edge so that her hair lifted slightly in the updraft," again showing fearlessness—but a fearlessness indicative of ignorance rather than courage. Notably, the one other girl named by the narrator, while only briefly mentioned in the story, displays a similar quality. The narrator recounts that when the man called out "Aaron," the children were silent until, after some ten minutes, Grace called down, "What's your name?" as Arthur and little Jason had the days before. Once the man said Aaron's name, the time for playfulness was over, but Grace had no sense of this, and so, the narrator says, "someone pulled her back from the well, and we became silent again."

Like Wendy, Grace lacked the apprehension that might have kept her from moving too close to the well and from saying the wrong thing. Both characters appear to have been fashioned in the mold of the female child imagined by Freud: the girl who, having no fear of castration, acts carelessly, without regard for the fearsome power and authority of the father. Given this, perhaps it is not surprising that a girl's inclusion in the "fraternal clan" should lead to the children's undoing.

THE DEAD FATHER IN THE WELL

Let us turn now to the series of events that led to this undoing—events that, tellingly, are set off when the father is expressly named. On the morning of the second day, when the children returned to the well, the man asked them, "Did your parents get help?" Rather than answer, the children presented him with the food and water they had brought. The narrator recalls how he felt when Arthur dropped the bag into the well: "It hit the ground more quickly than I had expected; that, combined with a feeling that he could hear everything we said, made him suddenly closer, as if he might be able *to see* us. I wanted to be very quiet, so that if he *heard or saw* anyone, he would not notice me" (my emphasis). While the man at the bottom of the well could not possibly see the children, the "suddenly closer" dead father threatened to see and hear all.

It is in response to this threat that a father is first mentioned in the story. Once more the man asked the children when their parents would be coming:

> We all looked at each other, aware that he couldn't address anyone in particular. He must have understood this, because he called out in his thin, groping voice, "What are your names?"
>
> No one answered until Aaron, who was the oldest, said, "My father said he's coming, with the police. And he knows what to do." We admired Aaron very much for coming up with this, on the spot.
>
> "Are they on their way?" the man in the well asked. We could hear that he was eating.
>
> "My father said don't worry, because he's coming with the police."

Rather than name himself, Aaron (perhaps emboldened by how "thin, groping," and weakened the man sounded) replied by naming his father, who "knows what to do" and whose power and authority are reinforced by that of the police. In saying what "father said," Aaron spoke on behalf of patriarchal authority. Though the children were impressed by their friend's ploy, the illegitimate naming of the father, by a boy who was the oldest among his friends but still a child, would lead to their undoing when Wendy—who, as a girl, was still less qualified, in the patriarchal order of things, to take on the name of the father—repeated his lie at the cost of breaking the rules and giving away Aaron's name.

Wendy, less prudent for being less fearful of the man, spoke freely, whereas the narrator was silent and Aaron spoke with great deliberation.

(Can it be a coincidence that the biblical Aaron was the spokesman for his younger brother Moses and the enslaved Hebrew people?) Among the children, Aaron most understood the power of language—and thus the power of the voice from the man in the well—and accordingly spoke with much forethought and purpose. This is demonstrated not only when he named his father but also when he named the other children. When the man called out his name, Aaron first responded as the other children would after him: deeply afraid, he remained "very still" and "absolutely quiet" for some time. Only when he was addressed by the man a second time did he choose to reveal, in his "small, clear voice," the names of the other children so that he alone would not be known to the man.

The narrator recounts that he and the other children were powerless to act when Aaron said their names, starting with Arthur's, and when the man in the well repeated them:

> I could see Arthur was furious, but . . . nothing could be said or done without giving himself, his name, away; we knew the man in the well was listening for the changes in our breath, anything. . . . I remember the spasm of anger when [Aaron] said my name, and felt the man in the well soak it up—because the man in the well understood. . . .
>
> When he said my name, I felt the water clouding my eyes, and I wanted to throw stones, dirt down to crush out his voice. But we couldn't do anything, none of us did—because then he would know.

The words "water clouding my eyes" remind me of the narrator's previous mention of a "gathering of clouds" and the "turbulent wreck of the ocean," and I wonder if here the narrator is not also describing how he felt as a child hearing his mother weeping at night—if it is not a feeling of impotent rage that connects the man in the well to those upsetting months at home. As a child, might the narrator have wished to help his weeping mother and "crush out" his father's stubborn murmur? And was there nothing he could do because he was just a child, because he was afraid, because if he did or said anything his father would punish him?

The narrator indicates that the man in the well retained and repeated all the names Aaron gave him "because the man in the well understood" these were the children's names; he then states that he and the other children could not do anything other than stand very still and keep silent "because then he would know." What the man in the well "would know," what the children feared he *did* know, must have involved something other than what he already understood: namely, that Aaron had told him all of their names.

While, realistically speaking, there is little more the man could have known from hearing changes in the children's breath, the children were not thinking in rational terms. Readers must realize this for themselves, since the narrator refrains from assessing what he and the other children thought from an adult perspective; moreover, he recounts what they "knew" in such a matter-of-fact way as to make it seem reasonable—though it was not. For the children feared not the flesh-and-blood man trapped in the well but the phantasm they had made of him, a figure reminiscent of the dead father.

In Freud's account of the primal horde, the remorseful sons internalized the dead father. The children in the narrator's story sought above all to resist internalizing the dead father, to keep that authority out of their heads by consigning him to the well. Freud writes of the fraternal clan:

> After their hatred had been satisfied by their act of aggression, their love came to the fore in their remorse for the deed. *It set up the super-ego by identification with the father; it gave that agency the father's power,* as though as a punishment for the deed of aggression they had carried out against him, and it created the restrictions which were intended to prevent a repetition of the deed. (762, my emphasis)

In striving not to be heard or noticed, each child essentially sought to hide him- or herself from an externalized superego. The children's fear of what the man in the well "would know" if they "did anything" was a fear of the superego, a fear of what they might be made to know and feel about themselves. Normally nothing could be hidden from the superego, but, so long as the children could project the voice of conscience outside themselves, they could suppress their own bad conscience, their sense of guilt and need for punishment.

In my previous discussion of the short story, I similarly wrote of the children's efforts to keep the internalized eye of the overseer at bay. This similarity suggests that my Freudian interpretation is less a departure from my Canetti-Foucauldian interpretation than a rewriting of it, with the reversal crowd recast as the fraternal clan and the overseer recast as the dead father. Keeping in mind that a rewriting always diverges in form and meaning from the text it rewrites, Foucault's analysis of the Panopticon can itself be read as a rewriting of Freud's discussion of the superego, which Freud likens in one instance to a "garrison in a conquered city" that civilization sets up as an agency within the individual to watch over him (756).

This resemblance serves to remind us that while Freud may use the terms *superego* and *conscience* interchangeably, the Freudian superego is not necessarily a force for moral goodness directing the *ego*, or conscious self, to care for others and to do what is just. Rather, like the ruthless primal father, the superego may be aggressive, harsh, severe. It punishes with crippling guilt not only acts that violate social dictates but also "forbidden wishes" that are *not* acted upon (759)—and for Freud there is nothing more forbidden than the child's wish to supplant the father. Near the end of "The Man in the Well," we read: "Before we left that day, . . . [the man in the well] said, 'Why didn't you tell anyone?' He coughed. 'Didn't you want to tell anyone?' Perhaps he heard the hesitation in our breaths, but he wasn't going to help us now." In voicing these questions, the man aimed neither to help the children do the right thing, and thus help himself get out of the well, nor to find out why they did not tell anyone. No; like the harsh superego, like the vengeful dead father, the voice of the man in the well aimed to punish the children by instilling in them what Freud calls "a permanent internal unhappiness" tied to an irredeemable sense of guilt (759).

Several of my students contend that the children were able to mistreat the man only so long as they "ignored the fact that he was a human being with thoughts and feelings in need of help," as one puts it. Once they realized he was a human being, these students argue, the children could no longer face him. Carla makes this point by arguing that the children were able to deny the man his freedom because they and the man were "anonymous to each other"—until, that is, the man said Aaron's name. She writes:

> Names are the way in which people relate to each other and define themselves. The man in the well now has a piece of the humanity in the children who are holding him captive, and he forces them to consider his humanity as well. The man forces them to think about him as a human rather than a trapped toy, asking them by name, "Aaron, what do you think my name is? . . . Arthur. What do you think I look like? . . . How old do you think I am, Jason?"

Carla's interpretation is intriguing, her use of textual evidence is skillful, and her focus on the role and function of naming in the short story is perceptive. Still, she finds that "it is difficult to say why the children leave the man in the well."

My interpretation differs from Carla's and others that suggest the children came to recognize the man's humanity. I contend that neither when they refused him help nor when they were humiliated into silence did the children regard "the man" as an actual human being. Perhaps, like so many children, they were fascinated by the fact that adults—particularly one's own parents and teachers—have first names, and might even be addressed by them, and that by addressing the man as Charles or Edgar or David they might diminish his authority. Certainly, in asking the children questions, the man was throwing back at them what they had been asking him, in a reassertion of his authority. From start to finish, the children regarded the man in abstract terms as a figure of authority, a father figure who seemed both powerless and too powerful to face. But they never quite understood him as an individual, a person who existed apart from them. While in grade school, I once ran into my teacher while grocery shopping with my mother. I remember my surprise at realizing that this teacher had a life outside of school, an existence apart from the classroom, and my embarrassment—as if seeing my teacher out in the world was like seeing her naked. The children did not conceive of the man as a full-fledged human being, and for this reason were able to leave him in the well. An internal voice, a superego, a dead father cannot be killed, but one can try to run away from it, to leave it behind.

APPLYING THEORY TO LITERATURE

In his 2004 book *Why Read?*, Mark Edmundson laments the current state of literary studies, writing that in the classrooms and scholarship where literature is taught and analyzed, "one finds work that is best defined as out-and-out rewriting of the authors at hand" (38). I have been arguing that we always rewrite the literature we strive to analyze or interpret in our written work, and that we would do well to recognize this. For Edmundson, by contrast, rewriting is not inextricable from but contrary to the act of interpretation, and this because it involves "applying theory to literature" in a way that misrepresents literary works (41). To illustrate his point, he imagines a "current reading" of Charles Dickens's novel *Bleak House* that "recasts it in the terms of Foucault":

> Dickens is depicted as testifying, albeit unwillingly, to Foucault's major truths. In *Bleak House*, we are supposed to find social discipline rampant, constant surveillance, the hegemony of the police, a carceral society. Whatever elements of the novel do not cohere with this vision are discredited, or pushed to the margin of the discussion.... Thus the critic rewrites Dickens in the terms of Foucault. One effectively reads not a text by Dickens, but one by another author. Dickens's truth is replaced by the truth according to Michel Foucault ... and there the process generally ends. (38–39)

Well, this certainly sounds bad, and I cannot deny that such writing exists; in particular, it describes how students may write about literature when they first study literary theory and are assigned to "apply theory" to a text. But is this necessarily what occurs when writers draw on theoretical terms, concepts, and methods to analyze literature? Given that I draw on Foucault in my analysis of "The Man in the Well," I find myself implicated. Have I effectively read not a text by Sher, but one by Foucault, Canetti, and Freud? Have I replaced Sher's truth (whatever that may be) with the truth according to these theorists?

To move toward an answer, it will be helpful to review how I came to include those theorists in my discussion of "The Man in the Well." In reading the short story, I was strongly reminded of what I had read about reversal crowds and the Panopticon. Essentially, these intertextual associations made Sher's story seem thematically familiar to me. Whether or not I reference the ideas and terms I know from reading Canetti and Foucault in discussing or rewriting the short story, they have affected how I think about it. To my mind, not citing these sources would mean falsifying how I have come to interpret the story. In writing on "The Man in the Well," I have returned to Canetti's and Foucault's books in search of language that might help me better formulate my interpretation of the story, or put it into words.

I came to Freud less directly, as I was not reminded of the primal horde while reading Sher's story. Instead, passages in which Aaron named his father and Wendy repeated him to disastrous effect led me to recall the concept of the *Nom-du-père*, the Name-of-the-Father, formulated by Jacques Lacan, a French psychoanalyst whose notoriously difficult work essentially rewrites Freud. For a time I tried writing on "The Man in the Well" by applying Lacan's terms. While I was impressed by how well they fit the story, I grew concerned that my analysis was being overtaken by my explication of these complex terms, turning the short story into an illustration of Lacanian theory. Not wanting to abandon psychoanalytic theory, which so strongly influences how I make sense of the story, I turned to Freud's more accessible writings. Only after considering a number of them did I strike upon his account of the primal horde. My use of it reflects both associations I have made as a reader of Sher's story and decisions I have made as a writer anticipating an audience that might have little or no familiarity with Lacan.

In his book *Intertextuality*, Graham Allen states that just as a literary text is written or "built from systems, codes and traditions established by previous works of literature" and "other art forms and . . . culture in general," so it is read not in isolation from those other works, but in relation to them

(1). Reading in this way involves not recasting one text in terms of another, but recognizing what texts share in common. "To interpret a text, to discover its meaning, or meanings, is to trace those relations," writes Allen (1). That those relations exist between theory and literature is not a problem. The relation Krista draws between "The Man in the Well" and Hesse's *Out of the Dust* indicates that a text can be "recast" in the terms of a work of fiction no less than a work of theory. Why, then, is the use Krista makes of Hesse problematic in a way that my turning to Zunshine or Foucault is not? Whereas the connection to Hesse's novel serves to impose a setting on the short story that replaces the sense of time and place indicated by descriptive passages in the text, the move to writings by theorists (of literature, culture, psychology, neurology, etc.) is occasioned by what the text does not provide: concepts and terms with which to analyze and explicate the children's behavior in the story, the narrator's telling of the story, and the author's writing of the story.

Edmundson is right to warn against interpretive responses that discredit or marginalize whatever textual elements "do not cohere" with a given "vision" (38). Indeed, this book argues for paying particular attention to such disruptive elements, as they provide the means by which we may exceed the limits of a particular vision or interpretation of the text. Still, Edmundson may be faulted for identifying such blinkered vision with theory—"Foucault, or Marx, or feminism, or Derrida, or Queer Theory, or what have you" (38)—when literary interpretations of all but the briefest texts single out certain elements for discussion while pushing others to the margin and overlooking the vast majority of the text. It is not the application of a theoretical lens but the reduction of the potential text to any particular "truth" (including the truth according to the author) that threatens to recast a work of literature in greatly diminished terms. Certainly one may use Foucault to produce a procrustean reading of *Bleak House* (or use *Bleak House* to illustrate Foucauldian theory), but this hardly need be the case. More ideally, one might draw on what one has learned from reading Foucault to recognize and address elements of the novel that have gone largely unnoticed, or to rethink elements that have received considerable attention. Here one would aim not to present "Dickens' truth," but to add to the scholarly discussion of Dickens's novel by probing alternative interpretive possibilities.

This mode of interpreting literature is contrary to that espoused by Edmundson, who writes: "What I take to be worthwhile interpretation is centered on the author" (53). He contends that while we cannot discover what the author intended in writing a work, we should aim to arrive at "a version of the work that the author—as we imagine him, as we imagine her—would approve and be gratified by," one that "will make the writer's ghost nod in something like approval." This requires "operating with the author's terms, thinking, insofar as it is possible, the writer's thoughts, reclaiming his world through his language," and, for the teacher, making the voice of the author be heard in the classroom through an "act of inspired ventriloquism" (53). In calling the author "the writer's ghost," Edmundson suggests that the writer lives while the work is being written and dies upon its completion. His ghostly author bears a striking resemblance to the dead father: though no longer present to impose his intention upon us, he is the phantasmal authority we should strive to gratify. His thinking should be our thinking, his language our language. We should seek the author's approval, even if this means disregarding elements of the text that do not cohere with his vision as we imagine it.

AUTHOR, CONSTRUCTIVE AGENT, ORACLE, WRITER

In his devotion to the author, Edmundson is something of a throwback to "the early decades of the twentieth century," when, writes Lois Tyson in *Critical Theory Today*, "students of literature were taught that the author was our primary concern in reading a literary work: our task was ... to discover what the author meant to communicate—his or her message, theme, or moral—which is called *authorial intention*." Today, she adds, "among many contemporary critical theorists at least, the author is no longer considered a meaningful object of analysis"; we focus instead on the reader, the text, and the culture in which the text was produced (2). But if for Edmundson the author perseveres despite the death of the Author, the same may hold true for students and scholars who practice literary analysis of the kind Tyson describes. This is because the prohibition against taking authorial intention and agency into consideration shares with Edmundson's veneration of the writer's ghost a larger-than-life conception of the author. The thoroughness with which this prohibition has been enforced suggests that the author endures, haunting literary interpretation as a persistent threat that must be guarded against. Paraphrasing Freud, we might say that the dead author is stronger than the living writer could ever be.

Barthes's "The Death of the Author" concludes: "the birth of the reader must be at the cost of the death of the Author" (148). Jane Gallop notes that this ending has been taken as "the definitive statement" and "last word" on the author: "The author is the past; critics should no longer be concerned with the author; he should be dead to us" (30). While this accurately describes how Barthes's essay has been received, I want to suggest that Barthes's real target is not the author per se but the critic who reads in a certain way. He reviles criticism that "allot[s] itself the important task of discovering the Author ... beneath the work: when the Author has been found, the text is 'explained'—victory to the critic" ("Death" 147). Here, as in the distinction drawn between the writerly and the readerly, it is not the author's intention so much as the reader's certainty that is denounced. Barthes reproaches not the author who expounds upon his or her own work, but the critic who evokes the Author's truth to validate his or her own interpretation as singularly correct.

Believing that among critics "the *explanation* of a work is always sought in the man or woman who produced it" ("Death" 143), Barthes made the author a figure for criticism's attempt to assign the text an "ultimate meaning" ("Death" 147). An unfortunate consequence of his essay's influence is that literary theorists conceive of the author primarily in this way. The notion that critics might concern themselves with the author without assuming the text has a single true meaning, and without treating authorial intention as key to that meaning, has gone strangely missing in literary theory—at least for the most part. Scholars who take what Phelan calls rhetorical approaches to literary narrative offer a notable exception, as they "attend to the role of all three points of the rhetorical triangle—author, text, and reader—in the production of narrative meaning." Their approaches, he writes, "put special emphasis on the reader's share in the production of meaning even as they retain a strong interest in the textual signals that guide the reader's role and acknowledge the author as the constructive agent of the text" ("Narrative" 296–97).

An irony of Barthes's essay is that even as it announces "the birth of the reader" who is freed to make what he or she will of the text, it effectively prohibits readers from reading in ways that acknowledge that "texts are designed by authors in order to affect readers in particular ways" (Phelan, "Narrative" 300). In "The Death of the Author," Barthes seems unwilling to consider the author as a constructive agent, lest readers make of that agent an Author-God whose words give voice to a "single 'theological' meaning" (146). "To give a text an Author," he writes, "is to impose a limit on the text, to furnish it with a final signified [meaning], to close the writing" (147). And yet, critics hardly need evoke a text's author in order to impose such limits. As Edmundson might point out, critics can easily impose a limit by giving a text a Theorist, and Barthes himself writes that critics may explain a text with reference not to the Author but to "his hypostases: society, history, the psyche, freedom" ("Death" 147). Moreover, we might recall Appleyard's point that readers "may simply transfer the need for a single factual answer from the author to the text" (134). In short, the author is not the problem, as ultimate meanings may be assigned to texts based on textual evidence, cultural-historical context, theoretical framework, and so on. The author nevertheless persists as an ominous figure who threatens to define the text in unary terms that preclude and invalidate other interpretive efforts. Given this persistence, the author is not dead and gone so much as contained, like the man in the well, in a way that simultaneously denies his authority and invests him with a great deal of power.

Decades before Barthes proclaimed the death of the author, literary scholars in the United States, practitioners of the New Criticism that dominated literary study from the 1940s through the 1960s, argued that critics should not be concerned with what an author intended in writing a literary work. Most notably, W. K. Wimsatt and Monroe C. Beardsley coined the term *the intentional fallacy* to designate the error of seeking to know the author's intention in order to understand the work. And yet, they did not argue for disregarding the author altogether. In their 1946 essay "The Intentional Fallacy," they write:

> One must ask how a critic expects to get an answer to the question about intention. How is he to find out what the poet tried to do? If the poet succeeded in doing it, then the poem itself shows what he was trying to do. And if the poet did not succeed, then the poem is not adequate evidence, and the critic must go outside the poem—for evidence of an intention that did not become effective in the poem. (469)

Unlike Barthes, Wimsatt and Beardsley argue that the text, when it is well crafted, does convey its author's intention, that the successful poem shows "what the poet tried to do." What they argue against is looking outside the text, at the author's biography or commentary, for any indication of that intention.

Wimsatt and Beardsley conclude their essay by imagining a reader of T. S. Eliot's "The Love Song of J. Alfred Prufrock" who wonders whether or not the poem's mention of "mermaids singing" is an allusion to the "Mermaides singing" in a poem by John Donne. They claim that the critic who follows "the true and objective way of criticism" will analyze what the mermaids symbolize in each poem, perhaps concluding that this "resemblance between Eliot and Donne is without significance and is better not thought of" (486). Then there is the way of the critic who cannot abide the "very uncertainty" of the interpretive enterprise and, "taking advantage of the fact that Eliot is still alive," writes the poet to ask "what he meant, or if he had Donne in mind." Whatever Eliot's reply, they contend, "an answer to such an inquiry would have nothing to do with the poem 'Prufrock'; it would not be a critical inquiry. Critical inquiries, unlike bets, are not settled in this way. Critical inquiries are not settled by consulting the oracle" (487).

The oracle, like the Author, is a figure whose authority should not bear upon how critics interpret literature. But in refusing to grant this figure absolute power and authority, must we lose all sight of the writer who composed and designed the text with some intention in mind? In short, must the death of the Author entail the death of the writer? Or rather, why should it? Why not acknowledge the author as the writer and constructive agent of the text? Might not the author's reply to a critic's inquiry very well have something to do with the text he or she has written, and this without being authoritative or definitive?

At this point, I should confess that while teaching "The Man in the Well," my thoughts turned to the short story's author, Ira Sher. I cannot deny that I became curious to know "what the author meant" by the story and what he would make of my own interpretation and those of my students. But if I wrote to the oracle in the hope of having my own thinking validated, I heard back from a writer whose response opened up an ongoing dialogue that has led me to rethink the short story, its various interpretations, and the very concept of authorial intention.

TWO AUTHORS EMAILING

From: Gary Weissman
Date: Monday, February 20, 2006
To: Ira Sher
Subject: The Man in the Well

Hi Ira,

As I wrote in my last message, I'm hoping to write something engaging, thoughtful, and funny on teaching "The Man in the Well" and the issues of interpretation it has raised for my students and me. I have taught your story now three or four times, asking students to write a one-page paper answering the question, Why do the children act as they do in the story? Here are four answers taken from their papers: (1) The story is set during the Great Depression, and the children felt they could not afford the responsibility of saving and taking care of the man when their families were struggling; (2) The children followed the lead of the oldest child, Aaron, who was troubled, possibly owing to child abuse; (3) The children were able to act immorally so long as they remained anonymous, so that when the man learned their names they felt accountable and had to flee the scene; (4) The children sought revenge against the man because he had abused them in the past.

I've also gotten responses claiming that the man in the well is probably the narrator's mother's lover, and that is why she is crying at night, because her lover is stuck in the well (presumably put there by the father). And at least a couple of students have read race into the story, proposing that it is set during segregation and the man in the well is black. Such answers have led me to discuss with my students what makes one interpretation of a literary work more convincing than another. We distinguish between interpretations based on textual evidence and interpretations based on associations that have little or no basis in the story. I ask them to consider their investments in whatever interpretation they put forth, and how one interpretation may free us from considering more challenging ones.

My own opinion is that number 3 above is pretty astute, whereas 1, 2, and 4 are unsupported interpretations that avoid your story's more disturbing implications. If only the children were justified in seeking revenge against the man, then the story is not really about us, our capacity to act very badly, our ambivalent relation to the "good values" instilled in us by parental authority and enforced through fear rather than "good will towards men." But that is my interpretation, and, given that all reading is a negotiation between what is written by the author and what is projected onto the writing by the reader, I wonder where it loses its basis in the text. For instance, in teaching the story I've realized that I've assumed a male narrator although the text leaves this uncertain. I wonder if you meant to do that.

The part of the story that has most confused my students is the passage about how it was "at the time" when the narrator's mother was crying at night and the father was murmuring. I see a parallel with the man in the well (the parents down below, not visible, only voices can be heard) in terms of the breakdown or crisis of adult authority. I wonder how you explain or think about this part of your story. My students also wonder why the man in the well won't give his name, and why the children don't ask him about how he came to be in the well.

Lastly, I wonder how you feel about expressing or sharing any of your own intention in writing the story. As the author, do you know the meaning of most *everything that is in your story, or do you relate to parts of it more as a reader, wondering how to interpret aspects of what you yourself have written? Is there something in particular you want readers of the story to understand about children and moral/immoral behavior?*

Best wishes,
Gary

From: Ira Sher
Date: Tuesday, February 21, 2006
To: Gary Weissman
Subject: Re: The Man in the Well

Gary,

What I write often escapes me, particularly at the time it first goes to paper. I think of the process of writing as a kind of dream work. The ideas and threads tend to present themselves without my knowing why I've come up with them, during the process of writing, and it then becomes a matter of seeing how individual threads relate and how the whole thing should be contained when I sit down to edit. When I began writing "The Man in the Well" it was with no plan in mind: I began with the children playing in the field, in the summer with the insects and dust, and then they heard the voice from the well—very much as it's written. The well was such a powerful subject, the story really wrote itself around that. This is in many ways an odd piece, being written quickly, and just coming out (as people who don't write often imagine stories or essays occur, but as they in fact hardly ever do). I wrote it about ten years ago in a single afternoon, though I edited it once about a month later. I did not try to make sense in the moment of what was going on in the story, though I've thought about it since.

And so for this reason, there are many elements you've asked about—like the mother crying downstairs, the murmur of the father—that were for me tonal and not written with a rhetorical aim. I have had a number of screenplays written (by other people) based on this story, and in two of them those brief sentences swelled into whole second plots with their own scenes and dialogs. You're right to see a parallel between the man and the parents, hidden and downstairs, though this was not intentional. I do think there is a theme of secret and inassimilable hurt that was obviously presenting itself to me; it is an ongoing theme in my work.

As far as the information and lack of information exchanged by the kids and the man, this was also not premeditated, and even the use of the names was a fairly late discovery in the writing of the piece. I can see that information and revelation are full of moral vulnerability in the story, and the power dynamics are all about possession of knowledge (and through its aspect of surveillance, the ability to inspire guilt), but as I've noted, none of this was written by design. And the narrator—yes, I always assumed he was a boy! But funny there should be no real marker for that. It wasn't intentional, though it's entirely appropriate for a story by someone who seems to be telling this into a hole in the ground, with the hope that no one else might ever know what he took part in.

Something that readers seem to do automatically (and I myself as a reader/editor of the books I'm working on do the same) is create meaning and coincidence from things that have no intentional meaning at all. This is, of course, what we do with our lives. Many of the things I've written return to the way people build narratives for their lives from the stream of experience, and how sustaining, dangerous, and essential these narratives are. I would have to agree with you that a host of ulterior motives can also lead people to easier, thinner readings. The 3rd reading you mention in your note is really the only one I can find a place for in the narrative.

I'm glad you're approaching the subject and story with humor (this is such a dour little story). Let me know if you have any further questions or ideas, and good luck. I'd love to see what you write when you're done.

Take care,
Ira

THE AUTHOR IN THE WELL

Though asked about the meaning of "The Man in the Well," Ira responds by discussing "the writing of the piece." He stresses that he began drafting the story "with no plan in mind," remarking: "I did not try to make sense in the moment of what was going on in the story, though I've thought about it since." He notes how much of the story was not intentional, not premeditated, not written "with a rhetorical aim" or "by design"; even the importance that names take on when Wendy speaks Aaron's name, when Aaron reveals the names of the other children, when the man calls out to each of the children by name, was something he discovered "fairly late" in the course of drafting the story in one afternoon, a decade or so ago.

I have argued that theorists, in contending that the author should be dead to us, have made the author a figure akin to the man in the well, an authority both deposed and invested with superhuman power. Much as the man was left in the well by the fearful children, so the author has been left for dead by literary scholars. Yet in Ira Sher we find an author who effectively places himself in the well, voluntarily ceding his authority to assign an "ultimate meaning" to the short story he has written. He states that he wrote the short story without knowing what would happen in it, much less the meaning of its unfolding events, the significance of the narrator's recounting of those events, or the point the story might convey as a whole. He neither began writing the story nor ended it with a particular message in mind or moral for the reader to take away, and the theme he mentions, that of "secret and inassimilable hurt," is not specific to this story but broadly descriptive of his writing as a whole.

In the previous chapter, I proposed that "The Man in the Well" has the effect of placing readers in the well, a space of cognitive uncertainty that they may constructively explore as writers. Ira's remarks indicate that the author, no less than the reader, can be understood as a writer in the well, as he too enters unknown territory, giving up certainty and foreknowledge in an effort to make discoveries through writing. While not all fiction writers share his writing philosophy, it is widespread. In his 2005 study *The Author*, Andrew Bennett includes the conception of the author as "unknowing, as not, or as not quite, conscious of what she does" among "the most common forms of twentieth- and indeed twenty-first-century authors' explanations of their own work" (68). This conception prevails as well among teachers of creative writing. In her widely used textbook *Writing Fiction: A Guide to Narrative Craft*, Janet Burroway warns writers not "to write a story to illustrate an idea." Instead, she writes, "You'll begin with an image of a person or a situation that seems vaguely to embody something important, and you'll learn as you go what that something is. . . . Rather than 'putting in a theme,' you'll be looking back to see what you've already, mostly subconsciously, been doing all along" (346). This is just what Ira describes when he likens his writing to "a kind of dream work" in which "ideas and threads tend to present themselves without [his] knowing why [he's] come up with them." For Ira, looking back involves "seeing how individual threads relate and how the whole thing should be contained" when he edits his writing.

Burroway's discussion of fiction writing draws on John Gardner's 1984 study *The Art of Fiction: Notes on Craft for Young Writers*, once standard reading for creative writing students. She takes up his point that a theme should be "not imposed on the story but evoked from within it" (qtd. in Burroway

437), but without the emphasis he places on authorial certainty and control. The development of a story's theme, according to Gardner, is "initially an intuitive but finally an intellectual act on the part of the writer" (177). Describing this intellectual act more fully, he writes:

> What Fancy sends, the writer must order by Judgment. He must think out completely, as coolly as any critic, what his fiction means, or is trying to mean. He must complete his equations, think out the subtlest implications of what he's said, get at the truth not just of his characters and action but also of his fiction's form. . . . (7)

Today few fiction writers are likely to relate their process to that of a critic, and Fancy has gained pride of place over Judgment. Indeed, Gardner's conception of the writer's task has given way to a sentiment that Ron Carlson, a fiction writer who teaches creative writing, puts thusly: "It is not my job to explain the story or understand the story or reduce it to a phrase or offer it as being a story about any specific person, place, or thing" (100).

The notion that fiction writers should "think out completely" the meaning of their stories is upended by Robert Boswell in his book for young writers titled *The Half-Known World: On Writing Fiction*. Boswell writes that he neither tries to attach significance to his characters' actions nor looks for symbols. His method, instead, is to "listen to what has made it to the page":

> Invariably, things have arrived that I did not invite, and they are often the most interesting things in the story. By refusing to fully know the world, I hope to discover unusual formations in the landscape, and strange desires in the characters. By declining to analyze the story, I hope to keep it open to surprise. Each new draft revises the world but does not explain or define it. I work through many drafts, progressively abandoning the familiar. (4–5)

Boswell would have fiction writers render characters and worlds that can be only half-known by their authors and readers. "When the reader's experience of a story results in a world that is too fully known, the story fails," he contends (20), since "to make something fully known is to make it unreal" (7). In reality people are complex, inconsistent, and only partly knowable (hence the pervasiveness of "mind misreading"), and so in fiction "any character that is fully known" is an unrealistic, simplistic type—a stereotype (7).

According to Boswell, "the most common failed story" is written by a writer who knows too much, who "comprehends where the story is going too correctly" (22). Its narrative is dull, in large part because "the characters tend to be motivated by explicit and logical reasons and nothing else," so that "the unexplainable, the quirky, the unconscious" is ignored (22). It occurs to me that some of my students rewrite "The Man in the Well" as a failed story in this sense. Providing "explicit and logical reasons" for the children's actions that disregard less explicable narrative elements and depend on stereotypes (the troubled kid, the stranger), they have yet to appreciate that, as Boswell puts it, "a crucial part of the writing endeavor is the practice of remaining in the dark" (24).

Carlson treats fiction writing quite similarly to Boswell in a compelling little volume titled *Ron Carlson Writes a Story* (17). He describes writing as "a strange activity done alone in a room mostly" (23) and the writer as *"the person who stays in the room"* although it is difficult to stay there, "especially when you are not sure of what you're doing, where you're going" (24). To stay in the room is to remain in the dark, exploring what Boswell calls "terrain you only half-know" (23). "Beginning a story without knowing all the terrain is a not a comfortable feeling," writes Carlson, but it is necessary:

> Even in stories where you think you have control of all the elements, there are going to be surprises and turns in the writing that you didn't anticipate. If there aren't, then the story is not going to be as solid as it should be. Simply, and others have said this: *if you get what you expect, it isn't good enough.* (14–15)

Ira seems to have avoided this problem entirely by beginning the story that would become "The Man in the Well" with no expectations, "no plan in mind."

"The single largest advantage a veteran writer has over the beginner is this tolerance for not knowing," claims Carlson. He explains: "An experienced writer has been in those woods before and is willing to be lost; she knows that being lost is necessary for the discoveries to come" (15). In much the same vein, Blau remarks that "one of the principal differences between expert readers and those who appear less skilled is that the more accomplished have a greater capacity for failure" (213). What is this capacity for failure, if not a willingness to be lost in the woods, to remain in the dark, to stay in the well? In Blau's words, this capacity is what enables readers "to read a text a second time after feeling bewildered or blank in a first reading, and then to reread again when the second reading is hardly more satisfying than the first" (213). The experienced reader, like the veteran writer, has a tolerance for not knowing.

As readers of literature who are also writers of interpretive "readings," we can make the greatest discoveries by allowing ourselves to be lost yet again when writing on the text, using the occasion to reread and discover interpretive possibilities unknown to us before we sat down in the room to write. "Writers use language as a tool of exploration to see beyond what they know," states Donald Murray in his 1978 essay "Internal Revision: A Process of Discovery" (74), which concludes with dozens of statements by fiction writers, poets, and dramatists who equate writing with discovery. These quotations—such as novelist Cecelia Holland's remark, "One of the reasons a writer writes, I think, is that his stories reveal so much he never thought he knew" (86)—show how long-lived and pervasive are the views Boswell and Carlson theorize at greater length. Still, Murray is less interested in literary authors than in student writers who analyze literature, his point being that they too should use writing "to discover and develop what they have to say" (77).

Let us dwell on this point a moment, given that critical writing as a process of discovery is so seldom addressed in literary scholarship. In a notable exception, Derek Attridge remarks that while he sometimes experiences writing as "a trying-out of different words" to express ideas he already has in mind, at other times he "seem[s] to be composing new sentences out of nothing, or rather out of a largely inchoate swirl of half-formulated thoughts and faint intimations" (17). In drafting, deleting, and reworking these sentences, Attridge resists his mind's "tendency to process any novelty it encounters in terms of the familiar" so that he might exceed the limits of what he has "hitherto been able to think" (18). Here again writing involves gaining knowledge by resisting the comforts of familiarity and certainty.

Whereas Attridge describes this act of writing as "creative" (18), creative writing is typically conceived in opposition to critical writing. Thus Burroway remarks in *Writing Fiction*: "Theoretically, an outline can never harm a paper for a literature class: This what I have to say, and I'll say it through points A, B, and C. But if a writer sets out to write a story to illustrate an idea, the fiction will almost inevitably be thin" (346). Perhaps because it conflates college-level writing on literature with the five-paragraph theme many students are instructed to write in grade school, this remark wrongly depicts literary analysis as a cut-and-dried undertaking. Borrowing Carlson's words, I would tell the literature student whose paper does little more than present points A, B, and C that "*if you get what you expect, it isn't good enough.*" Surprises and turns in the writing should involve literature students in a process of discovery, a process that is impeded if we stick to reporting what we had to say before sitting down to write. "To write a story is to stay alert and open to the possibilities that emerge as each sentence cuts its way into the unknown," states Carlson (14). The same can be said of what it means to write *on* a story: critical writing, no less than fiction writing, is a process of discovery and realization through writing.

"Writing a story is really going into something pretty blind," Ira wrote me in a message over three years after we began our conversation, when I was *still* asking him about decisions he might have made when drafting and revising "The Man in the Well." "Often it just doesn't work, but when it does, you realize afterward what's strong, and go back and try to strengthen that further." In what follows, I will discuss this "strengthening" in terms of the writer's decision making. After completing a story, Ira writes, "what I'm left with is something for me to figure out as a reader, too." Even when he casts doubt on certain interpretations of his story ("The 3rd reading . . . is really the only one I can find a place for in the narrative"), he does so by evoking not his authority as the author but his inability as a reader to find textual support for those interpretations. Still, while recognizing the degree to which Ira refuses the mantle of Author, we should not overlook his role as the constructive agent of the text.

INTENTION AS SOMETHING-OTHER-THAN-MEANING

"The Man in the Well" is "really about us, our capacity to act very badly, our ambivalent relation to the 'good values' instilled in us by parental authority and enforced through fear rather than 'good will towards men'"—or so I wrote in my February 2006 email to Ira. I must have felt unfulfilled by his response to my interpretation, for soon after receiving his reply I wrote him the following:

> I don't know if I said it clearly in my first email to you, but a lot of what I take from your story is that ethical behavior is instilled in us as children through fear of authority—that at the root of good values is a kind of authoritarianism, and that this may explain why we feel pleasure in defiance, in being "bad" and doing bad things (even as we feel guilty for doing them). I regard the children's thrill in disobeying the man in the well as a response to the fear they initially feel ("At first afraid to disobey the voice . . .").

Ira replied: "I like what you've indicated about morality finding its source in authoritarian fear, and I can see how the story speaks to that." In other words, while my interpretation might have interested Ira and made sense to him, the theory of morality I describe was not something he had in mind or thought to express in writing the story. What I "took" from "The Man in the Well" was not something its author knowingly (consciously, intentionally) put there for the taking.

My claim is not that Ira writes without intention but that his intentions bear on something other than the meaning of the story he writes. Peter J. Rabinowitz notes that the term *authorial intention* need not refer to intended meaning. "We can talk intelligently (even if not definitively) about the (intended) meaning of a word or a phrase or perhaps a paragraph," he writes, but not of a literary text: "'What's the meaning of *Hamlet*?' simply doesn't make any sense as a question." What else might authorial intention concern? "Intention as something-other-than-meaning takes many shapes," writes Rabinowitz, including "intending the audience to do something: to feel something, to react in some particular way" ("Shakespeare's" 358). Culler has also discussed intention in terms of the impact a text is designed to have on readers, stating,

> Choices between words, between sentences, between different modes of presentation, will be made on the basis of their effects; and the notion of effect presupposes modes of reading which are not random or haphazard. Even if the author does not think of readers, he is himself a reader of his own work and will not be satisfied with it unless he can read it as producing effects. (*Structuralist* 116)

Conceived in broad rhetorical terms, intention concerns all such writerly choices an author makes in composing a text. Each word, punctuation mark, turn of phrase, bit of dialogue, paragraph break, and section break is the inscription of a decision, however fleeting or worked over, made by a writer.

Ira makes this point when discussing writers' efforts to manipulate the pace with which a story may be told by a narrator and experienced by readers:

> There is a certain micro-level of that pacing that happens all the time on the sentence level for writers. There are a lot of ways to say what needs to be said, and part of what you think about when writing has to do with line pacing, so dialogue breathes right, and you have some measure to phrases—some consistent cadence. You avoid repetition. You choose moments of lyricism to hold a reader and spread out time, and then condense language and strip it down to move things along. And this affects

narrative, too. It creates language choices that might seem to be about saying something a particular way from a critical perspective, but which actually originate in style—not to draw too hard a distinction.

Pacing, breathe, measure, cadence, lyricism: these terms, more evocative of poetry than literary narrative, concern the sounds of language and the duration of reading. In using them, Ira emphasizes choices that affect readers through style rather than plotting. For an example, let us turn to a "moment of lyricism" in the story that has most confused my students, the aforementioned peculiar paragraph in which the narrator recalls his weeping mother, murmuring father, and the feeling of a time he cannot describe without "resorting to the man in the well, as if through a great whispering, like a gathering of clouds, or the long sound, the turbulent wreck of the ocean." Why at this point does the narrator pause in his account of the children's encounter with the man in the well to mention "those days, months actually," when his mother was very upset? And why is this recollection conveyed in such lyrical terms?

Ira explains that he meant "to slow the reader down and create tone" with this passage. Having ended the previous section with Wendy and the character narrator fleeing from the well after she spoke Aaron's name, he wanted to offset that action with a moment of lyricism. "I had a moment of drama, and then I needed to let the reader breathe before bringing things to a conclusion," he writes. "And a side effect of that decision, of course, is that some narrative *is* created, but that isn't the guiding impulse. That becomes part of the accidental discovery process—what material comes out when you're *not* focused on the narrative. What narrative you get when you're looking at the subject a bit awry, wanting to solve a different problem."

The problem Ira sought to solve with what he calls "the passage about the ocean" was one of pacing, not narrative meaning. And yet, as he notes, the inclusion of moments of lyricism affects the narrative in ways that bear on its meaning. In addition to slowing down the reader and creating tone, the passage introduces the character narrator's parents and home life, providing a larger context for the current story about the children's involvement with the man in the well. "In a story," writes Carlson, "much narrative evidence concerning character appears in exposition, that is, in periods of time before the current story" (37). The passage about "those days, months actually," is exposition in this sense, though it provides only a slight indication of who the character narrator and his parents are as people.

Ira mentions two screenplays based on his short story in which this brief passage swells into "whole second plots with their own scenes and dialogs," and in speaking to me he has described the narrator's mention of his home life as a second story that exists apart from, or in relation to, the primary story of the children and the man in the well. Most fiction that works, he tells me, has a second story that "crosses" the first, and this is what makes the narrative "tick." That the short story ends by returning home to the mother ("That night it rained, and I listened to the rain on the roof and my mother sobbing, downstairs, until I fell asleep") suggests Ira was consciously crossing the two stories—but not that this crossing had, for him, a specific meaning. He could not tell me, for instance, why in the end the mother reappears without any mention of the father. "There's a lot of discovery and accident," he writes, "things in your own work which you discover and then interpret in much the same way as any other reader."

AUTHORIAL CHOICES

In *Ron Carlson Writes a Story,* Carlson holds that writers, while drafting stories, should not be concerned with the effects their choices will have on readers. Rather, choices should be made on the basis of what allows a writer to stay in the room and keep writing. Consequently, no mention of impacting the reader through line pacing appears in Carlson's discussion of one of his own short stories. He remarks of a sentence in this story: "It's good. It's okay for a reader, but I don't care, I can't even think that way here. It's good for the writer because it creates what I'll call inventory—there's something in it" (23). This something is a stock of details or story elements that can be used to generate the narrative. "I'm constantly looking for *things* that are going to help me find the next sentence," writes Carlson (23).

Here he describes one such thing:

> You write something, for example, "a blue and white wool sweater," and what you want is a real sweater, something a character would really wear, something that might help us see and believe him a little bit. What you don't know is that five pages from creating the sweater as a realistic item of your inventory, it is going to help his sister find him at the Garfield County Fair late that night. You didn't plan that, but when it happens it will seem only necessary; and staying in the room will allow it to happen. (25–26)

When Carlson writes that the wool sweater should "help us see and believe" in a character, this "us" refers not to readers but to writers who need to "create something real enough" to "believe and hold onto" as they write (35). Still, in the transition from the singular *you* (what "you want") to the plural *us* (what "might help us"), I detect the ghostly presence of readers in the room, or in the writer whose belief in her characters is inseparable from her sense of whether or not her readers (or the Reader she has internalized) would find them credible.

In another instance, Carlson discusses a sentence from his story in which the character narrator recalls, in passing, a night his wife took him to a western bar where they "watched all her young lawyer friends dance with the cowboys" (81). He comments: "I see that that I drop into exposition when I'm trying to delay, avoid, prolong what is happening in the current story. Looking at the entire paragraph, you can see my uncertainty about what will happen" (82). Carlson sees, and instructs his readers to see, evidence of writerly indecision: uncertain where his story was heading, the writer employed exposition as a delay tactic. Moreover, he writes that "a close reader"—one who reads "to understand the writer's choices" (68)—will see the writer's "uncertainty about which way to go" in the writing (77).

I imagine very few readers would take the narrator's recollection of the western bar as a sign of the author's uncertainty about what might happen next in the story. Still, I am intrigued by the notion that, whatever story it tells, a literary text also tells about its own coming into being as writing—at least when it is interpreted as a record of writerly choices. Take, for example, the western bar sentence, which Carlson describes as "exposition offering a tiny look at who these people are via their history" (82): it can be interpreted not only in mimetic terms (what it conveys about the characters), synthetic terms (how it serves the narrative structure), and thematic terms (how it contributes to issues), but also in writerly terms (what it intimates about the drafting process). While I question our ability to mind read from the text what a writer felt while composing its sentences, I like to imagine that writerly uncertainty may be inscribed there, particularly given a critical tendency to conceive of authorial intention in terms that overstate the writer's conscious control of textual form and meaning—a propensity, in other words, to regard the author as an authority and not as a writer.

Scholars interested in the choices authors make when writing and revising their work might examine drafts of their published writings when these are available. Less may be gleaned from the published works themselves because, as Joseph Harris notes, "finished texts tend to conceal much of the labor involved in writing them" (99). Even so, a literary text may be read as the end result of a writer's (and in many cases an editor's) myriad choices, only some of which will be observed and interpreted. Whereas Phelan, Rabinowitz, and Culler observe reader-based choices, decisions bearing on how an author has designed a text to affect readers in certain ways, Carlson observes writer-based choices, the decisions a writer makes in order to "figure out ways not to stop" writing (22).

Ron Carlson Writes a Story marginalizes the reader because it focuses on the hard work of writing the first draft of a short story, with almost no attention paid to revision work, and because Carlson regards reader-based decision making as an impediment to the "discovery process" writers must engage in "while wading through the draft" (96). In choosing to represent fiction writing in this way, he obscures what Barbara Tomlinson calls "the socially shared assumptions and practices that establish writing as a collective, cultural, and trans-individual activity" (13). Her point is that writing, even when done in solitude, is a social practice constituted by communally established ways of using language to communicate with readers. Rabinowitz makes this point as well, writing:

> In a trivial sense . . . authors can put down whatever marks they wish on the page; readers can construe them however they wish. But once authors and readers accept the communal nature of writing and reading, they give up some of that freedom. Specifically, once he or she has made certain initial decisions, any writer who wishes to communicate—even if he or she wishes to communicate ambiguity—has limited the range of subsequent choices. (*Before* 23–24)

Carlson essentially opposes this conception of writing. Having defined the writer as the person who stays in the room, he describes the room as a space "the naked writer gets to enter alone and unmolested by convention" (30)—that is, as a space outside the social or communal realm.

Carlson's tale of how he stayed in the room and "survived the writing" of "a story [he] wrote in one long day several years ago" (17) fits Tomlinson's description of the "metanarrative of writing" that "encourages us to focus attention on the special selfhood of the heroic author . . . rather than . . . the social nature of composing" (2). That Carlson appears to have written the story in one go is part of this heroic narrative. Tomlinson writes:

> Precisely because writing and revising require actions too small to support heroic narratives—revising sentences, re-arranging paragraphs, changing punctuation, looking up the meaning of words, adjusting the rhythm of phrases and the pace of paragraphs, lengthening or shortening chapters that previously seemed to be completed—they generally remain hidden from view, therefore mystifying the processes of writing and allowing both

advanced and beginning writers to believe that no one else has to struggle with writing in quite the way we do. (4)

Literary scholars who attend to the author's reader-based choices, to the exclusion of writer-based ones, are also unlikely to address these "small" actions.

While these scholars and Carlson offer opposing ways to think about the choices an author makes, these ways are not necessarily or entirely incompatible, nor are they the only ways to think about writerly choices. For instance, I recently came across the following conception of the writing process in a piece by Myra Jehlen:

> Through a series of essays, I've been pursuing an idea that writing—the work of finding the right word, refining sentences, fixing tone—is an effort to find out, to understand: an epistemological process start to finish. Finding the right word and putting it in the right place so that the sentence finally strikes the definitive note of beauty is how a writer figures out the point of a sentence or a novel. Form pursues content. (4)

While Jehlen, like Carlson and a great many other writers, describes writing as a process of discovery, she offers a quite different account of what is discovered. Jehlen's writer discovers not what comes next in the story (content), but the right words in the right place (form) and, through that, the point of his or her writing. Here writing involves not finding the right words to convey a preestablished point, but finding out meaning by composing sentences that strike "the definitive note of beauty" or that feel right aesthetically. This conception of writing locates discovery less in the initial drafting of a story than in the work of revising (refining and fixing) what one has drafted.

THE AUTHORIAL UNCONSCIOUS

Ira describes his own writing process as chiefly concerned with aesthetic form. He states:

> To try not to intentionally shape something theoretically is important for me. Even in the editing process, my attempts to shape are generally aesthetic. The final product of this process, though, gives me something, when I'm satisfied with it, that I can feel is very sound, aesthetically but also

theoretically, because it comes from a place I haven't given myself power to entirely censor.

Here the theoretical refers to what his story might mean from a critical perspective, whereas the aesthetic concerns what fiction writers typically discuss in terms of craft: word choice, characterization, dialogue, tone, pacing, and so on. Ira writes that while he loves critical theory, he does not trust it as a "tool to shape fiction"—not, at least, when it is consciously employed. He explains:

> I feel that if I wrote from theory, I would at best arrive at a very good illustration; what I have the other way is a possibility of thinking the theory out behind my own back. I might come to conclusions I don't even like, and might have denied myself—so there's that idea of censorship again. There is such a layer of censorship in our apprehensions of everything, don't you think? There is so much authority.

Ira's description of his writing practice reminds me of Qualley's discussion of risky reading. "If the reader is not at risk," she writes, "his or her current understanding and (self-)awareness remain safely immune to further complication or illumination" (*Turns* 61). Ira suggests that the writer may or may not be "at risk" as well. In writing stories, Ira wishes not to illustrate his current understanding but to exceed the limits of his preunderstanding, at the risk of coming to uncomforting conclusions.

I was reminded of Ira's comments on theory when speaking to him more recently. I had been drafting part of this chapter on the place of "the father" in the story, and told Ira that I was struck by how well Lacan's theory—his concepts of the Name-of-the-Father and the Symbolic Order—apply to "The Man in the Well." Ira said he was not surprised to hear this: if I could have seen the books on his bedside table at the time he wrote the story, he told me, I would have found a book by Lacan and another on Lacanian theory. Ira surmised that what he had been reading found its way into his writing without his knowing it. I would like to think that this "happy coincidence" corroborates my interpretation, that in analyzing the story I have detected something of the author's unconscious intent. That said, one can produce any number of Lacanian "readings" or rewritings of Sher's short story, none of them dependent on or validated by the authorial unconscious.

Moreover, the authorial unconscious is not reducible to these terms. Long before we spoke of Lacan, Ira had discussed his story by referencing the work of the Swiss psychotherapist Carl Jung. "Jung was important in my family," he wrote me. "My mother was in Jungian analysis when I was in grade school and, after traveling though some other forms of analysis, is now an analyst herself. Over the years, I've read a great deal of material as part of our ongoing conversation." Jung, unlike Lacan, is not required reading for literary theory students, and so I had little idea of what Ira meant when, in the course of our dialogue, he referenced Jung's Puer/Senex paradigm to propose that the character narrator ("the eternal youth") and the man in the well ("the eternal old man") might be "one and the same, merely at different times of life," such that "the angry young man (taking pleasure, his very meaning, from his stance toward authority) will become that loathed authority." Imagining I might draw out this interpretation, I purchased a short introductory book on Jungian psychology; it remains unread. I might enjoy reading a Jungian rewriting of "The Man in the Well," but, given the foreignness of Jung's theories to my ways of thinking, it is not mine to tell.

Over the course of our dialogue, I have continued to pester Ira with questions about what he did and did not intend in writing his short story. Did he assume that readers would judge the children negatively for their actions? Did he think them immoral for leaving the man in the well? Was the age of the narrator ("I was nine when I discovered the man in the well") a meaningful choice? As will become clear in the next chapter, although Ira had no message or moral in mind when writing his story, certain intentions and understandings did inform how he wrote much of it. Even so, a caveat is in order. What a writer says about his or her intentions in writing a text provides readers with a tool they might use to reexamine the text from another angle, but that tool is itself also a text calling for examination.

Noting changes over time in Ira's explanations of certain story details, I wrote him that I was interested in exploring the impact of reader response on what might be called the author's retrospective intention, or authorial intention after the fact. He replied, "I do think 'retrospective authorial intention' happens all the time, and in ways generally unperceived by authors (who, I think, often don't set out to write about something, but find that they have when they're done, and elaborate what they set out to write about from hearing people discuss their work)." He pointed to the unspecified sex of the character narrator in "The Man in the Well" as an example: "The sexlessness of the narrator ... wasn't something I wrote with intention, although it's the sort of thing I might one day assume I had, or speak of as if I had. One forgets, after all, almost everything about what one has already written after a while." Unbound by time, the authorial unconscious may continue to shape authorial intention long after a text has been written.

IMAGINING THE WELL

Around two years after I first emailed Ira Sher to ask him about "The Man in the Well," I began writing on my experiences of teaching the short story. Wanting to illustrate the challenge Sher's minimalist writing poses to understanding, I decided to write on the story's second paragraph. Although I had read this paragraph countless times, in the course of writing on it I was surprised to find much I had not noticed before. Most notably, I was struck by the paragraph's protracted last sentence:

> Because of this, I never went very close to the lip of the well, or I only came up on my hands and knees, so that he couldn't see me; and just as we wouldn't allow him to see us, I know that none of us ever saw the man in the well—the well was too dark for that, too deep, even when the sun was high up, angling light down the stones like golden hair.

Something seemed amiss. The character narrator either never went very close to the lip of the well or he did, crawling up to it on his hands or knees. Well, which was it? And if he never looked down into the well, lest he be seen by the man, how could he know that sunlight angled down the stones "like golden hair"? Or that if he or the other children *had* peered down into the well, they would have seen only darkness?

As I wrote on the passage, I felt uneasy. Intermittently while rereading the paragraph and drafting my own, I imagined (as I must have when reading the story in the past, only now I did so consciously) a boy on his hands and knees by the stone column of the well, peering up at the lip. Something was wrong with this picture. Why should a child approach the well on his hands and knees if he could walk up to the stone wall without a chance of being seen? What if, I wondered, there was no stone wall, no aboveground well structure at all? This was a difficult thing for me to wonder, because from the first time I heard "The Man in the Well" I had imagined an old stone well, and later on I imagined a picture of an old stone well on the cover of this book. Could the well merely be a hole in the ground? Searching the text for other descriptions, I read: "We sat down around the mouth of the well on the old concrete slab, warming in the sun and coursing with ants and tiny insects." If the children sat around the well's "mouth" or "lip," wouldn't the well's opening be a hole in the concrete slab on which they sat, more or less at ground level?

Sensing that I had erred in imagining the well as I had for so long, I wrote Ira to ask if he had pictured the well "as a stone structure of some height above the ground (taller or shorter than those children?) or more as a hole in the ground." He replied: "I do have a physical idea about how I see it, though there's not an enormous amount of detail given, and I can imagine people drawing a different conclusion. I see a 'hole' as you've described it, with a broad cement rim, flush with the ground. I see it as a very functional object, not made of stone and handsome in any way as an old stone well can be." I replied in turn that "because the hole-in-the-ground well wasn't in my mental storehouse of images" I had not imagined it as a possibility, and I asked Ira if his image of the well draws on an actual well he has seen or if it is a "purely imaginary construct." He answered: "No, I've never seen such a well. There might not be such wells, but they seem possible—that is to say, it's imaginable."

A colleague has since told me that she imagined the well in Sher's story as a hole in the ground because, having grown up in Oregon surrounded by farmland, she knows that farm wells *are* holes in the ground. Farmers are practical, she said, and economical in their labor, and for this reason wells on farms are more likely to be covered with a wood board (which may eventually rot away) than to be surrounded by a stone wall, like a village well. Lacking such real-world knowledge, I had imposed a stock image of a well on the short story, neglecting or underreading textual descriptions that, while minimal and largely "inexplicitly noncommittal," do point to its inaccuracy. Not unlike Krista supplementing the text with images of the Dust Bowl, I drew upon ready-made imagery instead of imagining the unfamiliar but "imaginable" well described in the text. Ironically, the well *sans* stone wall is a better fit for my Freudian interpretation of "The Man in the Well": not handsome (masculine) and old (patriarchal), this well is a hole with a lip (feminine), flush with the ground (castrated). But if this well serves my rewriting of the story better than the old stone well I had pictured, it also overturns how I have long imagined the short story when reading it and recollecting its storyworld.

Now I picture the well as a hole in the ground with the children gathered around it. I imagine Aaron and Arthur standing by this hole and Wendy crawling to its edge, and in picturing them I draw on the *World Book* comic strip that has long intrigued me. I cast its two schoolboys as Aaron and Arthur, and picture Wendy rendered in the same style. Relating the "back then" time of the narrator's childhood with the setting of the dated cartoon, I rewrite the short story and the comic strip, combining them in an image drawn from the story but visualized in terms of the strip:

This image, arising from an intertexual assocation peculiar to my own experiences, does not depict how I would expect others to visualize the short story. Rather, it depicts an instance in which I like what I am able to make of "The Man in the Well."

My mental images of the farm-lot, the well, the children, the man in the well: these are part of what might be called my mental construal of the short story or its storyworld, the interpretation that precedes and informs my rewriting of the short story. What does it mean that for so long my mental image of the well was at odds with the well described in the text, if not that my written "reading" of the "The Man in the Well" has rested on a misreading of the short story's central image, the titular well? I recall a question a student posed in her response paper: "Honestly, who really falls in a well?" At the time, I found her question amusing but had little to offer in response. Now I might answer that her skepticism is understandable if the stone lining of the well extends upward several feet to form a protective wall around the well opening; but if the wellhead is a flat concrete slab with an uncovered opening, the answer to her query is that anyone traversing the untended field without care might fall in.

Having theorized "the well" as a space occupied by deposed and internalized authorities, as a space of uncertainty occupied by readers willing to engage confusion and uncertainty, and as a space occupied by authors willing to remain in the dark, I will close this chapter by observing a fourth conception of the well, one specific to my experiences of interpreting and teaching "The Man in the Well." In its belated transformation from an old stone structure to a hole in the ground, the well symbolizes for me that whatever authority I am granted as a teacher or scholar, my interpretation of the short story, like that of its author, is inevitably a work in progress.

CHAPTER 3
GENRES

ON AUTHORIAL READING

If we grant, as I believe we should, that there is no single correct interpretation or right reading of a literary text, and that our interpretive efforts are never fully completed so much as halted at some point deemed "good enough" (for now), still we might ask if there is, among the myriad interpretive possibilities that comprise the potential text, a most necessary interpretation, one that implicitly or explicitly provides the foundation upon which other ways of construing the text build upon and rely. Might some basic understanding of a text underlie and inform other ways of interpreting or responding to it? And might the lack of such foundational understanding account for misreading?

Rabinowitz argues as much, contending that because an author writes with a more or less specific audience in mind, a proper understanding of a literary text begins, or should begin, with an effort to read it from the standpoint of that audience, with the relevant knowledge that audience would bring to the text. He notes that while authors cannot foresee who will actually read their work, their writing reflects choices they have made based on what they presumed to be the knowledge and beliefs of their readers. For example, Washington Irving assumed readers of his 1819 tale "Rip Van Winkle" would know that "during the Revolution, the American colonies became independent of England" (*Before* 21); consequently, the reader who does not know this history will have an impaired understanding of the tale. Rabinowitz calls the imagined, ideal readership for whom the author designs his or her text the *authorial audience,* and he calls the reader's effort to join this audience *authorial reading.*

Authorial reading is presented as a "necessary first step" but certainly not the only or last step readers need take when interpreting literature (Rabinowitz and Smith 52). Rabinowitz writes, "I would be disappointed in a student who could produce an authorial reading but who could not . . . move beyond that reading to look at the work critically from some perspective other than the one called for by the author" (*Before* 32). He describes authorial reading as a "provisional testing, not a permanent adopting, of a perspective," one that enables rather than hinders "vigorous disagreement with an author or a text," for the simple reason that "without prior understanding, there is nothing to disagree *with*" (Rabinowitz and Smith 14–15). Authorial reading, in short, provides the necessary means for understanding a text as its author likely intended it to be understood, and for pushing against or beyond that understanding. Just how necessary? Rabinowitz contends that "in order to read intelligently, we need to come to share the characteristics of the authorial audience, at least provisionally, while we're reading. To the extent that we do not, our reading experience will be more or less seriously flawed" (Rabinowitz and Smith 5).

Nearly two centuries after Irving wrote "Rip Van Winkle," we may safely assume that readers will bring at least a rudimentary knowledge of the American Revolutionary War to their reading of the tale. Still, there is much they are unlikely to know, such as what a "curtain lecture" was or, more central to the story, what it meant to be a Federal or a Tory (Irving 457). Readers today are also unlikely to recognize that what Rip takes to be "a tall naked pole, with something on top that looked like a red nightcap," is a liberty pole with liberty cap; indeed, most readers will have no knowledge of these once-pervasive "symbols of liberty" (Irving 463). Footnotes appended to the tale in academic anthologies explain these arcane references, as editors effectively rewrite "Rip Van Winkle" for their own authorial audience. These footnotes reflect the editors' belief that students will lack much of the knowledge Irving expected of his readers and, more to the point, that a sufficient understanding of the tale requires having this knowledge. The preponderance of annotated texts used in literature courses implies that, whether they know it or not, educators widely share Rabinowitz's belief that, while a gap will always exist between the authorial audience and actual readers, "the smaller the gap, the better the reading" (Rabinowitz and Smith 6).

A practice akin to authorial reading has been advocated by philosophers who defend a view of literary interpretation called *hypothetical intentionalism*. In "Intention and Interpretation in Literature," Jerrold Levinson writes that a work's "core of literary meaning ... is not the meaning (the many meanings) of the words and sentences taken in abstraction from the author, or ... the meaning that the author actually intended to put across, but our best *hypothetical attribution* of such, formed from the position of intended audience" (179). Like Rabinowitz, Levinson holds that readers should endeavor to construe a text in the manner its author intended it to be construed by readers. He distinguishes "two kinds of intentions relevant to the production and reception of art: *categorical* intentions, on the one hand, and *semantic* intentions, on the other" (188). Semantic intentions involve the meaning of words, phrases, and historical and cultural references—or, more precisely, the author's presumption that readers will know those meanings. Categorical intentions are another matter. They involve "an author's intention that [a text] be *classified* or *taken* in some specific or general way" (188).

Intentions are categorical when they concern how a writer frames or categorizes his or her work for a projected audience. Levinson calls "the intention that something be regarded as literature" the "most general of categorical intentions" (188). To regard a text as literature, or more specifically as a poem, or more specifically still as a sonnet or a limerick or an ode, is not to know what it means but rather to know how to go about construing its meaning. Categorical intentions, states Levinson, "govern not what a work is to mean but how it is to be fundamentally conceived or approached" (188), and "thus indirectly affect what it will resultingly say or express" (189). In other words, an author cannot directly inscribe meaning in the text but can design the text in a way that indirectly leads readers to construe that meaning ... or something like it.

Levinson writes that "whatever meaning the text-as-work ends up possessing, this will not be independent of whether it is properly construed as in one category or genre or medium rather than another" (188). That is to say, its meaning will differ depending on how the text is categorized by readers. Rabinowitz similarly remarks, "We do not read so much as *read as*—texts are always seen as instances of broader or narrower genres, and genre placement determines how they are read and, to a certain extent, what readers will find in them" (Rabinowitz and Smith 63). Because literary texts are typically categorized in terms of genre, Rabinowitz refers not to categorical intentions but to genre placement. Emphasizing its central importance, he states that "knowledge of genre is a prerequisite to authorial reading. In order to participate as part of the authorial audience, a reader needs to know (explicitly or implicitly) the genre of the text in question" (Rabinowitz and Smith 60).

Modifying Levinson's terms by drawing from Rabinowitz, I would refer to semantic intentions and generic intentions. My scholarly edition of "Rip Van Winkle" suggests the importance of having readers recognize both, as it not only explains arcane terms and historical references but also identifies the text by genre, describing Irving's tale as the satirical retelling of a German folk-legend (Irving 455n1). What a reader makes of "Rip Van Winkle" will vary greatly depending on whether it is read as a modernized folk-legend, a political satire, a historical allegory, a comic sketch, a fairy tale, or something else entirely. Likewise, what a writer makes of the tale in writing about it depends on the generic terms in which it is rewritten.

GENRES AS AGREED-UPON RULES

Genres are typically defined in terms of textual attributes. This is the case in this book's first chapter, where I write that a genre is a category of cultural text marked by the use of particular storytelling methods and conventions. Rabinowitz provides an alternative conception, stating that "genre is best understood not as a group of texts that share textual features but rather as a collection of texts that call on similar sets of rules, that invite similar interpretive strategies" (Rabinowitz and Smith 60). Taking this a step further, he remarks that a genre comprises not texts that call upon certain sets of rules but the sets of rules themselves. Rather than collections of texts, "genres are collections of rules the readers are accustomed to find together" (Rabinowitz and Smith 69). And just as these rules constrain how readers interpret texts, so they constrain how authors write them. This is true even when texts belong to a genre as broadly conceived as the short story. Authors do not, after all, reinvent the short story each time they compose a work of short fiction. Much as they follow rules of grammar and syntax, so they follow conventions for rendering thought and dialogue, characters and narrators, time and place, beginnings and endings. As George Hughes puts it, "Writers do not just sit down to write: they try to write something of a certain kind, or genre" (7). Even Carlson's "naked writer," who enters the room "alone and unmolested by culture" (30), would not sit down to write a short story if the short story genre did not already exist.

Rabinowitz proposes that "rather than think about writing as an individual's act of pure creation," we should think of authors and readers as "people who are engaged in a common project, one that requires prior agreements about the way the project is conducted. Genres, in this scheme, are the agreed-upon rules of conduct that make the activity possible" (Rabinowitz and Smith 63). If the activity in which authors and readers are engaged is communication through literary narrative, genres are the common languages in which this activity is conducted. Authors utilize genre conventions with the presumption that their readers will recognize these conventions and interpret what they have written accordingly. For an illustration of this point, let us briefly return to the *World Book* comic strip discussed in the introductory chapter.

What characterizes the strip's authorial audience? We can safely say its author assumed his readers would recognize that the characters are schoolboys, that they are carrying books because they are coming from school, and that history is a subject taught in school. Though such knowledge may seem to "go without saying," I can imagine a future in which readers will neither recognize the curious objects the boys carry nor know that history was once a subject taught in schools. I note too that the author took the precaution of writing the word *school* on the building drawn in the first panel, as if to ensure that readers will identify it as a schoolhouse and, by extension, the books as schoolbooks and the boys as schoolboys.

So much for the cartoonist's semantic intentions and the mimetic content of the strip; an authorial reading of the cartoon also requires having familiarity with its synthetic components through recognition of genre. The authorial audience knows to regard the text as a comic strip and, more specifically, as a two-panel gag cartoon (and not as a political cartoon commenting on the state of public education, or an autobiographical account of an episode from the cartoonist's childhood). It knows the relevant rules, such as that panels are read sequentially and chronologically from left to right, that dialogue appears in word balloons, that the first panel presents the setup for a joke and the second delivers the punch line. The authorial audience recognizes too what Rabinowitz calls the "degree of realism" operative in the text (*Before* 103). It understands, for instance, that the characters function as simple types rather than complex individuals with rich interior lives, and that a squiggly line in the second panel represents grass.

What of readers who, unaware of the rules, fail to join the authorial audience? Inspecting the wood fence rendered in both panels, I see what appears to be one or more planks, totaling maybe five feet in length and somehow held vertically in place to no apparent purpose. I might ask, What kind of "fence" is this?—except that my knowledge of the comic strip genre, of how strips work and are meant to be read, involves knowing not to pose such a question because it is beside the point. The minimally rendered fence serves to convey locale with an economy of detail. Like the grass, the sketchy fence is indicative of a visual shorthand that is less realistic than "cartoonish"; to expect it to appear and function more like an actual fence is to misread the genre and the strip. Another uninformed reader might misconstrue the minimal background detail and absent horizon, seeing it as evidence that the boys inhabit a boundless white void littered with random objects—a fence fragment here, a schoolhouse over there. The authorial reader knows better than to read the strip so literally.

For all my knowledge of the cartoon-strip genre—indeed, because of that knowledge—I knew as a child that some deficiency in my understanding prevented me from joining the authorial audience of readers who get the joke as the cartoonist presumed they would. I am reminded of another joke that baffled me as a child: Two elephants are taking a bath when one says, "Pass the soap." The other says, "No soap, radio." Here the supposed joke is on the unwitting recipient who, wanting nothing more than to join the authorial audience, takes the bait and laughs at the "punch line" despite its incoherence. This recipient errs in pretending to get the joke, but that is not all; like the recipient who responds not with laughter but with embarrassed confusion, he or she fails to discern the correct genre: "No soap radio" is an exemplary prank joke. Assuming the comic strip is a proper gag cartoon, I imagine that something in my disposition continues to impede me from reading it in the particular way "shared by the author and his or her expected readers" (*Before* 22). Either that, or the author has violated the rules by writing a gag cartoon that fails to deliver on the joke.

One can speak of authors violating the rules because, as aforementioned, writing is a rule-governed activity. Just as readers knowingly and unknowingly process texts in accordance with "rules for reading," observes Rabinowitz, so authors knowingly and unknowingly write in accordance with "rules for the proper construction of texts" that vary according to genre (*Before* 196). Of course, writers often craft texts that bend, twist, or defy the rules, but this does not free them or their readers from knowing the rules themselves. Indeed, knowing the rules is a precondition both for subverting them and for recognizing when they have been subverted. Arguably, texts that defy convention (jokes that purposely lack logic and humor, comic strips that feature nonsequential panels or nonsynchronous words and pictures) reaffirm genre norms (the exception proves the rule) while modifying them and contributing to the establishment of new genres or subgenres (the prank joke, the avant-garde comic). Joining the authorial audience entails not only discerning what a text's author presumed her or his readers would take its genre to be, but also observing how the text follows and subverts the rules of that genre.

DETERMINING GENRE

How are readers to ascertain the genres within which authors expect their work to be read? Typically it is the paratext—the material accompanying a text, such as book-jacket artwork and copy, blurbs, a title page, and possibly an introduction or preface—that informs readers of a text's genre, and readers accept this classification unless, in the course of their reading, they find reason to think otherwise. In *Chicago Review*, "The Man in the Well" is listed on the contents page under fiction (the two other headings are poetry and essays), and on *This American Life*, the host tells listeners that "The Man in the Well" is a work of fiction. Hughes writes that "the paratext sets up, in effect, an agreement, or contract of reading, between text and reader. Information given in the paratext helps us decide what category to place a text in, and the choice of category will affect our reading and evaluation of the text" (15). Still, how can we know if the author, who seldom writes the paratextual material, would have signed on to this contract?

Rabinowitz suggests that authorial reading is largely a matter of recognition. He writes that "literary conventions are not in the text waiting to be uncovered, but in fact *precede* the text and make discovery possible in the first place" (*Before* 27). Writers and readers both make use of these preexisting conventions, writers to compose texts and readers to interpret them. Given the importance placed on originality, some commentators deemphasize this aspect of literary writing. For instance, Carlson remarks that whereas "genre writers" traffic in cliché, "a good fiction writer is creating her own conventions" (34). And yet, *Ron Carlson Writes a Story* can be read as a primer in the conventions of writing genre fiction of a certain kind: the American minimalist short story, which includes "just enough data for us to apprehend the contours of the story that are suggested by what's on the page" and no more (Carlson 62). Recognized as such, Carlson's book illustrates Rabinowitz's point that genres are sets of rules for writing—in this case, rules for knowing "what is left out" when writing minimalist fiction. We as readers will apply a corresponding sets of rules when interpreting this fiction only if we recognize the genre conventions a writer has adapted—and in the absence of such recognition we will still construe the text in generic terms, though they may be misapplied. As Rabinowitz states, "Some preliminary generic judgment is always required even before we begin the process of reading. We can never interpret entirely outside generic structures: 'reading'—even the reading of a first paragraph—is always 'reading as'" (*Before* 176).

In the course of reading a text as one thing, we may come to read (or reread) it as another. Rabinowitz writes that "the attempt to read as authorial audience is ideally a process of matching presuppositions against unfolding text, and revising strategies if the text moves in unanticipated directions" (*Before* 189). This is ideally what takes place, but readers "predisposed to finding . . . meanings and values that the author did not intend" might not "run against stumbling blocks in the text" that cause them to rethink their determinations of genre, or they might cling to their presuppositions even if they do (*Before* 190). In sum, genre placement will vary greatly depending on the qualities of both readers and texts. Some readers are more informed and adaptable in their reading practices than others, and some texts are more easily categorized than others.

Likewise, some genres are more familiar and thus more readily perceived than others. As Rabinowitz notes, "genre categories can be broader or narrower," ranging from broad classes to smaller groupings to "ever more precise categories," some of which lack generic names (*Before* 178). He refers, for instance, to "a genre that has flourished especially since the 1950s: the ironic-grasping-at-straws-in-the-meaningless-abyss-novel" (*Before* 179). Obviously, readers are far less likely to recognize this genre than to recognize more broadly defined, popular, and long-established genres. I assume that all of my students would recognize "The Man in the Well" as literature, that the vast majority would classify it as fiction, and that most would identify it as a short story (while some would misidentify it as an essay, an article, or a novel). But very few, I imagine, would read it as a work of literary minimalism or minimalist fiction, most being unaware of this pared-down style of writing associated with American short story writers Ernest Hemingway and Raymond Carver, among others. While this hardly exhausts ways of categorizing Sher's story, we can already see that "The Man in the Well" may be placed within several genre categories.

Rabinowitz notes that "genre categories can overlap. Depending on *what* rules we choose to focus on, a given work may appear to fall into several different generic classes" (*Before* 177–78). It is arguably the case that genres always overlap, given that all texts simultaneously fall within broader and narrower genre categories, and that, as Douglas Hesse observes, a "precise boundary line" between genres may not exist (86). Hesse writes that "few works, finally, are generically pure. Classifying them is more a matter of specifying which emphases count than positing a set of qualities that exclude all other classifications" (85). Here we again confront the hermeneutic circle, for while the rules that we apply and the textual elements that we emphasize determine a text's genre, it is also the case that a text's genre determines which rules we apply and which textual elements we emphasize.

Genre designation seems fairly straightforward in cases where the paratext informs readers of a text's genre and the textual cues affirm this categorization. But uncertainty characterizes our determinations of genre in less straightforward cases, those marked by what Rabinowitz calls "generic ambiguity" (*Before* 193). Holding that "misreading follows in the wake of erroneous placement," he finds that less easily categorized texts are particularly "open to misreadings" (*Before* 177, 193). Might generic ambiguity account for my students' misreadings of "The Man in the Well"? Beyond its classification as a short story, is this text difficult to classify? Is its genre ambiguous, uncertain, difficult to name? I believe so, though due not to a lack of generic signals or cues in the text, but rather to how little known is the genre in which it participates. That is to say, I believe my students' unfamiliarity with the genre of Sher's short story accounts for why so many of them interpret the story in ways that conflict with the rules or conventions for reading a text of its kind. And what kind is that? For reasons I will next discuss, I take Sher's short story to be a modern parable.

THE ALLEGORICAL FIGURE IN THE WELL

What I am calling the modern parable is a seldom-noted, undertheorized literary genre that lacks a single established name. I take the name *modern parable* from Howard Schwartz's 1991 collection *Imperial Messages: One Hundred Modern Parables,* which largely includes works dating from the 1960s and 1970s, though it opens with short stories by Franz Kafka that serve as archetypes of the form. In an introduction titled "Kafka and the Modern Parable," Schwartz observes that contemporary short story collections feature, alongside "more conventional short stories," an increasing number of "short prose allegories," "usually brief works" that bear "a strong resemblance to the parables of the ancient past, due to their use of a central or extended metaphor which has obvious allegorical implications" (xxi). Allegory is the rhetorical device of using characters, actions, or settings to represent abstract ideas and symbolic meanings. Referring to brief literary narratives that make considerable use of allegory, Schwartz remarks, "Now that so many authors have successfully written in this allegorical mode, it is obvious that the parable has been resurrected as a genre" (xxi).

Reason to question Schwartz's term of choice can be found in Paul March-Russell's 2009 study *The Short Story*, where the parable is defined as a narrative that aims "to instruct the reader according to a higher religious or moral purpose" (3). The parable is often paired with the fable, a closely related genre that uses anthropomorphized animals and things instead of human beings as characters. March-Russell states that the fable is also distinguished by a use of ironic humor that "often unsettles a consistent or overarching morality," making the moral of the story less evident (3). He writes that "whereas Christian parables such as the Good Samaritan have a clear and instructive meaning, Aesop's *Fables* are more ambiguous, especially the shorter fables that are scarcely more than epigrams" (4). For this reason, he finds that although short stories such as those by Kafka "appear to have a parabolic structure, in that they seem to portend some deeper meaning, the narrative form is closer to that of the fable" (4).

John Gardner and Lennis Dunlap, in their 1962 textbook *The Forms of Fiction*, similarly apply the term *modern fable* to such short stories. Unlike March-Russell, however, they propose that it is the fable that has a clear and instructive meaning, whereas the parable "need not be cynical or ironic, and its meaning need not be instantly apparent" (26). Indeed, they contend that the main difference between the fable and the modern short story is "the fable's very obvious moralistic purpose, the degree to which it instructs" (26). Accordingly, the fable became "modern" by becoming less clearly instructive and more like the parable, so that "no distinctions between the two any longer need to be made" (26).

Whether one identifies the parable or the fable as more ambiguous and open-ended, the genre's qualifying elements would appear to be symbolically resonant characters and settings, morally freighted scenarios, and—perhaps most important—meanings that are not didactic but enigmatic. Ian Reid, in his 1977 study *The Short Story*, writes that fables and parables can only "enter the territory of the genuine short story" when they "no longer insist on a narrowly didactic point" (37). Schwartz likewise distinguishes the modern parable from its "ancient moralistic form, primarily associated with religious teachings, and in particular with the parables of Jesus," by noting that it is no longer limited to "religious and moralistic ends" (xxii), for while "the element of drawing a moral" remains, there is no longer an explicit moral to the story (xxvii).

Rather than offer clear and instructive meanings, the modern parable, "deriving much of its subject matter and imagery from unconscious inspiration" (xxiii), describes truths that are "complex and not fully accessible to consciousness," according to Schwartz (xxvii). He states that these truths concern the psyche, or inner self. Much as dreams present us with "images from the world around us," rendering them in ways that refer "not to the world from which they were taken, but to the psyche itself," so the modern parable, through a "use of symbolism, so close to that found in dreams," conjures a minimally realized but nonetheless realistic world in "an attempt to map out a great unchartered area, the human psyche" (xxiv).

I read "The Man in the Well" as a modern parable because I recognize its adherence to the rules of that genre. I see these generic rules reflected by the story's economical form, its sparsely rendered characters and setting, its use of the well as a highly symbolic central metaphor, and its enigmatic quality. I recognize that its realistic storyworld feels otherworldly because of its allegorical resonance: a dry well on an abandoned farm-lot may seem unremarkable, but in the story this setting exists as if center stage, surrounded by darkness. I recognize that the narrative evokes in readers a sense that a moral is or should be forthcoming, yet ends up providing little sense of what this moral might be, and that the story seems to say something inexplicit yet profound about the human psyche. And I recognize the man in the well as an allegorical figure, a character who is not a flesh-and-blood person but a symbolic entity.

Allegorical figurers are hardly limited to parables and fables. In his 1995 study *The Short Story*, Charles E. May writes that, prior to the nineteenth century, short fictional texts "such as folktales, short romances, fables, and ballads were for the most part allegorically code-bound rather than realistically mimetic" (21). He holds that this changed with the rise of realism in the latter half of the nineteenth century, in the form of literary narratives that use "specific detail and real-time events to provide a verisimilar version of the everyday world" (21). This realist turn presented a challenge to writers of short fiction. "In the older tale or romance," writes May, "characters functioned as psychic projections of basic human fears and desires; in the new fiction, however, the characters had to be presented as if they were real" (47). This proved difficult because, according to May, "the short story is too compressed to allow the creation of characters through multiplicity of detail and social interaction, as is typical of the novel" (52). He theorizes that early nineteenth-century writers of short fiction, finding themselves unable to match the realism of the novel and unwilling to "accept the supernaturalism that formed the basis of the older, allegorical short forms," combined the narrative conventions of these older forms with the new "verisimilar techniques" of realistic forms, creating a new genre that would come to be known as the short story (21–22).

May illustrates how differently short stories have mixed romantic and realistic conventions by contrasting two early works: Edgar Allan Poe's "The Fall of the House of Usher" and Herman Melville's "Bartleby the Scrivener." While both stories are told by "as-if-real" character narrators, May posits that they combine allegorical and realistic elements in opposing ways (32). Poe's character narrator enters a metaphoric world (the House) dominated by a metaphoric figure (Usher); Melville's character narrator resides in an as-if-real world (the law office) until a metaphoric figure (Bartleby) enters it and "transforms reality into metaphor" (47). In short, Poe has an as-if-real character enter a metaphoric world, whereas Melville has a metaphoric figure enter an as-if-real world. Sher's short story is more like Melville's, insofar as it features a character narrator who tells a story about as-if-real characters (the children) who reside in an as-if-real world (the farm-lot) where they encounter a metaphoric figure (the man in the well) who transforms the realistic setting into the symbolic terrain of the character narrator's psyche.

May writes of "Bartleby the Scrivener":

> The story seems so firmly grounded in social reality that it is difficult to take Bartleby as a purely symbolic character; at the same time, if we take him to be an "as-if-real" character, we have difficulty understanding what motivates him to act in the perverse way he does. We want to ask Bartleby, "What is the matter with you?" but we gradually begin to realize that he has no matter—which is to say, he can only react as a two-dimensional representation of passive rebellion. (38)

I would assume that readers of Sher's story would ask the children, and not the man, "What is the matter with you?" except that so many of my students are less troubled by the children than by the man in the well. I propose this is because they do not know what to make of a character who "has no matter," a character even more purely symbolic and less defined than Bartleby. Like Bartleby, the man in the well is a two-dimensional representation, though of patriarchal authority rather than passive rebellion. Readers who want to ask him, "Why are you in the well?" or "Why not tell the children your name?" have yet to recognize that he is not an as-if-real character but a metaphoric figure and a narrative device, a synthetic part of the story's generic structure.

How did the man come to be in the well? He was never *not* in the well; he was always already "the man in the well." Why was he in the well? For the same reason the well was on the farm-lot: to present the children with a dilemma. The story is not about the man—who he was, how he came to be in the well, what he might have done had he gotten out. It is about what the children chose to do when they discovered the man in the well, how the narrator recounts what they did, and the moral implications of both. Now, to answers such questions in this way is to break the mimetic illusion by referring to the synthetic component of the narrative. Why did the children never ask the man how he came to be in the well? That they never asked suggests the limits of their own as-if-real characterizations: ultimately they behaved as characters operating within the conventions of the modern parable, and conventions dictate that such a question would not be asked of a metaphoric figure.

THE IMPLIED AUTHOR AND IRA

Did Ira intend for "The Man in the Well" to be read as a modern parable? Yes and no—which is to say, no, not really ... but still, in a way, yes. A year after we began corresponding, I asked Ira if he regarded his short story as "a kind of parable in the modern parable tradition (of Kafka, Borges, etc., as opposed to biblical parable)." He replied, "I do tend to think of 'The Man in the Well' as operating much like a modern parable, although I did not set out to write such a thing. Something left open-ended enough often has that feeling." Ira did not knowingly set out to write a modern parable, or necessarily even know the genre by name, but what he wrote nevertheless fits its conventions due to his familiarity with how the modern parable operates—a familiarity gained from having read short fiction by Kafka and Borges, among others. I suspect that this familiarity accounts, in no small part, for why Ira was able to draft "The Man in the Well" so quickly, in one afternoon. Knowing how a story of this kind operates, but without knowing how much he was drawing on this knowledge, he might feel as if "the story really wrote itself."

In reading the short story as a modern parable, I presumed that its author intended for it to be read in that way. My realization of the story involved, in other words, forming a particular impression of its author. I took Sher to be the author of a modern parable, although I was not fully aware of this until my students' differing interpretive responses led me to reflect on my own. When my students treated the man in the well as an as-if-real character, questioning who he was and how he came to be in the well, I found myself thinking that surely the author never expected readers to respond to "the voice of the man in the well" in this way. Surely, I thought, Sher expected his readers to question the children's behavior, not the man's character and presence in the well. Much as I had conceived of the man and the children and the character narrator and his mother and father in particular ways, so I had characterized the author, ascribing to him a sensibility and expectations concerning how "The Man in the Well" would be read.

Narrative theorists have a name for this persona: he or she is (or they are, in the case of multiauthored works) *the implied author.* Distinguished from the narrator who tells the story and *the flesh-and-blood author* who actually wrote it (alternatively called *the real author, the historical author,* or simply *the author*), the implied author is a conception of the writer conveyed by or inferred from the text. Since Wayne Booth introduced the term in his 1961 study *The Rhetoric of Fiction,* its precise meaning and utility have been hotly contested. While some narrative theorists call for abandoning the implied author altogether, claiming the concept is incoherent and unnecessary, others defend the term's relevance while offering more fine-tuned conceptions of its meaning. This back-and-forth has generated a large and steadily growing body of scholarship, including a recent essay in which Susan Lanser writes: "For the past few years, I've wandered around narrative conferences muttering, 'Please, not another talk about the implied author.' 'Can't we banish arguments about the implied author from the conference?'" She explains that "those cranky comments were calling not for the erasure of a term but for the admission of a stalemate," given that "the longstanding debates about the implied author had reached a point of diminishing returns" (153).

Why has the implied author proven so controversial? Debates over the term's validity are rooted in questions concerning what grounds literary meaning. As Abbott puts it, "the continuing argument regarding what exactly the implied author is and what role this concept should play attests to a persistent need to anchor the interpretation of literary texts in some version of an intending source" ("Reading" 464). Booth introduced the implied author partly in response to the New Critical assertion of the intentional fallacy and emphasis on the work itself. Whereas Wimsatt and Beardsley wrote that a poem is "detached from the author at birth and goes about the world beyond his power to intend about it or control it" (470), Booth would call attention to the work of fiction as the creation of an intending source, "as the product of a choosing, evaluating person rather than as a self-existing thing" (*Rhetoric* 74). But in identifying this person as the implied author, he made the nature of this intending source unclear. Who or what implied the implied author? Is the implied author a self-existing thing or the product of a choosing, evaluating person? And, if the latter, is that person the author, the reader, or both? In fact, Booth suggests all of the above, identifying the implied author first with the "implied version of 'himself'" the author creates (*Rhetoric* 70), then with "the picture" the reader has of the author (*Rhetoric* 71), and finally with "the core of norms and choices" that compose the work (*Rhetoric* 74).

Narrative theorists have sought to improve on Booth's concept by identifying the implied author with either the text, the author, or the reader. For example, Seymour Chatman asserts that the implied author, "a silent source of information" (85), is "nothing other than the text itself" (86); Phelan holds that the implied author is neither the text nor "a product of the text but rather the agent responsible for bringing the text into existence" (*Living* 45); and Lanser contends that the implied author is "necessarily a *reading effect*," for "without a reader, there is no implied authorship" (154). I am reminded of the story of the blind men who present incompatible descriptions of what an elephant is because each takes as definitive that part of the animal he touches: a leg, a tusk, a trunk. Abbott provides a picture more closely approximating the animal as a whole:

> Of course, when the real living and breathing author constructs the narrative, much of that real author goes into the implied author. But the implied author is also, like the narrative itself, a kind of construct that among other things serves to anchor the narrative. We, in our turn, as we read, develop our own idea of this implied sensibility behind the narrative. So the implied author . . . could as easily be called the "the inferred author" and perhaps with more justice, since we often differ from each other (and no doubt the author as well) in the views and feelings we attribute to the implied author. (*Cambridge* 84–85)

The parts played by author, text (narrative), and reader are all represented here. Still, Abbott stresses what readers infer over both what is inferable in the text and what the author has implied when he deems *the inferred author* a more precise term than *the implied author*.

Finding use for both terms, Patrick Colm Hogan writes: "Anyone who has ever taught anything realizes that there is always some student who will come up with a different interpretation, who will infer a different author, even in cases that we find straightforward. This is where the difference between an inferred and an implied author comes into play. The implied author is, so to speak, the correct version of the inferred author" (26). I recall my students' misreadings of "The Man in the Well" and think that it is far easier to single out an erroneous conception of the author (say, one that equates him with the narrator) than to determine "the correct version." In fact, the correct version of the implied author will prove as elusive and contestable as the right reading of the text. Instead of providing an anchor for the interpretation of a literary text, the implied author is part and parcel of the interpretation it would anchor. It is an important part, insofar as it calls us to attend to how a literary text has been designed to affect readers in particular ways. Still, we might ask, is the implied author necessarily part of this authorial design?

In a recent contribution to the implied author debate, Jeroen Vandaele contends that much as readers of fiction "assume by convention" that the narrator is fictitious and not to be confused with the flesh-and-blood author, so they should accept that a fiction writer "creates an ethical position, an authorial voice" that differs from her own (165). Consequently, he argues, "any authorial voice or values inferable from the text" should not be identified with her "in a straightforward manner—as if she were producing nonfictional discourse" (165). In fact, readers of nonfiction should also recognize this disjuncture between writers and the authorial voices they achieve in writing. As Carl H. Klaus puts it,

> the "person" in a personal essay is a written construct, a fabricated thing, a character of sorts—the sound of its voice a byproduct of carefully chosen words, its recollection of experience, its run of thought and feeling, much tidier than the mess of memories, thoughts, and feelings arising in one's consciousness. (1)

Moreover, an essayist or critic may "try on" an ethical position, pushing it as far as he can; despite ambivalence or uncertainty, he may adopt the authorial voice of one wholly committed to a position, if only to see where it will take him.

That said, I imagine that personal essayists are more mindful of constructing implied versions of themselves in writing than are fiction writers, precisely because they expect their readers to assume a shared identity between author and narrator. That fiction writers consciously create implied authors strikes me as less likely. But then a reader's conception of the implied author may be supported by considerable textual evidence regardless of what the flesh-and-blood author has intended. Indeed, for Booth the possibility that "the author's expressed intentions, *outside* the text, could be in total contrast to the intentions finally realized in the finished text" only points to "the importance of the implied author/author distinction" ("Resurrection" 75). Part of this distinction, as I see it, concerns the writing process. Simply put, the implied author reflects not this process but its end product, the finished text. And just as "finished texts tend to conceal much of the labor involved in writing them" (Harris 99), so the implied author inferred from a finished text conceals the drafting process through which meaning is discovered and evolves, offering in its place the illusion of a simple and direct causal relationship between authorial intention and textual realization. Given this, it is no wonder that the flesh-and-blood author and his or her readers may offer different descriptions of "the intentions finally realized in the text."

Wary of becoming lost in the weeds of the implied author debate, I have largely avoided the terms *implied author* and *flesh-and-blood-author*, referring instead to Sher and Ira. Students sometimes refer to authors by first name in their papers. For teachers, a reference to Jane or Toni, rather than to Austen or Morrison, designates either a naively informal or a falsely intimate relation to a flesh-and-blood author (though it also may indicate a student's intimate connection to the implied author of a text that has powerfully affected him or her). In referring to Ira, I play on this distinction between the first-name and last-name author. Whereas Sher is a textual figure, born of a text authored by a writer and interpreted by readers, Ira is the actual person who wrote "The Man in the Well" and with whom I have discussed the story over email, on the telephone, and in person. But is Ira the flesh-and-blood author who wrote "The Man in the Well" twenty years ago? Not exactly. No doubt, what Ira tells me differs from what the flesh-and-blood (first-time) author would have said or written in 1995, in response to questions concerning the creation and conception of his story. What Ira tells me reflects the development of his thought on fiction writing to date, his experience as a short story writer and novelist, and the imprecision of memory. "I wish I could provide more information on the drafting process behind 'The Man in the Well,'" he wrote me in one instance, "but it was quite a while ago."

Because the author exists in time, there is no single flesh-and-blood author. The text is certainly more stable, though it too is altered with every revision, annotation, new edition, and recontextualization. However, unlike a person, the text does not have intentions, views, and feelings—all attributes of the implied author. Because there are any number of nondefinitive, more and less persuasive interpretations of this "sensibility behind the narrative," there is no single implied author. Nevertheless, it is often useful to distinguish between the flesh-and-blood author and the implied author of the text one is discussing. With these terms I can reflect on how, when I first contacted the flesh-and-blood author of "The Man in the Well," I addressed my questions to the implied author I had inferred from that text. At the time, Ira Sher was for me the flesh-and-blood incarnation of that implied author. I presumed him to be the author of a modern parable, and I expected that he would judge the children harshly for their immoral acts.

Not surprisingly, Ira has proven to be unlike the author I imagined. Whereas I inferred an implied author who expected readers to take the children's immorality as a given, Ira has described writing his story in such a way as to make the children's moral character more ambiguous: perhaps these boys and girls were not immoral so much as *a*moral, lacking in moral understanding. Now one may ask, whose conception of the implied author—Ira's or my own—is more in line with the ethical position or intentions "finally realized in the finished text"? My sense is that textual evidence can be cited to make a compelling case for either view, and the question cannot be answered conclusively.

MAYBE THE MOTHER KNEW THE MAN

If the implied author of "The Man in the Well" adhered to the rules of the modern parable, Ira did not consciously do so. This may explain why he did not think to mention certain decisions he made in crafting the short story—not, that is, until I asked about them. Chief among these was his decision to treat the man in the well as something other than an as-if-real character. After asking Ira if he considered his story as a kind of parable, I asked if he regarded the man in the well as a MacGuffin, a prop that exists to drive the story with a minimum of narrative explanation. Did he think that sophisticated readers, being more conversant with literary conventions, would understand that questions regarding the man's backstory are irrelevant to the moral drama posed by the story? He replied:

> As far as the man goes, you're entirely right: I didn't think of him as a fully articulated character—that much I do remember. How the man came to be in the well is not, for me, meant to be a question that engages the reader. I hadn't considered that someone might become caught in this MacGuffin, might run with it and find it full of meaning. I've seen such a thing happen with the parents, too, in some readings. Clearly, I do, as you suggest,

assume that a more sophisticated reader will be on the same page as me about such stage-setting devices.

In writing "The Man in the Well," Ira had not imagined that readers would question how the man came to be in the well. Now familiar with how readers respond to his story in ways he had not anticipated, he recognizes acts of overreading through which readers provide "missing" narrative explanations. Not part of the authorial audience, these readers invent backstories to account for why the man was in the well, why the mother was crying in the night and the father was murmuring, why the children chose not to help the man.

It is worth noting that while Ira did not regard the man in the well as "a fully articulated character" or even "a person, with a history, a trajectory" while he was writing the story, neither did he think of the man as an allegorical figure or symbolic character with a specific meaning. "He's more like a mirror or lens that the other characters are reflected in/captured by," he writes. "And then he is, I suppose, literally, a feature of the landscape." Elaborating on what he makes of the man in hindsight, Ira remarks:

> Very few of the characters have much to flesh them out, but the man really is more of a sounding board for the thoughts and actions of the children. He seems to say the most obvious things at the beginning, and then to mirror back to the children the things they've already said (which of course take on a different meaning when mirrored back). There is very little content in what he says, outside of the purely factual (the physicality of the well itself) and the obvious (get help, etc.) until the final scene, where he repeats the children's questions back to them, and asks, in a sense, why they didn't do the most obvious thing.

As Ira describes him, the man in the well is a device through which the children are made to face what they have said and done. This accords with May's conception of the modern short story as a form that relies less on plotted action than on having characters "confront a metaphoric embodiment of their dilemma" (73).

Of course, May's is a highly selective conception of the short story—one that, March-Russell argues, treats "lyrical short stories written within a post-Chekhovian mode such as [those by] James Joyce and Katherine Mansfield" as the norm, neglecting more accessible, popular, and commercial forms of short fiction (78). But given that Sher's story falls within this mode, this hardly diminishes the applicability of May's short story theory.

"The most obvious similarity between the stories of Chekhov and those of Joyce ... and Mansfield is their minimal dependence on the traditional notion of plot," writes May. Theirs are not "highly plotted stories" but "seemingly static episodes and 'slices' of reality" that "depend on unity of feeling to create a sense of 'storyness'" (16). I think of how Sher's narrator tells of "resorting to the man in the well" in order to convey an otherwise indescribable feeling, and of how much of the story he tells involves repetition and stasis:

> After waiting what seemed like a good while, we quietly came back to the well. We stood or lay around the lip, listening for maybe half an hour ... we were quiet for a bit ... we waited for a while, thinking about him waiting in the well. ... After an hour, he began calling again ... Only Wendy stayed by the well for a while ... After an hour everyone had left except Wendy and myself. ... We could hear him shouting for a while ... There was no sound for a while from the well ... we all waited for the man in the well to speak up ... We had to wait for an hour ... At last, the man in the well ... called a few of us ... Then he was quiet for a while.

Each day the children lingered at the well, silently waiting for something to happen, for the man to say something. I think of the children who, "after a while, ... went to town to sit in the cool movie theater." I read that they did so because it was hot outside, but I like to imagine they also went to the theater for the kind of highly plotted story they were not experiencing at the farm-lot.

My students who seek to understand "The Man in the Well" in terms of plotted action inevitably refer to the peculiar paragraph in which the character narrator recalls hearing his mother weep at night in her room downstairs, and the stubborn murmur of his father. As discussed in the last chapter, Ira regards this paragraph as a moment of lyricism intended "to slow the reader down and create tone." But for several of my students, and I expect a great many other readers, this paragraph provides the key to unlocking plot machinations. "Although in the piece there is no explicit correlation mentioned between the narrator's mother and the man in the well," writes one student, "I suspect that the mother's sobbing has to do with the man in the well. I think that she is upset because she is in a relationship with the man in the well (whether it is platonic or sexual I have no idea), and I think that she is grieving because she is missing the man in the well." The absence of any such explicit correlation between the man and the character narrator's mother constitutes a gap that many readers fill by forging plot connections.

Often this gap is addressed with notable uncertainty. "I wondered as I read the story if the man in the well had some connection to the narrator's family as he made reference to his mother weeping and his father mumbling at night during the time," one student writes, adding, "If there was such a connection, an argument could be made that the narrator had a larger moral responsibility to act and get help because of his personal connection to the situation." His classmate expresses greater confusion, writing: "The situations with the mother crying, was she missing someone? Did she know the man in the well? Maybe the people of the town put the man in the well and for this reason the mother was crying. Maybe the father put a man in the well and only the mother knew and for this reason she was crying. I never figured it all out." Other students explain why the mother was crying with more certainty. "The only textual connection that would explain these tears would be if the family knew the man in the well was missing and thus mourned for him," one comments; another remarks, "I think the mother must have known the man in the well. The man was probably a friend, family, or lover who went missing. We know that it isn't the boy's father because he is mentioned in the story. Whoever the man in the well was, the mother knew the man."

Recourse to a conventional adultery plot recurs in my students' interpretations. "I believe that the narrator's mother was having an affair with the man in the well. Moreover, the boy's father probably threw the man down the well," a student writes. She supports this belief by noting that when the character narrator ran away from the well on the second day, he "thought that . . . maybe [the man] had said he was sorry." What did the man have to feel sorry for, if not the affair? Another student speculates: "Maybe the mother knew the man in that well. The two could have shared an intimate relationship. The narrator's father could have found out the two had an affair and threw the man in the well. Did the man in the well commit a crime and that was his punishment? While falling down the well maybe he hit his head and had a case of amnesia." Here one formulaic plot point leads to another.

READING LITERALLY AND LITERARILY

The allure of familiar plot motifs among my students runs counter to a claim made by Peter Brooks that, somewhere in the course of our schooling, we learn that "reading for the plot" is a "low form of activity." He explains: "Plot has been disdained as the element of narrative that least sets off and defines high art—indeed, plot is that which especially characterizes popular mass-consumption literature" ("Reading" 202). I wonder if Brooks does not overstate the case, given that my literature students do tend to read for the plot. Qualley writes that students are most familiar with two kinds of reading, neither of which is "particularly useful for the kind of analysis and critical questioning college requires": they read either "for pleasure—to experience, escape, enjoy"—or "for the main idea (the gist), which entails reading for information" ("Using" 103). While my students might not read for the plot as they would when reading for pleasure, many read as if the story's main idea is revealed through plot machinations.

Are they wrong for reading the story in this way? Does "The Man in the Well" not engage readers on the level of plot? One might argue that the story's third sentence, "I think it's important that we decided not to help him," indicates the plot's minimal significance by revealing its outcome to readers. Yet the statement need not be taken as indicative of what the children decided to do in the end, nor need it dissuade first-time readers from reading on to find out if the man managed to escape by some other means, perhaps outwitting the children. My own sense, given that the children's decision did prove final, is that the sentence should serve primarily to redirect the reader's attention from the matter of whether or not the children would help the man to that of *why* they decided not to help him. This is a question the plot does not answer.

No doubt, students tend to read for plot because, being far more practiced in consuming mass media than in analyzing literature, they read works of "high art" as they would "popular mass-consumption literature." Like most readers, they are significantly less versed in what Carlson calls "the literary story" (100) than in "genre fiction," a category in which he includes thrillers, romances, and science fiction as well as "television stories" (10, 34). Though I would again note that the minimalist short story he favors is also a form of genre fiction, Carlson reserves the term for "fiction where plot rules the characters" (42). He writes: "Character serves event in genre fiction. They hold up the plot points like banners and march them around" (51). "Character, the human heart, is paramount," by contrast, in the literary story (51); actions and events matter to the extent they concern "unnamed emotional facets of the human heart" and similarly complex "states of mind" (100). Similarly, Rabinowitz writes that when reading "popular fiction" (as opposed to "serious fiction") we are likely to interpret a textual detail "in terms of what it may tell us about plot outcome, rather than in terms of what it may reveal about the inner states of the characters" (*Before* 185). Students who approach works of "serious" literature as they would more plot-oriented works of "popular" literature are likely to miss the emphasis placed on characters' mental lives, and may feel frustrated by the lack of eventfulness in the stories they are assigned to read.

The distinction between genre or popular fiction, on the one hand, and literary or serious fiction, on the other, recalls Barthes's distinction between readerly and writerly texts. Much as Barthes writes that "the commercial and ideological habits of our society" would have us consume a text in one reading "so that we can then move on to another story, buy another book" (S/Z 15–16), Rabinowitz remarks that "our current cultural context encourages us to zip through popular texts carelessly" (*Before* 185–86). The cultural context to which he refers was that of the 1980s and 1990s; today the act of zipping through texts is associated less with popular fiction than with digital technology—with the Internet and "hyperreading" as opposed to "typical print reading" (Hayles 66). Forgotten is the fact that, as Keith Oatley notes, literary reading as a "mode of extended concentration on a piece of fiction or non-fiction is, and always has been, a minority interest" (175). In other words, typical print reading has never been synonymous with the close reading of literary fiction. Students who zip through assigned literary texts, reading them quickly and just once even when writing on them, can be accused of laziness or diagnosed as digital natives with a diminished capacity for "deep attention and close reading" (Hayles 72). The real problem, however, may be students' lack of awareness that these texts are designed to be read and reread with extended concentration. In reading them hurriedly, students mistake the genre of both text and task.

Amy J. Devitt writes that knowing a genre entails not only or even primarily recognizing its textual conventions, but rather "knowing one way of responding appropriately to a given situation" (16). While genre may be determined in terms of textual attributes, authorial intention, reading practices, and paratextual markers, the "given situation" or context in which a work is read is also determinative. Any text read "for school," whether drawn from the literary canon or the current best-seller list, belongs to a genre we might call the *study text*. Though at one time only canonical literature merited study in the classroom, the academic study of popular texts and popular culture is now commonplace, while an emphasis on *what* we read has ceded ground to an interest in *how* we read. While at one time only "serious" literature would have been regarded as literary, this is no longer the case. Here I recall Patricia Harkin's remark that "what makes a text literary is the kind of reading a reader gives to it" (*Acts* 56). This kind of reading—what she calls "reading *literarily*, rather than *literally*" (*Acts* 57)— entails two acts: first, looking for places in a text where one has "difficulty constructing meaning" (*Acts* 55–56) and, second, seeking to "construct meaning from figurative language" (*Acts* 228).

A text need not be literary in order to be read literarily, as my analysis of the *World Book* cartoon illustrates. Literary theorists, as Culler notes,

> have come to insist on the importance in non-literary texts ... of rhetorical devices such as metaphor, which have been thought crucial to literature but have often been considered purely ornamental in other sorts of discourses. In showing how rhetorical figures shape thought in other discourses as well, theorists demonstrate a powerful literariness at work in supposedly non-literary texts, thus complicating the distinction between the literary and the non-literary. (*Literary* 19)

I made meaning of the comic strip by considering some of its details (as you may recall, the boys' hats, their books, and the schoolhouse) in metaphoric rather than literal terms, and I used my difficulty in making sense of the strip as a point of entry for rereading and writing on it. In doing so, I applied my training in literary analysis to a popular text. When readers respond to a text such as "The Man in the Well" as if it were a straightforward, almost factual recounting of events, they make the opposite move of reading literature literally, neglecting its "powerful literariness."

My students read literally rather than literarily when they treat the children in Sher's story as they would real people rather than as text-based creations, claiming to understand them based primarily on what they know of their younger siblings, their work as babysitters or nannies, or their own childhood memories. Culler refers to "a certain kind of attention that we might call literary: an interest in the words, their relations to one another, and their implications, and particularly an interest in how what is said relates to the way it is said." This attentiveness to language, he explains, should move us to ask of a sentence not only what it means but also "How does this language work? What does this sentence do?" (*Literary* 24). A response to "The Man in the Well" that considers the text only in relation to the reader's own life experiences bypasses any such consideration of language, paying no attention to "how what is said relates to the way it is said" by the narrator and written by the author. Neglecting rather than engaging the words of the text, such a response cannot properly be called literary analysis.

Students also fail to read literarily when they draw narrow plot-based meanings from language, characters, and events that might be treated metaphorically or symbolically. For instance, many imagine that the rain mentioned at the end of "The Man in the Well" caused the well to flood, more than likely drowning the man—unless, as one enterprising student has it, the rainfall enabled the man to swim out of the well. Ira accounts for the rain in more symbolic terms, stating:

> I think I see the rain as a release for the story. It seems physically unlikely the man has drowned, but many people do read it that way. What I take as important is the possibility of this death existing (or escape—the question as to whether the man was waiting for rain as a good thing or a bad thing), and I think for the boy signifying resolution. The man is in a way dead for him after the rain in at least that he may no longer return and add meaningfully to the story. Consequences have run to their end.

While my students are not wrong to interpret the ending of the story in terms of death or escape, they might do so in terms that are meaningfully evocative rather than starkly literal. Problems arise when they do not choose a literal interpretation over a metaphoric one but instead assume a high "degree of realism" in the text without considering figurative meanings.

While not all of my students disregard symbolism and metaphor, a penchant for reading literally persists. Some, having learned to identify the "hidden meaning" of a literary work with its symbolism, read figurative language in highly literal terms. One student writes, "I'm sure there is some underlying meaning for the children, the man, and the well, but I don't really know what it is. I am guessing the children represent the human race and the man in the well is morality. . . . So I guess that makes the well the gray area between the right and wrong thing to do. I honestly have no idea." Another ends her paper: "Out of pure frustration I explained this story to my roommate and she agreed that the man sounded metaphorical. She came to the conclusion that maybe the man in the well is symbolizing misery. . . . She thinks that maybe it is like we live in misery . . . We do not climb out of the well or the misery . . . and eventually we are consumed. The rain in this theory may be . . . the end of the misery." Engagement with figurative language is limited to the reductive move of equating one term (such as the man) with another (such as morality or misery), as if literary interpretation is a matter of solving for x in an equation.

Literalist thinking culminates in the presumption that "The Man in the Well" is based on actual events in the author's life. One may be excused for reading literally if, in fact, the author wrote this short story because as a child he "literally" encountered a man trapped in a well. In that case nothing in the story is symbolic, nothing a metaphor used to explain one experience in terms of another. Alas, Ira writes, "I myself never had an experience that corresponds closely to anything that happened in this story (I've had to reassure so many people about this!), and I think that's true of almost everything I've written." He holds, moreover, that writing so directly from experience would impede rather than enable his process: "I generally feel that if I am working with biographical material, I have to change so much about it, to defamiliarize myself from it to such an extent, that I can re-approach it again as something I don't know."

The very familiarity Ira seeks to overcome in writing fiction is what so many readers seek when they look to ground their interpretations in something more literal, more factually true, than literary writing. In actuality, even narratives that have an autobiographical or biographical basis are shaped less by actual events than by literary convention and the act of writing. Simply put, while "what is said" may be largely determined by real-world events or the author's recollection of them, "the way it is said" reflects writerly concerns, or the choices made by a writer utilizing, playing with, or pushing against the rules of a given genre. This too is why we should read literarily and not literally, grounding our interpretations in knowledge of literary genres.

A STORY TOLD INTO A HOLE IN THE GROUND

Lest we become too comfortable with the notion that "The Man in the Well" is a modern parable, at least according to an authorial reading of the short story, I would like now to consider an alternative determination of its genre placement before turning, later in the chapter, to two more genre designations that I find less compelling. To begin, let us return to the first email message I received from Ira in 2006, to that part in which Ira addresses the narrator's curiously unmarked gender. It reads: "I always assumed he was a boy! But funny there should be no real marker for that. It wasn't intentional, though it's entirely appropriate for a story by someone who seems to be telling this into a hole in the ground, with the hope that no one else might ever know what he took part in." These words struck me as odd, for at no time had it occurred to me that the narrator was telling his story "into a hole in the ground"; indeed, why would he tell the story at all if he wished no one to know "what he took part in" that summer when he was nine?

I expressed these thoughts to Ira, adding that when I read or listen to "The Man in the Well" I assume the narrator is speaking to a narratee, and, in placing myself in the position of that narratee, I feel that the narrator is telling his story to *me*. Could he elaborate on what he meant? Ira replied:

When I spoke of speaking into a hole in the ground, I meant that I have a sense of the narrator as someone who tells this story reluctantly, without naming himself, barely placing himself (to the point where, as you pointed out to me, his sex is in fact ambivalent) as a physical person in the scenes at the well. He is willingly confessing a terrible moment from the past, but simultaneously seems bent on removing himself from the scenario, from identification, much as the children sought to do at the time of the story. His attitude at the end feels to me entirely unchanged from what it would have been in childhood: that determination, having brought things to a head, to never go back. The retelling of the story is exactly that return to the well, then (as if to tell the story puts him right back in that place, a place he never fully escaped; and as if the man, doomed and all-knowing as he is, is the only one he could ever tell the story to in the first place). On the level of psychoanalysis, I suppose the telling of the story is the recapitulation of a trauma.

While the idea that the narrator might be telling his story to the man in the well still eludes me (it was in clarifying this idea that Ira cited Jung's Puer/Senex paradigm), I now observe something in Ira's statement that I long overlooked. A year later, I would ask Ira if he regards his short story as a modern parable, and he would reply that he does "tend to think of 'The Man in the Well' as operating much like a modern parable," though he did not "set out to write such a thing." But here, at the start of our dialogue and with little prompting, he discusses his short story as a confessional narrative.

Given that, as Rabinowitz writes, "readers who make different initial generic assumptions . . . may find that they are reading what appear to be different texts" (Rabinowitz and Smith 61), let us consider how differently "The Man in the Well" might appear when read or rewritten as a confessional narrative. In describing his short story as the narrator's confession of a "terrible moment from the past," Ira emphasizes the narrator's simultaneous willingness and reluctance to tell his story. He emphasizes as well the narrator's effort to obscure his place in the very story he tells by providing his reader or listener with little sense of his identity and diminishing his presence in recounted scenes. For instance, because dialogue is provided for Arthur, little Jason, Wendy, Aaron, and Grace but not for the character narrator, when we read "We all asked such stupid questions, and he wouldn't answer anyone," we can only wonder what he might have asked the man. This is a confession that hides as much as it discloses—and in this regard it is like many other literary confessions.

In his description of the genre, Peter Brooks writes: "The confessional tradition in fictional narrative often dramatizes a narrator who tells us something that he or she might in normal social circumstances prefer to keep hidden—and has perhaps hitherto kept hidden." This is not to say that "the speaker or writer [who] wishes or even needs to reveal something that is hidden, possibly shameful, and difficult to articulate" will be entirely forthcoming; for as Brooks explains, "the confessional narrator may be self-deceptive in ways detectable by the reader" and "the rhetoric of the genre may involve a kind of hide-and-seek, where the reader finds that what is confessed by the narrator is not the whole or the pertinent truth" ("Confessional" 82). In Sher's short story, questions concerning the reliability of the character narrator's confession are intertwined with questions regarding the behavior of the children in the story he tells. The question of why the children decided not to help the man in the well is bound up with that of whether the character narrator is confessing all he knows when he states, "I don't remember if we told ourselves a reason why we couldn't help him, but we had decided then."

Then there is the question I put to my students: "Why do the children act as they do in the story?" In asking them to write in response to this query, I put the children's decision not to help the man, and ultimately to abandon him to his fate, at the center of the text. This, after all, is the central question posed by the short story when it is read as a modern parable. But it is also in many ways a deceptive question, one that—my students' rewritings have led me to see—greatly limits responses to "The Man in the Well." I might have asked, "Why did the children act as they did in the story told by the narrator?" Instead, the present-tense construction and wording of the question I did ask have encouraged my students to respond to the story as if it is told by a third-person narrator describing events as they unfold. Other questions would no doubt elicit responses quite different from those I've received. I might have asked: "Why does the narrator tell this story? Who is the narrator telling this story to and why?" To ask or answer these questions is to treat the short story as a confessional narrative.

A FANTASTICAL STORY

Tellingly, my one student who interpreted "The Man in the Well" as a confessional narrative was not asked to account for why the children act as they do in the story. Unlike the other students whose responses I have discussed, Tara encountered Sher's short story in my course Introduction to Critical

Theory. Assigned to analyze a short story or poem through a theoretical lens, and given an array of texts and theories from which to choose, Tara opted to write an analysis of "The Man in the Well" using psychoanalytic theory. What she wrote reflects a Freudian interest in exploring how dreams, childhood memories, and life stories are shaped—or perhaps misshaped—by repressed fears, conflicts, and desires. As such, her response focuses less on what happens in the story told by the narrator than on the narrator's *telling* of this story.

"The narrator," writes Tara, "tells us this fantastical story of an experience he had so many years ago to avoid the truth of what really happened. All the information is there, but he is avoiding it by sharing it through a fantastical story." The fanciful, perhaps untrue story of the man in the well is here distinguished from the truth of what happened to the character narrator when he was nine; yet, at the same time, this truth finds expression in the story he tells about the children's encounter with the man in the well, albeit in censored form. Because "what really happened" is untellable, it can be conveyed only indirectly through dreamlike symbols. Tara writes that "the narrator's family dynamic has nothing to do with the literal story he is telling about a man in the well, but it has everything to do with the real story." Taken literally, the man in the well has nothing do with the narrator's family, but read symbolically, the man in the well is a "fantastical" stand-in for the narrator's parents.

Tara rewrites the fantastical story told by the narrator to get at the "real story" it conceals. In her rewriting, the character narrator "cannot get what he needs from his mother," who, "weeping at night in her room downstairs," is in the "enclosed, dark space" of the well. And the character narrator's father is there too. Tara explains:

> His father is there in place of the water. Therefore the well is dry. She has nothing to give him. She is not nurturing, and for that the boy resents his father. . . . He cannot face this head on so he displaces his anger on the man in the well. The problem is, the man in the well is not only his father. It is the father's relationship with the mother as well as their relationship with the narrator.

There is a well-established name for this relationship defined by a rivalry between a father and son for the mother's affection: it is what Freud termed *Oedipal*. Freud theorized that the male child desires to take his father's place as the object of his mother's affections. Perhaps averse to such theorizing, Tara postulates instead that the narrator's father abused his mother, writing of the nine-year-old boy the narrator once was: "He cannot get what he needs from his mother because his father hurts her." I think of a child's capacity to misperceive consensual sex as a violent, hurtful act, to hear cries of arousal as shrieks of pain.

This, however, is not what Tara means to suggest. Her argument is that the abuse the character narrator's mother suffered at the hands of his father made her unable to care for him, and this explains why, in his fantastical story, the character narrator and the children (who, in their diversity, represent his "mixed feelings") abandon the man in the well. Tara writes:

> There was no way he could save his mother, but there was no way he could go on listening to her cry. He ran away from the whole situation, and as he did his mother asked, "Why didn't you tell anyone? Didn't you want to tell anyone?" He has lived with that guilt every day since then. He will never return to the well. He will never revisit those issues.... Even when he writes this he is unable to share the real facts. He must... avoid the truth of what really happened.

In telling "the real story," Tara rewrites "The Man in the Well" as a confessional narrative about the character narrator's guilt for having abandoned his abused mother. At the same time, she rewrites a more familiar scenario involving abuse within the family: a father abuses a child whose mother, failing to intervene, enables the abuse to continue. Tara's story evokes this scenario with a twist: she reverses the roles of mother and child.

Does the confessional narrator know that the story he tells about discovering the man in the well is not "what really happened"? Tara does not say whether he knowingly spins a tale to represent metaphorically what he cannot speak of directly, or if he believes this fantastical story to be true. If the latter, his remembrance of the man in the well is what Freud terms a *screen memory*, a fantasized or actual recollection from childhood, "often distorted from the truth, and interspersed with imaginary elements," that serves to conceal an associated, distressing event (Freud 419). But whereas screen memories are typically banal or unremarkable, the story the character narrator tells is darkly disturbing. If his recollection of the man in the well does serve to screen or conceal the memory of still more distressing events from childhood, one can only imagine how deeply troubling his home life must have been.

Inspired by Tara's interpretation, I asked Ira what the narrator means when he remarks that he cannot describe the feeling of "those days, months actually," without "resorting to the man in the well." Does the narrator mean to suggest that the story of the man in the well is secondary to another story he cannot bring himself to tell? Ira replied:

> In thinking about it, especially in conjunction with the distress of the parents, this must have been a difficult, lost, and in some way traumatic time for the narrator, and the encounter with the man in the well must have captured in some way a sense of personal failure or a feeling of things gone irreparably awry. None of this was considered directly in my choice of language or plotting, but so much of choosing elements in narrative has to do with the way things feel rather than a direct understanding of how they relate. If I'd understood what I was writing very clearly, it would have hampered my ability to put it all down, if that makes sense.

Tara proposes a more decisive answer. Her highly symbolic interpretation of the short story overlays what is, in effect, a starkly literal backstory: the character narrator's father abused his mother. While we should question the textual basis for this backstory, Tara's idea that the story of the man in the well is a cover for a less tellable, more disturbing story—one the narrator only hints at when referring to his weeping mother and murmuring father—is intriguingly counterintuitive. In any case, Tara's response to Sher's short story contributes greatly to our consideration of the potential text by drawing attention to the confessional narrator and to questions regarding the truthfulness of what is confessed. Did the author presume readers would question the character narrator's account? Does joining the authorial audience require such questioning? Though readers cannot access Ira's psyche, they may find that the text follows the conventions of the confessional narrative. If one rule of this genre is that narrators may deceive themselves and their narratees, it follows that an authorial reading of Sher's story involves consideration of the confessional narrator's reliability.

If an authorial reading of "The Man in the Well" can treat the text as a modern parable *or* a confessional narrative because it falls into both genres at once, one might ask which genre designation is more correct, more true to how the author expected readers to experience the short story. But this question may overestimate the stability and discreteness of genres, as well as the extent to which an author is conscious of writing in accordance with the rules of any one genre. In fact, neither the author's conscious intention nor generic purity need be demonstrated by a text. Without knowing the precise genre in which its author intended to write, we can ask what kind of response the text appears designed to elicit from readers, knowing that our answers will involve some degree of reasoned guesswork.

INTENTIONAL, SYMPTOMATIC, AND ADAPTIVE READING

Scholes remarks that major twentieth-century theoretical approaches to analyzing literature associated with New Criticism, reader-response theory, deconstruction, and cultural studies all "undermine the notion of authorial intention as a feature of the reading process." They are all, he writes, "in various degrees and respects, . . . right and useful, but only if reading for authorial intention precedes them" (167). Is this so? Is Rabinowitz similarly correct in arguing that "our reading experience will be more or less seriously flawed" (Rabinowitz and Smith 5) if we do not first interpret texts as their authors intended them to be read? These points may justifiably appeal to teachers whose students show a readiness to criticize or dismiss texts in ways that mischaracterize those texts. After all, the idea that readers should not disagree with a text without first understanding "what it is saying" seems only reasonable. Still, I would argue that, in practice, authorial reading does not precede other ways of construing a text. Rather, it accompanies them.

What are these other ways of construing a text? While the possibilities are endless, Abbott provides useful terms for describing three broad approaches to interpreting literary narratives. *Intentional reading* involves the effort to understand a text in accordance with the sensibility of its author. The intentional reader assumes that "a single creative sensibility lies behind the narrative" and tries to draw from the text "ideas and judgments" that are "understood to be in keeping with" that sensibility (*Cambridge* 102). *Symptomatic reading*, by contrast, concerns elements of the narrative that escape the control of this governing sensibility, ideas and judgments "the author had no conscious intention of constructing" but that nevertheless find expression in the text (*Cambridge* 105). Much as a doctor might read physical signs as symptoms of a condition unknown to her patient, so elements of a text can be taken as symptoms of latent meaning, as traces of received beliefs or repressed fears and wishes the author has unknowingly written into the text. Symptomatic reading involves, in short, analyzing how ideological and unconscious meaning shapes the narrative in ways unintended by the author.

Before turning to Abbott's third category of narrative interpretation, I would distinguish intentional reading from authorial reading. These terms may seem synonymous, but they are not, for the reason that authorial reading incorporates aspects of symptomatic reading. It does so by concerning itself with aspects of the authorial audience's mind-set that the author might have had no conscious intention of finding in his or her readers. Rabinowitz suggests as much when he states that "no author can make any rhetorical decisions (conscious or unconscious) without relying on prior assumptions about precisely what values, experiences, habits, and familiarity with artistic conventions his or her readers will bring to the text" (Rabinowitz and Smith 5). Authors, he writes, "design their books rhetorically ... based upon these assumptions—conscious or unconscious—about readers" (*Before* 21). Whereas an intentional reader does not concern him- or herself with the author's unconscious decisions and assumptions, these will concern us when we join the authorial audience (*Before* 25). This is not to say that authorial reading involves distinguishing between deliberate and unconscious authorial choices. On the contrary, according to Rabinowitz, authorial reading frees us from such concern by treating "the reader's attempt to read as the author intended, not as a search for the author's private psyche, but rather as the joining of a particular social/interpretive community" (*Before* 22).

Joining this community involves temporarily adopting both its conscious and unconscious (unexamined or repressed) "beliefs, engagements, commitments, prejudices" (*Before* 26). To illustrate his point that "you cannot step *beyond* the authorial audience without first recognizing it" (Rabinowitz and Smith 13), Rabinowitz writes that readers "can't begin to explore the macho ideology" of a Hemingway short story "without first taking account of the beliefs and attitudes" Hemingway expected to find in his readers (Rabinowitz and Smith 14). This is not to say that Hemingway consciously expected his readers to subscribe to a macho ideology or meant for his story to espouse it. (Indeed, ideology, in a Marxist sense, concerns culturally instilled beliefs sustained by motives and presuppositions that are misrecognized by those who hold them.) A symptomatic reading might show, through close textual analysis, that a macho ideology underlies Hemingway's story regardless of—and even contrary to—the author's assumed or stated intentions, or the expression of a countervailing ideology in the same story.

Whereas intentional and symptomatic reading involve constructing evidence-based interpretations, what Abbott calls *adaptive reading* entails creating one's "own version of the story by adapting it" (*Cambridge* 108). I have proposed that we always create our own versions of the texts we analyze, that all our interpretations are adaptations of the texts we rewrite. Abbott, by contrast, reserves the term for an interpretive response that exercises poetic license to the point that it qualifies less as commentary on a literary narrative than as a "new creation" in its own right (*Cambridge* 109). I readily think of graphic novel, radio, and film adaptations of short stories and novels, and of works of fiction that rewrite older works of fiction, but

Abbott has in mind works of literary criticism. "From time to time, we have all had this uneasy feeling in reading criticism," he writes. "We feel that an interpretation purporting to be either intentional or symptomatic has crossed the line and become an adaptation of the tale itself with its own life" (*Cambridge* 108). Still, he notes the difficulty of drawing this line, given that "all interpretation involves some level of creativity" and collaborative meaning-making (*Cambridge* 108).

There is value in recognizing differences between adaptive, intentional, and symptomatic approaches to interpreting literature. But there is value as well in recognizing that most rewritings of literary texts incorporate aspects of all three approaches. And my sense is that they should. Our interpretations should strive to be critical as well as creative, evidence-based as well as inventive and exploratory, responsible to the texts they gloss while telling their own stories. Further, our efforts to expose a literary text's "unconscious"—its latent meanings and ideological premises or underpinnings—should adjoin efforts to understand how that text has been purposely and intuitively designed by an author writing to facilitate a particular reading experience and to communicate in anticipatory, purposeful ways with readers. Further, our analyses of text and author should be accompanied by efforts to recognize our own interpretive proclivities as readers, our investments in construing a text in some ways and not others. And we might recognize as well the cultural contexts in which we encounter a text and how they shape our reading experiences and interpretive efforts. This is not to say that a single interpretation, or a single writer, need attend to all this—author, text, reader, and context. Rather, this is the purview of a cumulative and collaborative interpretive practice.

I agree in spirit with Rabinowitz's contention that "while authorial reading without further critique is often incomplete, so is a critical reading without an understanding of the authorial audience at its base" (*Before* 32), but with two caveats. First, while authorial reading serves as the base for symptomatic reading, so symptomatic reading serves as the base for authorial reading—for often it is in the course of interpreting literary texts symptomatically, or analyzing their subtexts, that we come to more nuanced understandings of how their authors expected readers to experience those texts. Authorial and symptomatic reading are ongoing endeavors, crossing, impinging upon, and reshaping each other. Second, although a scholar will finish writing a piece on a literary text, that hardly means work on that text has been completed. Rather, her published writing simply adds to the material that others may take up when discussing that text or related ones. Particularly if it is successful—that is, influential—her work will occasion more, not less, critical readings and rewritings of that text. The work of interpretation remains fundamentally open-ended and incomplete.

MORAL COMPETENCE AND LITERARY COMPETENCE

With its elusive character narrator and enigmatic telling, "The Man in the Well" is unlike traditional narrative forms—the fable, perhaps, or the parable—that make narrowly didactic points. A desire to regain certainty may nevertheless lead us to append to the story, if not a moral lesson, then a clear sense of what the reader's moral response to it should be. Following a talk I once gave on my students' responses to Sher's short story, an English professor in the audience asked me what, when all is said and done, I thought of my students who absolve the children of wrongdoing and blame the victim for his predicament. Were their responses not morally reprehensible? Were they not immoral in justifying the children's abandonment of the man? Ethically speaking, were they not little better than the children in the story?

In the classroom (as in this book) I have made the moral implications of such responses a topic of discussion. The tendency among my students (and, I expect, many other readers) to absolve the children is troubling, and yet I would not characterize any of my students as morally immature, much less immoral, based on their responses to the short story. To do so would entail treating "The Man in the Well" as what it is not: a moral dilemma, a thought experiment or hypothetical problem of the kind discussed by moral philosophers and employed by psychologists to evaluate respondents' moral thinking. (Moreover, it would entail treating moral dilemmas as adequate measures of moral character—a point to which I will return.) Moral dilemmas confront us with hypothetical situations in which all choices are unsatisfactory. A notable example is the Trolley Problem, which has been debated extensively and greatly expanded upon by philosophers over the past five decades. A recent article summarizes the problem and one of its many variants as follows:

> A runaway trolley is about to kill five workmen who cannot move off the tracks quickly enough; their only chance is for a bystander to flip a switch to divert the trolley onto a side-track, where one workman would be killed. In a parallel scenario, the bystander's only chance to save the five is to push a fat man off a bridge onto the tracks: that will stop the trolley, but the fat man will die. (Di Nucci 662)

Should the bystander flip the switch, saving five men but killing one? Should the bystander push the fat man off the bridge, again saving five men but killing one? An extensive and ever-growing body of literature addresses how these questions have been, and arguably should be, answered.

Rewritten as a moral dilemma, "The Man in the Well" might read:

> Children at play discovered a man trapped in a well. He asked them to bring a rope or a ladder, or to tell their parents he was in the well, but they decided not to help him, other than to bring him food and water over the next two days. They did not know the man's name, but he found out their names on the third day, after which they left him in the well and never went back. Should the children have done that?

One might regard Sher's short story as a moral dilemma in this way, but it would be a mistake to do so—and not only because the actual dilemma is unclear, given that helping the man hardly seems an unsatisfactory choice. Reducing the text to this brief narrative badly misrepresents the character narrator's more complex, layered account, which concerns not only the story of the children's encounter with the man in the well but the manner of its telling. In fact, the character narrator is omitted altogether, replaced by impersonal third-person narration that presents a hypothetical scenario rather than a haunting memory.

While the study of literature should lead us to grapple with moral principles and ethical rules of conduct, works of literary fiction are not moral dilemmas through which a reader's *moral competence*, or "capacity to make increasingly sophisticated moral judgments," might be measured in an objective, credible sense (Wark and Krebs 229). More so than moral competence, responding to literary texts requires what Culler calls *literary competence*, an engrained understanding of how to read texts as literature. As he puts it, the competent literary reader, having "internalized the 'grammar' of literature which would permit him to convert linguistic sequences into literary structures and meanings," has "implicit knowledge" of the generic conventions by which texts are read (*Structuralist* 114, 116). Competent readers, like the authorial audience, share the author's implicit understanding of the "system of conventions" or set of rules for a given genre (*Structuralist* 104). They share in the knowledge that informs the author's generic intentions.

Simply put, my students' responses to Sher's story are far more indicative of their literary competence than of their moral competence. This is not to say that their evaluations of the children's actions as recounted by the narrator express nothing about their facility with moral reasoning or their "moral orientation," but any such evaluations are significantly complicated by their varied abilities, as readers, to decipher seemingly opaque language, construe metaphoric meaning, fill gaps, recognize genres, observe their conventions, and parse what authors communicate to readers through the stories that narrators tell narratees. In short, the moral judgments made by readers of literature are bound up in their "struggle to interpret elements that flout principles of efficient communication" (Culler, *Literary* 27). Insofar as they respond to those elements as well as the dilemmas faced or posed by characters, their moral judgments are an inextricable part of that struggle.

Unlike literary narratives, the moral dilemmas devised by philosophers and psychologists are designed to maximize efficient communication, reducing any "noise" that might complicate responses to the quandaries they pose. Nevertheless, they are not free of literary elements. To illustrate, I will turn to the Heinz dilemma, which should be familiar to anyone who has encountered Lawrence Kohlberg's theory of moral development in an introductory psychology or ethics course. Kohlberg developed his influential theory based on interviews conducted with adolescents who were asked to comment on "situations ... in which acts of obedience to legal-social rules or to the commands of authority conflicted with the human needs or welfare of other individuals" (9). The Heinz dilemma is the best known of the situations Kohlberg devised. First presented in his 1958 doctoral thesis, it continues to be discussed by scholars and used in psychological studies, including one reported in a 2014 article that charts the "moral motivation" of college students (Kaplan 336).

The Heinz dilemma reads as follows:

> In Europe, a woman was near death from a special kind of cancer. There was one drug that the doctors thought might save her. It was a form of radium that a druggist in the same town had recently discovered. The drug was expensive to make, but the druggist was charging ten times what the drug cost him to make. He paid $200 for the radium and charged $2,000 for a small dose of the drug. The sick woman's husband, Heinz, went to everyone he knew to borrow the money, but he could only get together about $1,000 which is half of what it cost. He told the druggist that his wife was dying and asked him to sell it cheaper or let him pay later. But the druggist said: "No, I discovered the drug and I'm going to make money from it." So Heinz got desperate and broke into the man's store to steal the drug for his wife. Should the husband have done that? (Kohlberg 12)

Based on the responses of his adolescent subjects, Kohlberg defined three successive levels of moral reasoning, each consisting of two stages. Briefly, emphasis is placed at the first level on avoiding punishment and benefiting one's self; at the second level on pleasing others and conforming to social rules and laws; and at the third level on making judgments based on individual conscience and universal principles.

In her 1982 book *In a Different Voice*, Carol Gilligan charges that Kohlberg's theory, "based empirically on a study of eighty-four boys," is genderbiased (18). In making this argument, she examines responses to the Heinz dilemma provided by two eleven-year-old children, Jake and Amy. Asked if Heinz should steal the drug, Amy replies that he should not but neither should his wife die. She says that if Heinz stole the drug he might be put in jail, "his wife might get sicker again," and he would be unable to help (28), whereas "if Heinz and the druggist had talked it out long enough, they could reach something besides stealing" (29). Gilligan writes that Amy replies to the dilemma "in a way that seems evasive and unsure" (28), whereas Jake is "clear from the outset that Heinz should steal the drug" because "a human life is worth more than money" (26).

Jake voices certainty, whereas Amy appears uncertain; he applies abstract logic to a hypothetical situation, whereas she appears caught up in its particularities; he uses deductive logic "to differentiate morality from law" (27), whereas she seems unable to "to think systematically" about either (30). Consequently, writes Gilligan, "her moral judgments appear to be a full stage lower in maturity than those of the boy" (30). Yet the real problem, according to Gilligan, lies not with her thinking but with Kohlberg's theory, which impedes us from seeing that Amy's moral thinking is not inferior to Jake's but so different from it that "most of her responses fall through the sieve of Kohlberg's scoring system" (31). Whereas Jake "abstracts the moral problem from the interpersonal situation, finding in the logic of fairness an objective way to decide who will win the dispute" (32), Amy attends to the interpersonal situation itself, treating "communication as the mode of conflict resolution" (30). Gilligan argues that Amy's moral orientation, based in concern for and connection with others rather than abstract logic, reflects an ethic of care that Kohlberg's theory, informed by an ethic of justice, is unequipped to recognize, much less evaluate.

Whereas Gilligan addresses Amy's and Jake's responses to the Heinz dilemma in terms of their ethics, their differing responses may also be explained in terms of genre and authorial reading. I suspect that while Jake is no more familiar with moral dilemmas than Amy, he implicitly understands the genre in a way she does not because he has been socialized to share Kohlberg's predilection for abstract logic over reasoning in relationships. Gilligan writes that Jake "construct[s] the dilemma, as Kohlberg did, as a conflict between the values of property and life" (26), whereas Amy "constructs the problem differently" because "Kohlberg's conception completely evades her" (29). Put another way, Jake succeeds at joining the authorial audience where Amy fails—and in this unusual case the author is uniquely situated to judge her effort. That is to say, Kohlberg does double duty as both the author of the story and as the authority who dictates how responses to it should be evaluated.

Jake's authorial reading of the Heinz dilemma regards it as "sort of like a math problem with humans" (Gilligan 26), whereas Amy's misreading (arguably an adaptive reading) fails to distill the problem from its narrative trappings. Imagining Heinz, his wife, and the druggist as full-fledged characters, Amy effectively rewrites the dilemma, making it "not a math problem with humans but a narrative of relationships that extends over time" (Gilligan 28). She imagines what might have happened if Heinz stole the drug and was caught, if his wife got sick again when he was in jail, and if Heinz had appealed once more to the druggist. To the extent that she mistakes props in a word problem for as-if-real characters, we can fault her for overreading. We might even charge her with embellishing upon the narrative so as to avoid facing the dilemma it poses in stark terms. Was it not made clear that the druggist would not accommodate Heinz in any way?

JUDGING MORAL JUDGMENTS

Still, we might ask, why should a response to the Heinz dilemma that largely ignores the elements it shares with literary narrative, including its use of characters and evocation of a storyworld, be privileged over one that addresses those elements? The Heinz dilemma is not, after all, a math problem, but a fictional narrative. Why did Kohlberg present children with this fictional narrative—the story of a woman in Europe who is dying from cancer, her cash-poor husband Heinz, and a druggist who not only sells the one drug that might cure her but is himself responsible for discovering and manufacturing it—rather than simply ask them if it is morally permissible to commit a theft in order to save a life? Moral dilemmas serve to make such abstract queries more concrete, while also testing the respondent's ability to discern the broad moral principles that underlie particular cases. Yet they do so at the cost of introducing narrative elements that open up the abstract dilemma to unforeseen interpretive possibilities. Rather than addressing the problem, respondents may respond to its narrativization by engaging in imaginative speculation or by questioning the author's construction of the narrative.

For instance, rather than leave the matter of the woman's illness vague, Kohlberg introduces the notion of a "special kind of cancer" and a special drug treatment "recently discovered" by "a druggist in the same town." Although these odd details are clearly intended to preempt certain responses (such as that Heinz should buy a different drug, or buy the one drug elsewhere), they may prompt others that are equally undesirable. Given the emphasis on the uniqueness of both illness and cure, for example, Amy might be excused for imagining that the drug might not prevent recurrence of this "special" cancer. More striking still, Kohlberg poses the problem in highly gendered terms, through the story of two active men (Heinz and the druggist) and one passive woman (the sick wife) whose fate lies in their hands. In view of this, one might wonder if there is not something misleading, if not disingenuous, about moral dilemmas. Is there not some trickery involved in presenting a moral logic problem in the guise of a story about people who might exist in a world like our own, and then faulting respondents for responding to the specifics of that storyworld rather than the abstract problem it is meant to represent? Empathizing with Amy, I want to ask Kohlberg how he could know for sure that the druggist wouldn't have relented had Heinz "talked it out" with him "long enough."

Gilligan's critique of Kohlberg's model implies that what the Heinz dilemma tests above all is the respondents' implicit or explicit understanding of the moral dilemma genre. By that measure, a correct response to the Trolley Problem entails that we not inquire about the identities of the various workmen (taking into consideration their health, ages, families, etc.) but treat them as interchangeable figures, varying only in number, and that we do not consider the fat man as anything more than a figure distinguished by fatness and his placement above the tracks. What if the fat man's body mass proves insufficient to stop the trolley? What if he is a person of some significance? What if fat prejudice colors our decision making? Responding correctly entails *not* posing such questions. Similarly, a correct response to the Heinz dilemma entails that we recognize that the woman, her husband Heinz, and the druggist are not as-if-real characters but what Ira calls stage-setting devices, and that the European town in which they live is not an as-if-real world but a stage on which only one of two outcomes was ever possible: Heinz either stole the drug for his wife or he did not and she died.

Amy recognizes the inevitability of neither outcome. Gilligan remarks that Amy considers "not *whether* Heinz should act in this situation (*'should*

Heinz steal the drug?') but rather *how* Heinz should act in response to his awareness of his wife's need ('Should Heinz *steal* the drug?')" (31). By imagining that Heinz might act in some other way, Amy breaks the frame of the moral dilemma. To propose other courses of action, identify alternative outcomes, or consider complicating situational factors is to defy the rules of the genre. Following such rules, however, has little to do with moral decision making in everyday life. Reflecting this point, the authors of an article on psychological studies of morality comment: "It is somewhat disconcerting to consider how much we have learned about people's judgments about Heinz and his dilemma, and how little we have learned about real-life moral judgment" (Wark and Krebs 220–21).

If responses to the moral dilemmas used in psychological studies arguably provide little indication of how participants make moral decisions in their daily lives, surely teachers should hesitate to judge their students' moral competence based on their written responses to literary texts. Rather than pronounce such judgments, teachers should have students discuss their moral evaluations of characters and actions, analyzing the moral implications of their own interpretations. Literary texts, after all, provide us with rich opportunities to exercise our moral thinking skills, and Sher's short story is noteworthy in this regard. Not unlike the Heinz dilemma, "The Man in the Well" confronts us with a wrongful act (the refusal to save a life by providing help), albeit one that is more difficult for mature readers to justify or explain. Indeed, whereas Kohlberg designed his moral dilemma with a specific notion of what constitutes the best—that is, most morally developed or principled—response to the narrative, Sher crafted his story to heighten its moral ambiguity.

I became aware of Ira's intention in this regard only when I asked him if the character narrator's age when he found the man in the well was a "meaningful choice." He replied: "I did think about that at the time. It was a very real issue to be dealt with, and I probably played with a range of ages for the narrator in my mind before settling on something that seemed to have the right degree of agency." He elaborates on this point as follows:

> What the children did could be judged as either immoral or amoral. I think I chose nine because it leaves that open, particularly as the group is mixed-age with children who have more and less agency or sense of morality. Perhaps it is best to say that at a young age the moral frontier still seems a place children cross with relative ease, and without entirely understanding what it is they leave behind. As a writer I am aware that this slipperiness is available to adults, though with less sympathy given by readers.

Ira's remarks have led me to realize that he does not share my belief that the children certainly acted immorally. I have long regarded my students' claims that the children lacked moral understanding or agency as an escape route from confronting the immorality of their refusal to help the man, but here Ira grants these claims some merit. When I asked him about this, he replied, "I do see the children as creatures with agency—I think the story would have no tension otherwise. I think they have a loose grip on that agency, though." Again, what mattered for Ira was leaving this ambiguous: "The possibility that someone might choose to deny the children agency . . . is for me important in what makes the story work. If the situation was clear cut, then we would have simple sadism, or in the opposite case, a lack of comprehension." Here I would protest that asserting the children's agency neither explains their motivation nor reduces it to simple sadism. When the question of whether the children chose to act as they did is answered with a simple *yes*, the question of why they chose to take those actions remains open.

That said, I have come to question my investment in presuming that the children acted with a profound awareness of the moral gravity of their actions from the moment they decided not to help the man in the well. Ira tells me, "The narrator isn't making decisions in a consciously immoral way for much of the story, although he eventually is forced into the moral enormity of what is taking place, and he does what even much more mature people do in the face of moral enormity: he retreats." My concern is that *we* should not retreat from confronting this "moral enormity" by rewriting what took place in terms that exculpate the children. In response to such rewritings, I have perhaps gone too far in the other direction, dismissing the possibility that the children, while aware of the wrongfulness of their actions, might not have grasped that a life was at stake. In this way I may have favored a black-and-white view of their actions over one that peers into moral gray areas.

This discussion of moral judgment would be incomplete if I did not mention those responses to "The Man in the Well" that, far from excusing the children's behavior, abstract from it moral problems of global concern. "I believe it is really not a story about the man stuck in the well," writes one student. "It is a story about tragedy happening all around the world, and the nonchalant attitudes of the general population." This view is shared by another student who writes, "There are many horrible things going on in the world, like the genocide in Darfur or the civil war in Iraq, but we are not all running to help these people who are in danger, and overall to many people it is 'ethically' ok to not do anything. Instead, like children in the story, we just continue to ignore the problem and live our lives." For these students and others (including one who compares the children's "token gestures of help" to "a non-binding resolution from the United Nations that gives promises but in reality does nothing"), the character narrator and his friends represent an apathetic public composed of bystanders ("we are all those children who are ignoring the man calling for help from the well"), while the man in the well symbolizes oppressed and destitute populations around the world. "It is easy to feel detached and unconcerned about moral suffering that occurs in another land far from our own," a student remarks. "Whether it is war or epidemic that is destroying populations, all too often these human lives remain faceless and their voices simply die out in the darkness while we return each night safely home."

Such responses can easily be viewed as morally superior to those that absolve the children of wrongdoing. But as initial responses to a literary text, they are, by my estimation, less promising. While commendable on its face, the attention given to global injustices may serve as yet another escape route from grappling with the challenges posed by this particular literary text. The student who believes "The Man in the Well" is about a morally inadequate public response to global tragedy claims it must be interpreted in this more symbolic way because what it describes could never "literally happen," it being "unheard of" for children to "come together" as they did in the story; moreover, "no child would be capable of keeping a secret of that magnitude." But if these children acted as real children never could, they nevertheless "acted in a manner consistent with the world overall." In his own way, this student pardons the children, concluding that they acted wrongly only because they are not children but symbolic stand-ins for more economically developed countries.

For all of its ethical concern, the turn from attempting to make sense of the short story to condemning public indifference may be accompanied by a sense of relief. In reproaching themselves and others for doing nothing to ease the sufferings of poor and needy others, students may avail themselves of a ready-made cultural script, transforming the story of the children's dealings with the man in the well into a "main point" that, while only tangentially related to the narrative, can be expressed with moral certainty.

THE BOGEYMAN IN THE WELL

Whereas few students are well acquainted with modern parables and fictional confessional narratives, all will be familiar with fairy tales, which are "arguably the most powerfully formative tales of childhood and permeate mass media for children and adults" (Tatar xi). Not surprisingly, many read the story of the man in the well as a fairy tale. After all, like many tales of that genre, Sher's short story concerns children away from home who encounter a lone adult figure in a remote setting. If these children are like those young naïfs in fairy tales, it follows that the man in the well is like the wolf in the woods or the witch in the forest, a figure to be feared. Certainly many of my students define the man in these terms. One speculates that the children fear "the man will turn against them or that the man is . . . deceiving them into helping him out and then maybe hurting them after they help him out of the well." Another states, "The man in the well represents to me everything that we as children dared to dream about that was living in our closets. He represents the fear of what was living under our beds, in our basements, and in the dark." Another names this fear when he remarks that the man in the well "could have been the boogieman."

Boogieman, bogieman, bogeyman, boogeyman, bogey: for centuries and across various Indo-European cultures, these and related terms have designated a monstrous figure that preys on children. "Bogeymen and women are frequently imagined as single, anomalous outsiders—the Cyclops in his cave, the witch in her gingerbread house," states Marina Warner in *No Go the Bogeyman* (28). Whether or not the children in Sher's short story imagine that the unseen man in the well might be a bogeyman, some of my students do. I have suggested that many of them wish to suppress the immorality of the children's actions, retain a belief in childhood innocence, and deny the culpability of characters with whom they identify. Now I will add that these students' responses may result from reading "The Man in the Well" as a fairy tale. They may construe the children as innocent and the man as wicked not simply or only because they wish to excuse the children, but also because characters in the world of fairy tales tend to embody goodness or wickedness, with very little middle ground.

Furthermore, an inclination to forgive children their trespasses may be written into the fairy tale genre. Though the tales as we know them are intended for children, fairy tales are rewritings of earlier folktales that were told to adults and children alike. In *The Pleasures of Children's Literature*, Perry Nodelman and Mavis Reimer write that these tales came to be identified with children only after the Grimm brothers, whose 1812 collection of folktales was not widely read, published an edition of selected tales rewritten for children in 1825. With the success of these stories, which were less violent, horrific, and erotic than those the Grimms had originally compiled, "fairy tales achieved the status they still have as children's literature" (308).

As Nodelman and Reimer observe, the rewriting of folktales as child-friendly fairy tales has resulted in some peculiarities. Taking "Goldilocks and the Three Bears" as an example, they write,

With whom are listeners or readers supposed to sympathize, the nice family whose home is invaded or the nice little girl who has to deal with scary bears? The central character in early versions of this story was a nasty old woman, a vagrant who clearly was at fault for breaking into someone else's house. But as the association with fairy tales and children became established and, with it, the expectation that the main characters in fairy tales should be young innocents, the old woman became a girl in later tellings. That change made the tale as ambiguous as it now is, particularly when other tales, such as "Little Red Riding Hood" and "Three Little Pigs," assert the essential villainy of all hairy beasts, presumably including law-abiding bears. (312)

With whom are readers of "The Man in the Well" supposed to sympathize, the helpless man who has been trapped for days at the bottom of a dried-out well without food or water, or the deceitful children who decide to leave him there? In reading Sher's short story as a fairy tale, my students partake in a long tradition of regarding children as "young innocents" and positing the "essential villainy" of a figure who might otherwise be regarded with sympathy.

Still, the villainy of the man in the well is questionable. Whereas readers of and listeners to fairy tales do not ask why the witch, wolf, or troll should want to eat children, my students are full of questions regarding the man in the well. But then, "The Man in the Well" makes for an odd sort of fairy tale, as it is told by a character narrator and lacks a happy ending. It is also bereft of magic, as I noted after reading the following tender passage in Bruno Bettelheim's Freudian study of fairy tales, *The Uses of Enchantment*:

> Left alone for a few hours, a child can feel as cruelly abused as though he had suffered a lifetime of neglect and rejection. Then, suddenly, his existence turns into complete bliss as his mother appears in the doorway, smiling, maybe even bringing him some little present. What could be more magical than that? How could something so simple have the power to alter his life, unless there were magic involved? (72)

Nothing so magical altered the life of the nine-year-old child who, left alone in his room, heard his mother crying downstairs. The absence of "magic" in Sher's story may be tied to the absence of the mother, who did not appear in the doorway, and whose perceived failure to do so corresponds with responses to the story that blame absent parents for the children's failure to act responsibly.

Much as the mother never left her downstairs room, so the man never got out of the well. As a consequence, readers who suspect he is the bogeyman are left asking questions. Who was the man and why wouldn't he tell the children his name? Why was he in the well and what might he have done if he got out? Why did the man in the well act as he did in the story? I have argued that these questions are beside the point, that the man's intentions are no matter, and that the failure to realize this leads to misreading. And yet, given that authorial reading should be accompanied by considerations of the text from perspectives "other than the one called for by the author" (Rabinowitz, *Before* 32), why not ask about the man in the well?

I want to say that I had not asked such questions because I recognized the man as a device serving the narrative rather than as a full-fledged character (though it is hard to say that any characters are fully drawn in this minimalist story). Yet, this was an unconscious act, and one I came to realize only when confronted by my students' persistent questioning of the man's intentions and character. In short, I was made aware of my interpretive choice by my students' alternative choices, and in gaining this awareness I became more aware of and open to other interpretive possibilities. I still believe that critical readers of Sher's story should understand how the man in the well functions as a narrative device rather than as a character whose backstory should concern them. That said, interpretations that characterize the man in ways unsupported by or contrary to the text should not be rejected out of hand.

Misreadings are not simply errors to be discarded. Oftentimes they attend to peculiar textual elements that otherwise careful and discerning readers neglect when writing their sophisticated interpretations that would provide interpretive closure. While for some time I saw my students' concern with the man's character as an escape route from a meaningful confrontation with the children's disturbing behavior, their persistence has led me to recognize that something other than a resistance to risky reading informs their responses to "The Man in the Well." In positing that the man in the well might be a bogeyman—a figure who, at the very least, might be said to haunt their readings of the story—they are responding to the quite curious portrayal of the story's titular character.

A NARRATIVE FAULT LINE

What made the man in the well act as he did in the story? I have contended that the man is part of the story's setup, that he acted as he did so that the children could react, and that the story told by the character narrator concerns the children's decision making, their actions then and the narrator's sensibility in recounting them now. Here I will add that, whether or not this is so, my contentions do not adequately answer the question of why the man in the well acted as he did and not some other way. Whereas my answer does not address the specificity of his actions in the story, several of the students' responses do, including some of those discussed as misreadings in the first chapter. I recall, for instance, Cheryl's comment on the man's failure to "connect" with Wendy: "He didn't even ask her name; he simply answered her question about the existence of water in the well and focused on himself again." She concludes that the children "left the man there, in the well, because he was too preoccupied with himself and too demanding, and he was just a man in the well without a name and a face." While the man's preoccupation with his dire situation may be excused, his lack of a name and face and his too-demanding voice deserve further consideration.

The man's refusal to divulge his name is noted by many students, including one who finds it "very odd that the man isn't willing to share his name with the children," adding that "to the children this could be a possible sign that the man isn't friendly or nice." Another comments, "Perhaps if he had told them his name or answered any of the other questions the children asked, he would have become more familiar to them, . . . some of the fear associated with this person may have subsided, and the children may have sought help." Another proposes that the man seemed not only unfriendly and unfamiliar but also unreal, writing, "If the kids had seen the man or even knew his name, they might have realized it was a real person, not just a voice in the well." Developing this point in a follow-up paper, she remarks, "An interesting detail is that the man did not even attempt to humanize himself. He did not give up his name, age, or any details of his personal life. If the man in the well had told any personal information to the children, they may have realized they were dealing with a human and that he needed help."

Very possibly these students were themselves troubled by a sense that the man does not seem to be a real-enough person or human being, that something is mimetically lacking. "It was eerie that he was so calm day after day, and that he did not explain to the children who he was or how he got trapped down there," one writes. I have argued that to expect the man in the well to have acted more like an as-if-real person (and less like a metaphoric figure) is to misread the story's genre. Many of my students, being unacquainted with the modern parable and, more broadly, with uses of allegory in modern fiction, interpret the man's difference from the as-if-real world in which he is trapped as indicative of an uncanny, threatening otherness. They respond to what they experience as curious (because curiously unrealistic) aspects of the storyworld by giving them expression in "realistic" terms, whether that storyworld is imagined to be "real" like our own or more akin to the world found in fairy tales or gothic tales. Put another way, they respond to the synthetic component of the narrative in mimetic terms. If the man functions more as a symbolic figure or narrative device than as as-if-real character, this is because he is not real at all but a made-up figure in a children's game, or because he is an otherworldly figure, a bogeyman.

There is still another reason my students and other readers may find the man in the well to be a troubling figure. Cheryl addresses this reason when she describes the man as "too demanding" and unwilling to "connect" with the children. I have made much of the fact that the children initially went off to fetch a rope or ladder not out of a sense of moral responsibility or concern for the well-being of another, but because they were "afraid to disobey the voice from the man in the well." But this is only part of the story; it is also the case that the man neither appealed to the children's moral principles nor sought their sympathy. At no point did he encourage the children to take pity on him or "do the right thing." Instead, he tried to compel their assistance by voicing his authority over them, telling them what to do and ignoring their questions while pressing them for answers: "go get a ladder, get help . . . Go tell your parents there's someone in this well. . . . Just tell your parents. . . . . Are they on their way? . . . Are they coming now? They're coming, you said. . . . Right?"

More curious still, he continued to instruct them even after the failure of this strategy became evident. This has raised questions for my students. Had the man presented himself in more personal terms, would the children have empathized with him or related to him as a person and been motivated to go for help? Why did he cling to anonymity to the end, instead of switching tacks? I might ask as well: Did the man's strategy of presenting himself as an impersonal embodiment (or voice of) authority backfire, motivating the children to defy him? In the last chapter, I argued that the children perceived the man in abstract terms from their first encounter with him to their last, imagining him to be a threatening figure of paternal authority rather than a desperate, suffering individual, badly shaken from having been trapped in the well for days. And yet, given that the man only ever presented himself as the impersonal, commanding voice of paternal authority, one might argue that he was the fearsome figure the children perceived him to be even before they projected that identity upon him.

We can put such complicating factors out of mind by reminding ourselves that, as May says of Bartleby, the man in the well "has no matter": he is a narrative device. Yet in doing so, we may note a peculiarity of "The Man in the Well" that further complicates interpretive responses to the text. Phelan observes that "any character is constructed and has a specific role to play within the larger construction of the narrative, but the synthetic may be more or less foregrounded." When the synthetic is foregrounded, as in metafiction, characters appear as artificial constructs; when the mimetic is foregrounded, as in realistic fiction, characters appear to "act as they do by their own choice rather than at the behest of the author" (*Living* 20). Which is foregrounded in the case of the man in the well? Not the synthetic, since this would break the mimetic illusion, but also not the mimetic, since this might invite misplaced concern with matters irrelevant to the story, such as who the man is and how he came to be in the well. Unlike mimetic characters who appear synthetic when the author's hand shows, the man in the well appears neither as an as-if-real character nor as an artificial construct, but as something occupying an uncanny in-between space, indefinite and undefined.

In "The Difficulty of Imagining Other Persons," Elaine Scarry writes that although "the act of imaging oneself as another person is central to literature" (285), "literature prepares us inadequately" to feel compassion toward large numbers of others, or to believe in their reality, "since even secondary characters ... lack the density of personhood that is attributed to the central character" (286). What then of the man in the well, who, as Ira puts it, is less a fully articulated character than a stage-setting device? If the children are condemnable to the extent that the man was their innocent victim, what does it mean that the man in the well was also, at the same time, not a human being but a narrative device? How much sympathy or empathy can readers be expected to feel for a character so lacking "the density of personhood"? I think of a student who writes that "the narrator leaves us feeling disgusted at the complete absence of human compassion resulting in the death of the man stuck at the bottom of the well. . . . They completely ignored the fact that he was a human being with thoughts and feelings in need of help." Even as I approve of his ethical response, I question his humanizing description of the man in the well.

Recognition of the contrasting ways of construing the man in the well enables us to discern what I will call a fault line in the story's architecture—a conflict rooted in the text's narrative construction, concerning the man's double role as stage-setting device and innocent victim. The man-as-device and the man-as-victim make opposing, possibly irreconcilable demands on readers of "The Man in the Well." Insofar as the man-as-device represents the synthetic component of the text and the man-as-victim represents the mimetic component, we might say that the tension between the two, between the story's construction and its storyworld, runs like a fissure though the narrative. Whereas my analysis of how the children, empowered as a reversal crowd or a fraternal clan, turned against paternal authority is just one realization of the potential text, engagement with my students' responses has led me to stumble across a fault line in the narrative design that bears upon the structure of the potential text itself.

I want to say that all interpretations of the short story respond to this fault line in one way or another, whether by disregarding either the man-as-device or the man-as-victim, by attempting to resolve the tension between these two functions, or by treating this tension as generative of the story's effects and meanings. I think of the story I tell about a fault line running through Sher's story as a meta-interpretation of "Man in the Well," an interpretation that accounts for how the story has been and will continue to be interpreted by readers. But then, I suppose, there must be other ways to interpret the man's mimetic, synthetic, and thematic components, some of which will prove equally if not more useful for understanding how the text's narrative design affects readers.

LITERARY INTERPRETATION: THE GENRE

In his 1980 essay "What Makes an Interpretation Acceptable?," Stanley Fish answers the question posed by his title by arguing that an interpretation's credibility lies not in its fidelity to the text but in its conformity to "the unwritten rules of the literary game" (343). These are rules

> shared by everyone who plays that game, by those who write and judge articles for publication in learned journals, by those who read and listen to papers at professional meetings, by those who seek and award tenure in innumerable departments of English and comparative literature, by the armies of graduate students for whom knowledge of the rules is the real mark of professional initiation. (343)

The unwritten rules appear to be shared by everyone involved in literary study—everyone, that is, except for the undergraduate students who write on literary texts in far greater numbers than the professors and graduate students whose literature courses they take. Students who fail to follow the generic conventions of literary interpretation, or who enact them inexpertly, may violate the rules of the literary game in ways that prove instructive. Like Amy responding to the Heinz dilemma, they can call attention to "unwritten rules" by breaking them.

Fish observes that these rules (like those of any genre) are not "monolithic or stable," given differences that exist between "subcommunities" and that develop over time as "once interdicted interpretive strategies are admitted into the ranks of the acceptable" (343–44). He nevertheless describes as persistent and pervasive "the unwritten requirement that an interpretation present itself as remedying a deficiency in the interpretations that have come before it" (350). Refuting the perception that an interpretation breaks with the allegedly deficient interpretations it would remedy, Fish writes that "in fact it is radically dependent" on them (349). He explains,

> The discovery of the "real point" is always what is claimed whenever a new interpretation is advanced, but the claim makes sense only in relation to a point (or points) that had previously been considered the real one. This means that the space in which a critic works has been marked out for him by his predecessors, even though he is obliged by the conventions of the institution to dislodge them. It . . . is only because something has already been said that he can now say something different. (350)

From the space in which I work—a desk piled high with books and stacks of essays I have drawn upon in writing this book—I can see his point clearly. Yet, reading Fish's essay thirty-five years after it was published, I am most struck by how what he treats as the dirty truth of literary interpretation— the critic's radical dependency on what others have written—is taken by Harris to be the hallmark of academic writing. For Harris, the "generative paradox of academic work" is that critical writing, while rooted "in the work of others—in response, reuse, and rewriting," needs to "say something new and say it well" (2). Indeed, the *raison d'être* of literary interpretation is not, as Fish has it, "the discovery of the 'real point,'" but the presentation of a new point.

In describing literary interpretation in terms of "response, reuse, and rewriting," I have made four points that, if not entirely new, may yet inspire readers to think about and analyze literature in new ways. First, literary interpretation as practiced by students, scholars, and critics is less an act of reading than a genre of writing; second, authorial intention concerns a writer's manifold choices in drafting and revising a text more so than that text's overall meaning or message; third, a rewriting of a literary text does not replace that text or "remedy" other rewritings of it, but joins them in an ongoing dialogue occasioned by and about the text; and fourth, interpreting literature is a collaborative and cumulative undertaking in which misreading can play a productive part. Now I will add a fifth point, attested to by the proliferation, from the mid-twentieth century to the present, of literary theories. The point is this: in addition to interpreting particular literary texts, the work of literary analysis involves continually reassessing and developing the methods we use to interpret literature. As Fish puts it, an interpretation that presents "a more satisfactory account of the work" replaces "one set of interpretive principles" with another (352–53). In other words, in making an explicit argument about a text's meaning, an interpretation makes an implicit argument for a certain theory and practice of literary analysis.

The interpretive principles that Fish professes in his 1980 essay hold that nothing in a literary text "rules out some readings and allows others," that interpretations are validated not by textual evidence but "by the literary institution which at any one time will authorize only a finite number of interpretive strategies" (342). What then of interpretations that strike us as flagrant misreadings? Fish writes, "The fact that it remains easy to think of a reading that most of us would dismiss out of hand does not mean that the text excludes it but that there is as yet no elaborated interpretive procedure for producing that text" (345). Yet, given that those interpretations most likely to be dismissed rely on logical fallacies or result from a basic lack of knowledge concerning cultural-historical reference, literary convention, or linguistic meaning, it is hardly incidental that interpretive procedures for producing them have not been "authorized." The interpretive procedures used by scholars and critics are neither as random nor as prescribed as Fish suggests. While they reflect differing conceptions of what counts as evidence (the broadest distinction being between intrinsic, text-based approaches and extrinsic, context-based approaches), all entail evidentiary reasoning, or drawing reasonable inferences and conclusions from available evidence.

For an example of "a reading that most of us would dismiss out of hand," I will turn to a student's remark that "there's no way to prove [she] or anyone else in the class is incorrect," for "even if someone had decided that the children had previously been abducted by aliens and their brains controlled by evil beings from a different galaxy, there's no real evidence to support or disprove the theory." Actually, the sheer lack of evidence to warrant this theory, and the radical overreading it requires, does disqualify it as a credible interpretation of "The Man in the Well," while the failure to consider alternative theories for which there *is* ample textual evidence compounds the error. A reader is, of course, free to make what she will of a story, but for the abducted-by-aliens interpretation to have purchase with other readers, there must be something to warrant it. In other words, an interpretation requires a rationale. That said, rather than "dismiss out of hand" the theory of alien mind control (which is but a more extreme version of other interpretations that locate blame and agency for the children's "evil" actions elsewhere), I would ask my students to reflect on what motivates and gives shape to this misreading.

In contending that the text provides "no real evidence to support or disprove" an interpretation, my student echoes Fish's contention that "the text cannot be the location of the core of agreement by means of which we reject interpretations" (342). In addition to neglecting the central importance of evidentiary reasoning, this assertion neglects two attributes of the text. First, as Rabinowitz has argued, texts written in accordance with particular generic rules "invite similar interpretive strategies" from readers (Rabinowitz and Smith 60). For this reason, the relation between texts and interpretive strategies is less arbitrary than Fish proposes. A competent reader does not apply interpretive procedures to texts willy-nilly or at the bidding of the literary institution, but relies on paratextual and textual cues to determine which interpretive strategies apply. Recognition of a text's genre provides common ground for critics who otherwise view texts through very different theoretical lenses.

Second, literary texts are not putty in the hands of those who interpret them. To be sure, we as readers often find that texts prove difficult to understand using our familiar interpretive strategies and procedures. "Virtually all texts, to one degree or another, present some obstacles to the interpreter, some material that initially seems resistant to whatever translation schema [i.e., interpretive procedure] the interpreter is employing," states Phelan (*Narrative* 177). Austin Wright uses the term *recalcitrance* to describe the resistance readers encounter in trying to shape a text's material into a comprehensible whole, giving it cohesive and coherent form; recalcitrance is "what impedes or delays perception of that form" (116). He theorizes that we read literature with "a conviction that we are in the process of discovering a form, a belief that further contemplation or rereading will enable us to find a comprehensive principle of coherence" (116) and through it a "feeling of completeness, this sense that we understand the story" (122). But, Wright adds, this is not to say that we find it. "Generally, we do not—not as well as we think we could with a little more contemplation. It is better, therefore, to regard the form . . . not as a fully realized entity but as an emergent hypothesis of reading" (116).

Whereas Fish regards the literary text as the product of the interpretive procedure that produces it, Wright describes the literary text in its resistance to our interpretive efforts. "There is the original resistance of the language itself, which has to be understood, interpreted, before the story can be seen," he writes. "Then there is the dense substance of the fictional world itself, the multi-faceted resistances to our efforts to conceive the characters, what they are doing, and how they are to be judged, recalcitrance that increases as they depart from the stereotypes." Finally, recalcitrance "remains, after all our rereading and reflection is done," in "every ambiguity or obscurity that leads us to regard our perception of the form as hypothetical and incomplete, not definitive" (118).

Like Wright, Phelan cautions that "by always assuming everything can be explained, we overlook the possibility that sometimes recalcitrance may not be overcome" (*Narrative* 178). But whereas for Wright recalcitrance suffuses literary narrative and language, for Phelan it concerns the most reader-resistant material in literary narratives: *the difficult*, which impedes and delays but ultimately "yields to our explanatory efforts," and *the stubborn*, which "will not yield" (*Narrative* 178). The stubborn, like the resistant text theorized by Abbott, is intentionally designed to induce in readers persistent "states of unknowing" (*Real* 9). As such, the stubborn or resistant text epitomizes a quality that Wright treats less as an attribute of particularly dense or enigmatic works than as an aspect of all literary reading: necessarily recalcitrant, a literary text will involve and convey something more and something other than what each of our "interpretive strategies for producing the text" make of it (Fish 347).

While it overstates matters to claim that "only a finite number of interpretive strategies" are authorized by "the literary institution" at any one time, Fish is right to note that we typically interpret texts in accordance with a few most familiar theories and methods. By slowing down and interfering with the reader's process of understanding, more recalcitrant or resistant texts, like "The Man in the Well," can challenge us to revise our customary interpretive strategies or to deviate from them. Furthermore, the treatment of ideas and issues in literary fiction can lead us to reassess and modify our own feelings, beliefs, theories. The challenge that literature poses to understanding, and not our ability to apprehend literature within the limits of a preexisting interpretive framework, is what drives literary interpretation.

RETURN TO NEVER-NEVER LAND

Wright describes recalcitrance as a necessary component of literary reading—in moderation. "If a form comes into view too easily and ceases to evolve as we reflect on it, we find it banal," he writes, but adds that if "our quest for a form is too stubbornly frustrated, we find the work chaotic" (116–17). Iser, who holds that a literary text should "engage the reader's imagination in the task of working things out for himself, for reading is only a pleasure when it is active and creative," makes much the same point. Whereas a reader given "the whole story" will experience "the boredom which inevitably arises when everything is laid out cut and dried before us," a reader given too little will balk at the task of working things out. Thus, writes Iser, "the text may either not go far enough, or may go too far, so we may say that boredom and overstrain form the boundaries beyond which the reader will leave the field of play" (*Implied* 275). For me, "The Man in the Well" hits the sweet spot, going far enough but not too far, and this has kept me returning to its field of play.

Often I have returned to "The Man in the Well" with students, and over time my own understanding of it has been enriched and transformed by their perceptive and curious interpretations of it. Their rewritings and misreadings of the short story have allowed me to discern the limits of my own interpretation and have pushed me to peer beyond them. Now this is all well and good for me, but what can it mean for students? At the very least, it means that students of literature should be given opportunities to occupy the privileged position typically reserved for their teacher—the position of knowledge gained from reading and responding to what a significant number of other writers make of the literary text under discussion.

That literary interpretation is a communal activity bears repeating. A scholar would not write an article on a work of literature without first researching what other critics have written about it. While what she or he writes needs to "say something new and say it well" to merit publication, it should also show adequate awareness of previous work and join in relevant scholarly conversations. Literary interpretation is not, then, a solitary undertaking, although students may learn to regard it as such, and the act of writing "done alone in a room mostly" reinforces this belief (Carlson 23). Students would benefit from seeing how their classmates have interpreted the literature on which they have written, whether or not they struggled to make sense of it themselves. This involves, beyond reading a few notably probing or peculiar responses written by classmates, contemplating the broad sweep of their classmates' responses.

While I have gained much from examining particular students' responses, I have benefited most from taking note of claims and themes that recur across the many responses I have heard and read. Interpretations that initially struck me as eccentric misreadings—the claim that the children only pretended there was a man in the well, for instance, or the strong suspicion that the man was evil—took on greater meaning when I encountered them not once or twice but repeatedly. I came to recognize these now-familiar misreadings as particular categories of response, as rewritings of the short story that can be categorized in generic terms: the empty well interpretation, the bogeyman interpretation, the forbidden farm-lot interpretation, the kids-will-be-kids interpretation, the neglected or abused child interpretation, the mother's affair with the man interpretation, and so on.

I have encountered instances of what Rabinowitz calls "Quixotic or idiosyncratic reading—reading in which a reader applies rules that are not shareable, in the sense that there is no persuasive reason for anyone else to apply them to the text in question" (Rabinowitz and Smith 58). I think once more of Krista's Dust Bowl interpretation and her description of the rules she follows: she creates an "entire visual world" on the basis of "a few words, a sentence, or a tone" from a literary text and elaborates upon that vision "whether it is accurate or not." But I find that truly quixotic reading is unusual, as readers are less likely to create their own rules than to misapply established ones or resort to stock responses and familiar cultural scripts. Students will sometimes defend misinterpretations by asserting that what a reader makes of a text cannot be wrong because it is true to that reader's own experience of the text. However, the generic resemblance between misreadings speaks to Michael C. Smith's point that "literary reading is socially rather than personally constructed" (Rabinowitz and Smith 112). It indicates that what one makes of a text may owe less to one's "special selfhood" than to "trans-individual," shared acts of misreading (Tomlinson 2).

Shared acts of misreading can call our attention to recalcitrant aspects of a text that complicate and challenge our own "best" interpretations. Misreadings as well as interpretive responses that present themselves as unfinished, frustrated attempts to make sense of a text can place emphasis on textual elements that might otherwise escape notice—the paradoxical character of the man in Sher's short story being the foremost example discussed in this book. To realize this capacity of other readers' interpretive responses, we need to respond to them in ways that move far beyond pronouncements of agreement and disagreement. A meaningful response involves identifying what interpretive strategies and what elements of the text, including its gaps, account for certain ways of responding to the short story.

A classroom of students, or any community of readers, may take responsibility for each other's interpretations by producing an inventory that charts various categories of response, a typology of interpretive possibilities. Together they can determine what gap an interpretative move seeks to fill, and how it goes about filling it—whether through reference to textual evidence, intertextual association, personal experience, ready-made cultural beliefs, and so on. In this way, they would identify not only elements of the text but also the various *de facto* rules they have used to make sense of them. These findings may be recorded in the form of a diagram that offers a collaborative portrait of the potential text, charting, via categories and subcategories, similarities and differences in how a work of literature has been interpreted in writing by the class's many readers.

Beyond amassing interpretive possibilities, the work of literary interpretation involves the comparative work of assessing their validity. This entails distinguishing interpretations that participate in authorial reading—those that treat the reader as a member of the author's anticipated audience, and the author as the constructive agent of the text—from those that do not, and, crucially, exploring how they may relate. Against arguments that privilege "reading for authorial intention" (Scholes 167), Andrew Bennett writes that it might be

> a fundamental or constitutive uncertainty of authorial intention that distinguishes literature itself from other discourses, from philosophy, say: it may be that our reading of a poem or other literary text *begins,* in a certain sense, when we can believe that we have located something that the author didn't fully, consciously, properly intend, or that she intended only in the blink of an eye, in the periphery of a certain vision. (83)

While Bennett's remark speaks to my own interests in analyzing texts against the grain, it badly downplays the author's agency in writing a literary text, in large part because it equates authorial intention with overall meaning to the exclusion of writerly choices. Rather than choose between intentional and symptomatic approaches to literature, or treat them as separate projects, we should put them in dialogue and probe the porous border that separates them.

Our understanding is furthered both by determining the genre of a literary text and analyzing it in accordance with that genre's rules and conventions, and by considering the text through alternate genre lenses. For instance, recently while reading "Barefoot Boys and Other Country Children," an essay by art historian Sarah Burns, I learned of "a specialized literature both for and about children" that became popular in the United States following the Civil War. Corresponding with the rise in the 1860s and 1870s of paintings and illustrations that exalted "the beauties of childhood, rural childhood in particular," this literature took the form of novels and stories about boy heroes in rural settings who are "not paragons of virtue" but rascals and scamps "all the more likeable for their flaws." *Tom Sawyer*, published by Mark Twain in 1876, exemplifies this new genre, which flourished at a time when economic and social changes tied to urbanization lent rustic white childhood a nostalgic glow (26).

The American childhood depicted in these works clashes with "what was real life for hundreds of thousands of real children" at the time—namely, belonging to stigmatized immigrant groups, living in city slums, and working in factories (48). Against that reality, a sentimental, backward-looking image of childhood took shape. "All media contributed to a standardized iconography of country childhood nostalgia in the period," writes Burns (35). This iconography included the barefoot boy, who personifies the carefree existence of rural childhood, as well as "country boys and girls together, cooperating in happy, useful harvesting tasks or playing in barns and fields," (35) and "the American farmscape as a never-never land, where kindly old people exist mainly to keep traditions alive for the young, whose realm it is" (40).

I am interested in thinking about how "The Man in the Well," with its depiction of boys and girls playing in a field, relates to this late nineteenth-century American genre. For it seems to me that the abandoned farm-lot to which the character narrator "will never go back" constitutes another never-never land. Unlike the farmscape that invited readers "to burrow back into an ideal past, to be a child again, to shed the burden of adult responsibility for a retreat into a sheltered, pastoral never-never land" (Burns 48), the farm-lot of Sher's short story is forsaken. Its connection to an ideal rural past has already been lost, its well run dry. Lost too is the "enhanced status" that "childhood had acquired" by the 1860s "as a precious, magical condition, privileged in its immunity to the evils of the adult world" (Burns 26). The never-never land to which Sher's story returns us appears to play with the iconography described by Burns, referencing as well as subverting, by overturning, elements of the American rural childhood story tradition.

I expect this is why, although I was raised in the New Jersey suburbs, I find the story's "back then" setting strangely familiar. While I could not have identified the nineteenth-century popular literary genre that Burns describes, I recognize its attributes and can see traces of its mythic depiction of American rural childhood in more recent texts, including "The Man in the

Well." In proposing that Sher's short story can be interpreted as rewriting the kinds of stories that depicted barefoot boys and other country children over a century and a half ago, I am less concerned with Sher's conscious or unconscious intentions than with turning his story over to look at it from yet another side. This turning over and over of a text, through rereading, rewriting, and discussion, is what makes for discovery. The literary texts that are the best "machines to think with" facilitate such acts of discovery, deepening our capacity for realization and understanding.

Whereas Iser holds that no interpretation can exhaust a literary text because it is "infinitely richer than any of its individual realizations" (*Implied* 280), and Fish contends that our realizations are limited by the "finite number of interpretive strategies" we might employ (342), Qualley attributes a text's inexhaustibility to our limited habits of mind or ways of thinking. She writes: "Because understanding is . . . conditioned or constrained by readers' preunderstandings or 'prejudices,' a text can never be fully absorbed or disclosed by any one reader or any one reading" (*Turns* 65). This speaks to why we rely on others—beginning with the authors whose work we read—to broaden and deepen our understandings, our ways of interpreting texts and the world. In this book's introduction, I proposed that we like the texts that we like because of what we are able to make of them. I wrote "we" but was referring to what each of us does individually with texts, as in: I like "The Man in the Well" because of what *I* make of it. And yet, clearly so much of what I like about this short story is based on what my students have made of it. Or, rather, what I make of the text has become inextricably tied to what my students as well as its author have made of it.

Now I presume that what they and I have made of the short story has become an inextricable part of what *you* make of it, and that our respective and communal understandings will continue to develop as other readers and writers join us on this field of play, where time and again we have found the well, and then heard the voice of the man in the well calling out for help.

AN AFTERWORD IN TWO VOICES

Ira, one of the first things you wrote me after reading a draft of this book was "All those things I said!" The author is so often treated as a timeless figure, and authorial intention as his or her unchanging conception of a work—as if Mark Twain was the same person throughout his half-century-long career, and always conceived of Tom Sawyer *or* Huckleberry Finn *in the same way. Consequently, I'm interested in the idea that you might not recognize yourself in what you're quoted as saying about your work.*

It's part of the romantic vision of the author: All the classic tropes about the way ideas arise for an author, the way authors write, the way any kind of artist composes, and the solidity of those things. It's really striking when I go back and look at material that I've written, especially material that was fairly lightly worked, like correspondence. I probably passed through what I wrote to you once or twice and then I sent it, and so I basically don't remember any of it.

Even with something like "The Man in the Well," which I worked on as a story, when I read it now I am essentially in the same place as most readers are. I have bits and anecdotes about the way the material came to me, but when I'm actually reading it it's very much as if I'm a reader with anyone else. I think that's true about pretty much anything I've written. I think if I picked up my first novel now I would be entirely surprised by the material that's in it. I can't remember the trajectory of anything; I remember the most general outline, not really much better than if I was to think of any other novel that I've liked and read more than once.

Then you don't feel any ownership or claim to understand "The Man in the Well" based on having written it?

Well, there are certain things that have a kind of facticity, like I can say: This was what I was doing when I wrote this part. But I don't have a lot of ownership over the outcome of all that. I can tell you: The family scene, the pacing felt off there, the last section came too fast on the heels of the section before, and so I needed something to slow it down. I can say that I did that, and I can say that when I wrote it I liked the way it felt.

A lot of writing boils down to the feel of things. As you shape things you become aware that certain things need to be pushed and foregrounded and other things can be cut or backed off. At the end it has to feel right. In an odd way it has to feel true, which sounds like a dopey way of putting it. The parts of the story that come together in a particular passage have to feel like they resonate correctly, just like the different colors in a painting have to resonate. Sometimes you don't even know why the pieces resonate, but you leave it because you know that it works. And if it doesn't work you have this anxiety: It's not quite there, and you know it's not quite there.

Still, there are a lot of different scenes you might have written to slow the story down. Pacing only partly explains why you wrote the scene you did, introducing the mother and father into the story.

The poet Jack Spicer gave a number of lectures on how he saw poems coming together, and one of the things that he talks about is the furniture in the room. Whoever you are, you're not going to write like somebody else. You're going to write with the language you know, with the material that's in your head, with your own psychology. And that's essentially the furniture, the material that gets used. What you want is the essence of something that lies behind all that furniture. You try not to get in the way. You try to be smarter than you are by letting things come through without telling yourself what they should be in advance, because otherwise you get this predetermined outcome. You know what you know, and you get something that feels very flat.

●

When we first discussed "The Man in the Well," now over seven years ago, you stressed how unpremeditated it was. We've since discussed various decisions you made in writing the story, among them making the character narrator nine years old when he discovered the man in the well; granting the children agency, albeit with "a loose grip on that agency" to make their responsibility ambiguous; and rendering the man as a not-fully-realized character.

Although I've said this particular story came very quickly, with little editorial work on my part, everything would be too clear-cut if I was entirely a bystander and exercised no decision-making while writing. As much as this story came in a piece, that romantic vision of creativity in a purified form is not very useful. Even a short story is too long to rely on "first thought, best thought," at least for me. My main goal in shaping is to try not to get in the way of my own writing. I do try to bring forward the things that intrigue me about what I've drafted. I don't need to entirely understand these things, and probably do best not to, but I do need to recognize them and have reverence for them in the work.

As I pull a story together, there needs to be some connective material, and I feel I must bring out a shape, but it is a shape I feel I'm finding, not imposing. I think of the *soverchio*—the spirit in the stone—that a sculptor tries to draw from a block of marble. Writing is a very physical act, and every action creates and destroys other possibilities that otherwise don't exist. It isn't something to do in the head. I try to pay attention to what the piece I'm writing is trying to say as I write. After, in redrafting, I try to make decisions that keep this living part of the story alive, rather than decisions that tie it down and kill it with the set of meanings with which I was already prepared.

Can you speak more specifically about how you came to write "The Man in the Well"?

I can remember being in this Boston apartment—I was living in Somerville actually at the time—and I had just gotten back from India maybe six months before, and it was a nice writing period for me because I had not been able to write for about a year. I'd been in India and Indonesia, and I didn't have a computer with me. Before then I had actually not written very much, and it was not especially important to me. My parents are both visual artists; I'd assumed I would grow up to be a painter or a sculptor or something like that.

It wasn't that long after I'd been out of college. I'd lived in the city for a couple of years, and I basically saved up some money and went to Asia for a year. It was difficult to write when I was there; I was handwriting and literally cutting and pasting things. I have these crazy documents that are left over from cutting things up with a scissor and pasting them onto sheets of paper and then re-cutting the sheets of paper. My writing doesn't lend itself particularly well to just throwing it all out on the page. I move things around a lot, looking for the sound of the sentences.

When I got back and moved to Somerville, somehow just being able to write anything on a computer and edit it, and having the ease of that, really made me excited about writing. I think it was 1995. I wrote a handful of stories at the time, and "The Man in the Well" was one of them. It was almost like I'd been bottled up for all this time. The stuff I'd been working on before—I was very interested in experimental writing. I did a lot of Oulipo things where I'd leave out pronouns or have characters rotate through each other's positions, different kinds of games with structure. I was interested in *Hopscotch* by Cortazar at the time because I was interested in this idea of a book that could be shuffled, that did not have a predetermined structure. I was very interested in all of that.

But this wasn't the case with "The Man in the Well"?

That story came out in a piece. I wasn't attempting to do something experimental—it wasn't metafiction; it didn't have an analytical overlay. When I look back it's actually kind of funny. I had written this story in an afternoon, I went back over it the next day, I sent it out to the *Chicago Review*, and they took it. What I didn't know is that there's an etiquette to this. In the meantime I had redrafted some parts, and so when they called me and said it's great, we'll take the story, I was like, "Hold on, I've redrafted it. Would you take this version instead?" They were actually very nice about it. I know now that you don't really do that. You try to give people a finished product and let them choose it or not.

You don't have the earlier version anymore, do you?

No, I don't. I remember that one of the things I wanted to change, but which they didn't let me—and I think it was actually a good decision in the end—was I was going to open with a more descriptive setting of the well, and they didn't want that. You commented on how you imagined the well as one thing physically, and then realized at some point that it's not what you imagined. In the redraft, right at the beginning, I had some additional description of what the well was like. The initial paragraph was maybe three sentences describing the heat of the sun on the ground and the cement, and the insects on it, and the feeling of the summer air, and then the story began. It was a little tone piece about what that feeling was, that sort of summer feeling which, for me, is a childhood feeling. They took all the rest of the changes, none of which had to do with the structure or the plot; they were basically little tone bits and sentence shifts. But I think they liked the way the story just started. They liked that it opened very blank.

It's striking that you wrote this story, which is formally more traditional, so quickly at a time when you were interested in more experimental forms.

I was interested in experimental forms. At the same time I've always read widely and my favorite writers are not experimental writers. There are notable exceptions, but I think of avowedly experimental writing as a kind of masculine, analytic interest in story structure, which I still have. Probably for the same reason I feel that you have to be careful, when you're writing from the perspective of theory, not to have the work illustrate the theory, I feel that if you're going to work from structure it has to be loose, and you probably shouldn't understand your own structure too well.

●

Allowing the act of writing to be a process of discovery and surprise is important to both of us. I'm interested in how our interests and methods as writers—of fiction in your case, and of theory or criticism in mine—compare, and how they inform the ways we read.

When I'm done writing something I don't look at the work anymore. This is not to say that I don't think about what happened in a story or novel, but I don't look at the text. And so when I do have an opportunity to look at the words on the page again, I really do feel, particularly at a remove in time, that I become a reader along with everyone else. The story has gone off on its own, and if it still works it is still alive. When I read it I hope to receive that flash or jolt readers get when they read something that works, that just seems "true."

The whole reason for writing fiction is very much bound up with what makes a good story seem true or alive: that the reason I'm writing this thing is the thing I'm writing. Which isn't the case, for example, with what I'm writing now; now I'm trying to explain myself. But when I'm writing fiction, the reason for what I'm writing expresses more desire than certainty. Student work usually does not contain this motivation. Much critical work doesn't either, for that matter; and many works of art lack this life, too.

I've two main motives when I write, and I think they're not so different from your own. One is to understand something, to see it in a more perceptive way, to figure it out as much as I can. The other is to spin stories using compelling language. I want to write interesting stories about the things I'm interested in thinking about. If you're doing an analysis you have to tell a story about the text you're analyzing. And no matter what is going on in a text, in the course of writing a story about it things will happen that you don't expect, and they take you in unexpected directions.

I think the process is actually similar. If you're writing something, and you're writing to find out why you are writing about it, then the process is going to be much the same. But not if you're writing something that is just information. That's a jump that's hard for students to make at the beginning—writing not to report information but to discover something—because most of them don't have an inherent interest in exploring things through writing. And so when they write something they're writing really to satisfy someone else besides themselves.

Since students are writing to fulfill an assignment, we should wonder how much what they write reflects their actual reading experience and thinking about what they've read. It really helps if students write about a text or issue in which they take a genuine interest, and if they are encouraged to use writing to think through whatever leaves them feeling uncertain.

I was struck by how compassionate your way of approaching your students is. It's a very humane way of getting at the difficulties of writing about something that does demand literacy, and might demand a kind of literacy that they don't have—looking at the things they say not as lesser than your interpretation, but as different. There are going to be weaknesses, but then there will be things worth drawing out.

    You negotiate two schools of thought: the expansive notion that every reader is a collaborator in the text, and the more practical how-to of handling differences in reading, where clearly not all readings are created equal. I loved the way you looked for the kernel of something more curious and daring in what could otherwise seem very rote responses. It is how I think a writing workshop functions best, where you generally have a creative offering full of stock ideas and images—the sort of piece where someone is more describing what they have to say than saying it. And then there is a little moment, or something that seems almost broken, that is really where the energy is.

Looking at your story and my students' responses to it in such detail has led me to see that literacy can create blinders. Having read the man in the well in highly symbolic terms, I hadn't thought much about how he works structurally until my students, who "misguidedly" concerned themselves with who the man is and why he's in the well, got me there. At times it's freeing not to see within the genre- and theory-specific ways you've learned to see. As a teacher, you want to teach students to read in those informed ways, and at the same time to transcend them. Then you get in this funny situation, where students who haven't learned to read in those ways are, in effect, already transcending them.

I think of the woman who thought the story was set in the Dust Bowl, and that turnaround that you had in coming back to her, and then her actually very articulate discussion of her process—which was interesting because it was in some ways going to make it more difficult for her to approach the story. She was going to put material into the story that wasn't there. She seems sort of aware of that; she needs a story to have a kind of physicality or visualness to it, and without that she's going to supply the details. And that's part of the strength of what she does. She's a graphic designer, right?

Yes. Being so visual is a strength professionally, and adds to her reading experience, but it poses a problem when she can't distinguish her elaborations from the text itself. So I guess that for readers the thing to do, ideally, is become more self-aware. It's like being more conscious of the border between yourself and others.

My own reading habits are often very uncritical in a certain way. I approach writing or reading the way I would approach paintings in a gallery: If a painting speaks to me I'll stop and I'll spend some time, and then I'll think about the way that it relates to painting discourse. But if it doesn't I'm unlikely to linger over it, and maybe part of the reason is just that there's so much material in the world. It's a funny quest to find the things that speak to me as a reader, from this enormous cultural detritus. The critical part, the analysis, is almost a separate object for me. I like it, and it's an exploration that has its own interests, but it's different from my readerly self.

●

How does it feel to have your short story written on to this extent and in this detail? I wonder if you feel that anything is lost or gained when a work of fiction is examined so extensively.

I would be disingenuous to deny that I've been flattered by the attention you've given the story, and also that I learned a lot about it, myself, in the process. Can analysis kill a story? It was certainly something Nabokov feared psychoanalysis was doing to whatever work it touched, his own included. If the story is squeezed down to allegory, an illustration of an idea, it does die, at least for that reader. I think a good story is wily, though, and in pinning it down we have the suspicion that we've captured a picture but not the thing itself. Art is about compression, and is a mirror of consciousness—it is a real human fragment, and is elusive in its humanity. There is always some residue when a story is alive: its perfection is the imperfection of any group of vantage points. Its perfection can be its own imperfection.

I also think analysis can jump from that same moment that animates a work of fiction: that desire that's larger than certainty. As a lover of psychoanalysis, I understand Nabokov's fear, but believe what he feared was more the routine thinking that comes with any system, when the system is dead and it places everything it touches in one of its dead boxes. I can't number all the critics, philosophers, and psychoanalysts who have picked something up not to tie it down, but to open it up, so we can wonder at it together with them. In reading what you've done with "The Man in the Well," I don't feel as if you've killed it so much as allowed me to see more of it.

I'm gratified to hear that. Can you think of an example?

For me, the most obvious example is the sexlessness of the narrator. As I think I've told you, I admittedly always imagined a boy, but I was delighted (when you first brought this to my attention) to find that this was never directly stated. It really illustrates that idea of a good story being smarter than its writer.

Probably my favorite instance of apprehension, though, was when I encountered the notion of a "fault line" running through the story—this imperfect joint between two kinds of writing, relying on two differing forms of interpretation. That idea of different sorts of cultural literacy and different markers in a story throwing some readers is intriguing. I have been drawn to early novels from the eighteenth century, often precisely because they combine genres/conventions that don't entirely work together, but are memorable in their particular combinations. That disjuncture, I think, is also what has drawn me over the years to writers like Kafka, Melville, Schulz, and Walser.

And so I like where you go—for me very unexpectedly, with the question of "Why did the man in the well act as he did in the story?"—and with the idea that a multiplicity of readings reveals a sort of fault in the story's irreconcilable demands (between fable and realism, to some extent). This fault or rift isn't something I'd considered in this story, but I very much appreciate, and enjoy, the fact that there are irreconcilable demands made on the reader. I'd never thought of "The Man in the Well" as a hybrid of different modes of story telling, but I agree that makes sense.

I also hadn't considered that the story required a level of literacy—a certain voltage, if you will. I'd always considered it a simple, somewhat visceral piece: I knew why people were drawn to it, but had never thought it had much of an entry bar. I can see that without a certain literacy, though, the fault line is a barrier, not a capacitor. I've certainly been struck by that gulf in literacy when teaching, and was, honestly, humbled by the way in which you viewed it not only as a matter of the reader lacking knowledge but also of differing knowledge, where there's light to be shed from these other, what would be considered less-tutored, perspectives. The multiplicity of student voices, this cloud, gives us some real insights into the story that wouldn't exist if they were taken individually.

●

The idea of the flaw keeps coming up as I describe my response to your book. I believe the flaw or fault is often overlooked in creation in general—the flaw that is actually the most living part of a thought. When you were describing that fault line in my story, that is, in the end, what I felt: The fault line is, as much as a fault, a source of energy.

When we spoke last you related the fault line to the idea of "the garden in the jewel." You said that the garden in the jewel is your favorite metaphor for thinking about the flaw in a work of art or literature—the flaw being, if I'm not mistaken, the unplanned complication or contradiction that, far from detracting from a work, makes it compelling. You told me that you came across "the garden in the jewel" in Hopscotch, *a novel by Julio Cortazar, so after we spoke I searched through it and found this passage:*

> *Traveler had always been fascinated by that "—the—" which interrupted the rigorous crystallization of the system, like the mysterious* garden in a sapphire, *that*

mysterious spot in the gem that determines perhaps the coalescence of the system and which in sapphires irradiates its transparent celestial cross like a congealed energy in the heart of the stone. (And why was it called garden, *unless because of the influence of gardens of precious stones that appear in Oriental fables?) (515)*

I sent that passage to you, and you replied: "I like that the garden has always been synonymous with a flaw for me . . . but clearly he has something else in mind, more like a focal point."

I love the idea that you authored your favorite metaphor by rewriting Cortazar. I must confess that instead of realizing this I kept trying to read the flaw into the passage from Hopscotch, *though without success: here I find his writing somewhat impenetrable. I wonder if the idea exists elsewhere that a flaw in a jewel's crystallization may be what gives the play of light in it so much beauty, and if you folded that idea into Cortazar's "garden in a sapphire" by turning the "mysterious spot" into a flaw.*

You're very generous about my recollection of Cortazar! I often feel that my recollections are based on elaborations. Particularly with philosophical texts, I can easily remember what something reminded me of, rather than what it actually was.

The line between recollection and elaboration, or between remembrance and invention—like that between rewriting and misreading—can be difficult to draw. Anyway, if your recollection of Cortazar is flawed, it only speaks to your idea that the flaw is that chance place where ideas come alive.

●

Let's talk about something I did not include in the book (not, that is, until now). After you wrote me that many readers mistakenly assume your story is autobiographical, you added: "The moment the story reminds me most of in my life, in the sense of free association, is hearing my father weeping late at night during the time, I learned much later, my parents' marriage was in collapse. I was perhaps fourteen. I had no idea, in the moment, of what the content of that sound was, but it was very powerful."

I did not include that in the second chapter, just as I did not include my own personal association—that as a child I literally lay in bed listening to my mother weeping and my father's stubborn murmur downstairs. I was perhaps fifteen. My father would wake my mother and keep her up late into the night, arguing and harassing her. And more than once my brother and I woke up—we shared a room—we woke up and heard them downstairs. At least once my brother wanted us to go downstairs and intervene, but I was too scared and stayed in bed. Surely this bears on how I respond to your story and what I've made of it, but I do not mention it in my discussion of how I interpret "The Man in the Well." It has to resonate with why this story grabs me, but I'd list other reasons first: its parabolic quality, that it's about childhood, its darkness and moral ambiguity—

There are lots of things in the story that may have spoken to you, but maybe the thing that *is* most important to you is that connection to your childhood. I think about dreams, the way in which the thing a dream is trying to tell you is often not foregrounded. I've wondered why my favorite things to read are idiosyncratic; they're not the "great books," which I'm very aware are beautifully written and marvelously structured. Something in this other work must be speaking to me, through a channel I'm unaware of, about some part of me: a moment in my life, something durable which could be a feeling of being very young—I think it's often childhood things. It could be a moment of distress, hearing a parent cry, or it could be a place where I spent a lot of time, and a feeling of warmth there. When I read Proust I often think that's the thing I like most about it, even though I love the intricacy and depth. There are these moments of warmth that remind me—irrationally—of places in my own childhood. Even though it's silly, that might be what makes his books most drawing for me.

I have this image of something you can only see in the corner of your eye, in the periphery of your vision, and if you try to focus on it directly it disappears. But you don't mind that because it's so interesting when seen out of focus and off to the side. Maybe too there's resistance to seeing it straight on because it might prove less interesting or be transformed into something banal. Still there's part of me that wants to put things in direct focus by asking you if you think that, in writing "The Man in the Well," you transformed your weeping father into the narrator's weeping mother and stubborn father—and why you would do that.

If I want to use something direct from my life in a story, I have to change it in some way. That wasn't what was going on there, though sometimes you can do something like that without knowing. If hearing my mother weeping and my father's stubborn murmur had been a dream, and I was sitting with my therapist and he said what does this remind you of, I would have said it reminds me of hearing my father weeping. But it was nothing that I was doing on purpose. When something like that happens, if you're not doing it intentionally, it's because you want to get at it and you can't get at it properly. You can't get at it directly. So it's one of the reasons why you don't want to filter yourself or get in your own way too much. Because the only way I had to get at that material, otherwise, was probably not very productive for me, was not very . . . I couldn't learn anything from it.

Now that you're done writing the story, is there part of you that wants to try and figure out if and why you transformed that memory of your father in that way? Or do you feel like there isn't much there to figure out, or that you'd rather leave it?

As I writer I feel like I'd rather leave it. As a writer I feel like figuring it out isn't part of that story. As a reader, thinking about it . . . Am I curious about it, now that you've brought it up? I am curious about it. Has it been something that I've dwelt on before? No, and when you asked me about it I think that was my initial reaction. But it's a story about masculinity in many ways, and the mother weeping as a stand-in for the weeping father is a kind of interesting shift.

When I think about how the story resonates with my own experience, I think: Don't talk about that in the book because that's about me, not the story. Then I think that's dishonest, because that experience definitely informs how I think about the story. So my solution was: Well, I'm going to talk about it in the afterword with Ira. That way it's in the book but it's very decentered. It's food for thought rather than part of my analysis.

The inaccessible masculine principal that is authoritarian, but also essentially suffering, is the core of this. And in some ways it is very reflective of my associations with my father, who is a very lovely man, but is also very hesitant to say anything personal. And in some ways the figure, that man in the well, is very much . . . It's actually a kind of painful, lonely journey to make, if you're going to do that. It is a very masculine stance, the stance of: You keep it to yourself, you take care of yourself, and you take care of other people, but you don't depend on anyone. You don't allow yourself that luxury.

And you connect that to the way the man—

To the man's physical being. To his own detriment. That's my association, thinking about it right now.

Just recently when reading Eléctrico W, *a novel by Hervé Le Tellier, I encountered a scene in which the narrator describes standing in a dark room, listening to sounds coming from behind a bedroom door: a bed creaking, springs squeaking, a woman's voice "moaning, repressing a cry and then failing to contain it, like a cry of pain," and a man's voice, "unrecognizable, whispering such huge words, words that belong to moments no one should hear," words the narrator "can't even transcribe here" (152). I was immediately reminded of the part of your story where the narrator recalls hearing his parents downstairs. Suddenly it occurred to me that what he describes hearing, his mother weeping and the stubborn murmur of his father, might have been the sound of his parents having sex.*

Not that I think this is, in fact, what he heard, but that possibility opened itself up to me, and I wonder why it hadn't before. If what he heard was sex, that would turn the recollected moment into a primal scene in the Freudian sense. The sound of parental intercourse is misinterpreted by the child, who imagines a scene of violence.

Yes, I have thought about that (largely because, from screenplays people had made of my short story, I realized a great deal could be read into those few words). That wasn't what I meant to write, and it doesn't seem "true" to me in the sense of: That's what was happening. But it is true in the sense that it's in there, I think. There's a trauma in the interaction the parents are having, that the narrator is overhearing, that belongs to the same family as the primal scene: the excitement and the charge from this mystery that carries some violence.

●

My feeling is that my students' responses to "The Man in the Well" are not specific to young readers who are in the process of learning and maturing. Their interpretations are typical of those I've received from older readers, including professors. I'm wondering if that's true in your experience. What kind of responses have you gotten to "The Man in the Well"?

I've seen many variants on your students' responses down the years. A lot of people ask me if it's a true story. I can't count the number of times people have asked if it really happened.

Isn't that weird?

Yes. When you talk about a fault line in there . . . People like to know what they're getting. I think there's something about fiction as a construct that is slightly troubling, which is that it's not true. This layer of truth that you're asking people to participate in is a little removed, it's a little to the side, and I think people often just like to know if it's true or not. It would almost settle their minds over how they should feel about the story. They want to be told that it's not true, but they need to ask. Then there are some people it just makes uncomfortable; they don't like to read it. The subject, the fact that it has a dreadfulness to it, makes it hard for them to approach it.

And yet your story has received so much attention. "The Man in the Well" was featured on This American Life *and director Christopher Nolan has bought the film rights.*

That's right. It's being anthologized again right now in a college reader, which has happened a few times before. Over the past month I've had two more requests to turn it into a movie. It does receive this kind of rolling level of interest, which is very curious for me and is maybe part of the reason why I feel a certain amount of distance from it, in that it has a life of its own.

How do you account for this level of interest?

It is an archetypal story. You can see that it's talking about something significant, but you can't exactly name it. It's not an allegory—it's not exactly clear what the story is. And I think that gives it a lot of life. It's a very short story; it's pretty compressed. It's a funny thing: It's not like I could plan to write a story like that. You kind of can't plan what you're going to get; you just get things, sometimes. And this particular thing obviously speaks to people.

I think too that part of its appeal is that it involves childhood. Before you were relating the story to masculinity, which I see, but even more so, for me, it's about an experience of disillusionment in childhood with one's parents, when your parental home stops providing you with a sense of security and trust in the world.

That sounds right. There are things which it actually cannot protect you from.

Home itself turns out to be unstable. Drama lies in the realization of that instability, before which your parents define the world for you and, if you're fortunate, make it whole. For me, it's the tension between the parents in the story that marks the loss of this feeling of home for the narrator, and the loss of normalcy and law and order in the story.

Which is one of things that makes it curious that that piece about the mother weeping at night came into the story so incidentally. For me that piece in the story is almost like a found object. I think what you're saying is right, but it says a lot about the way the fiction writing process, as opposed to the reading process, can work—how unanalytical, in a way, the whole thing is.

•

I'm struck by how much we've talked about the character narrator's parents, and how little has been said about the children refusing to help the man. We haven't talked about that at all.

Well, that's almost the structure of the story. You know it at the very beginning, and to some extent my job is to tell the story and not spoil that. The essence of the story is these children find a man in a well and they decide not to get him out. I knew that was what was going to happen within the first paragraph or the second. I probably figured it out in the second paragraph. I knew that was the whole story right there. And I knew, in a sense, that I had to get close to it, but not too close to it.

Not too close to what?

Not too close to the idea that there could be a group of children that could find a man in a well and not get him out. I didn't want it to be about sadism. It wasn't supposed to be about that. I guess when I thought about the scenario of the children not helping the man, it seemed possible that this was within the range of human behavior. Was it remarkable? It was remarkable, but it wasn't inhuman. And so if you already know that's what the story is right at the beginning, the question is then how to figure out . . .

By telling readers from the start that the children decided not to help the man, you made it so there had to be something other than that (for both you and the reader) to discover. You set yourself the project of figuring out what that something else would be. That said, I still find myself questioning whether or not the reader knows from the get-go that the children didn't help the man. The narrator says "we decided not to help him," but does that necessarily mean they couldn't have changed their minds and saved him by the end of the story?

I want to believe that more seasoned readers would assume from the second paragraph on that the children never helped the man, but I'm sure some readers do read the story waiting to see if they helped him out of the well in the end. I think this is a matter of genre-based literacy, grasping from the start that they did not save him, and then the question becomes why. *Not "Will they help him?" but "Why did they decide not to help him?"*

Yes.

That question is tied to another, the question any story raises: How is it going to end? And you end it with the children being called out by name.

That was another found thing in the story. That wasn't something that I thought about at the beginning. It was suddenly like: Oh, this would actually do a lot of things. It's often like that when you're writing. You must have that feeling as you're working on something, a moment when you say to yourself, "Oh, if I look at this way, then . . ." In a way it's about economy. The use of the names condenses a lot of material into a discrete gesture: the namelessness of the narrator, the namelessness of the man in the well, the fact that there is this kind of shamefulness about the very nature of what's happened, and the fact that this person is telling the story.

Since you knew from the beginning that the children didn't get the man out of the well, you had to figure out how to allow that to happen in a way that seems possible, that would allow normal—not evil—children to do such a thing. And then you had this "oh" moment when you realized that the use of names would allow you to do that and tie everything together. Is that right?

I think there were many moments of discovering things while working on the story—it was, if anything, unusual for me in that things "worked themselves out" without breaks or returns through many drafts. But yes, the naming moment is pivotal, and allowed me to close the story, feeling the story had said what it had to say.

Okay, so what would it have meant for you to get "too close" to the idea that a group of children could find a man in a well and leave him there?

It would have meant flattening it out, someone saying, "I don't want to get him out—I'm scared of him" or "Let's exercise some power for once in our lives!" There are decisions that work because they're tacit, and happen through action rather than discourse or exposition. It is, in essence, the idea of showing rather than telling.

I've thought about how much the story would lose if you'd given the man in the well a name and an identity—if, for instance, he'd cried out, "God, get me out. I've been here for days. I'm Glen Johnson, a certified land surveyor, family man, and model train enthusiast. I fell into this godforsaken well while inspecting the property. They plan to build a new housing development here! Now go get a ladder, get help."

Making the man concrete is exactly that move of flattening out the story. Telling too much reduces the story to either sadism or comedy, robbing the story of its possibility to come alive. Think of how we do that in narratives all the time—taking an individual or group and essentially rendering them as less-than-human by making them either monstrous or ludicrous.

●

I recently read a piece by Phelan and Rabinowitz in which they discuss the "double logic of realism." They write that we respond to characters and setting "as if they were independent of any authorial construction"—that is, as if they are real—*even as we retain a "tacit awareness that the characters are doing the bidding of their authorial designer and that the setting is represented in the service of that authorial design" ("Narrative Worlds" 86–87). I find that your story, with its complicated depiction of the man in the well, tests or puts pressure on that double logic.*

The split between the real and the as-if-real is one of the reasons why I think fiction, and people's ability to hold that contradiction in their minds fruitfully, is valuable in a different way than nonfiction. There is an authorial layer to any writing, but one of the things I was often struck by in teaching young readers was the way in which they so easily collapse text into truth while reading nonfiction. They ignore the idea of authorial agendas and rhetoric. Political statements, advertising, news articles—all of these, in my experience, were generally accepted uncritically; or, just as unusefully, with a blanket lack of credence that led to what was essentially the same outcome: blanket acceptance.

The knowledge that one is reading fiction seems to imply a contract where suspension of disbelief is essential, and perhaps this is why some people resist fiction (although the idea that this same suspension isn't required in nonfiction is wistful). I feel that fiction exercises a muscle that needs a lot of work (in these times): the ability to hold the reality and irreality of a narrative together in mind. In fiction it leads to the choice to suspend disbelief, recognize certain aesthetic choices, think about structure, etc.

I think it paves the way to thinking about the authored nature of all writing, though, and the way in which you can be an active reader or a passive reader of what you're given and asked to take as "the true story" in any genre. Does that make sense?

Yes, and it certainly applies here, to our dialogue which is no less worked over, shaped, constructed, or authored than other parts of this book. What may appear as a straightforward transcript of our conversation is actually an amalgamation of email messages, phone conversations, and material added in the course of transcribing, condensing, revising, and editing this afterword over a period of weeks.

And all the while, look at the things that have come up, not just about the story but about ourselves—all from that split between something essentially true and untrue. All from something that might have been written by anyone, but happened to be written by me. I actually think, more than anything else, of seeing Arlo Guthrie in concert many years ago, and his remark that the songs we love are just in the air and, if you're a musician, sometimes you grab one. Followed by his wry remark that Bob Dylan, unfortunately, grabbed a lot of his songs first.

WORKS CITED

Abbott, H. Porter. *The Cambridge Introduction to Narrative.* 2nd ed. New York: Cambridge University Press, 2008.

———. "Reading Intended Meaning Where None Is Intended: A Cognitivist Reappraisal of the Implied Author." *Poetics Today* 32.3 (Fall 2011): 461–87.

———. *Real Mysteries: Narrative and the Unknowable.* Columbus: The Ohio State University Press, 2013.

"About Us." *This American Life from WBEZ.* Ira Glass, 1995–2015. Web. 17 May 2016.

Allen, Graham. *Intertextuality.* 2nd ed. New York: Routledge, 2011.

Appleyard, J. A. *Becoming a Reader: The Experience of Fiction from Childhood to Adulthood.* New York: Cambridge University Press, 1990.

Attridge, Derek. *The Singularity of Literature.* New York: Routledge, 2004.

Baron-Cohen, Simon. *Mindblindness: An Essay on Autism and Theory of Mind.* Cambridge: The MIT Press, 1995.

Barthes, Roland. "The Death of the Author." *Image, Music, Text.* Trans. Stephen Heath. New York: Hill and Wang, 1977. 142–48.

———. *S/Z: An Essay.* Trans. Richard Miller. New York: Hill and Wang, 1974.

Bartholomae, David. "Inventing the University." *Writing on the Margins: Essays on Composition and Teaching.* New York: Bedford/St. Martin's, 2005. 60–85.

Bennett, Andrew. *The Author.* New York: Routledge, 2005.

Bettelheim, Bruno. *The Uses of Enchantment: The Meaning and Importance of Fairy Tales.* New York: Vintage, 1989.

Blau, Sheridan D. *The Literature Workshop: Teaching Texts and Their Readers.* Portsmouth: Heinemann, 2003.

Booth, Wayne C. "Resurrection of the Implied Author: Why Bother?" *A Companion to Narrative Theory.* Ed. James Phelan and Peter Rabinowitz. Malden: Blackwell, 2005. 75–88.

———. *The Rhetoric of Fiction.* 2nd ed. Chicago: University of Chicago Press, 1983.

Boswell, Robert. *The Half-Known World: On Writing Fiction.* St. Paul: Graywolf, 2008.

Brooks, Peter. "Confessional Narrative." *Routledge Encyclopedia of Narrative Theory.* Ed. David Herman, Manfred Jahn, and Marie-Laure Ryan. New York: Routledge, 2005. 82–83.

———. "Reading for the Plot." *Essentials of the Theory of Fiction.* Ed. Michael J. Hoffman and Patrick D. Murray. Durham: Duke University Press, 2005. 201–20.

Burns, Sarah. "Barefoot Boys and Other Country Children: Sentiment and Ideology in Nineteenth-Century American Art." *The American Art Journal* 20.1 (1988): 25–50.

Burroway, Janet, Elizabeth Stuckey-French, and Ned Stuckey-French. *Writing Fiction: A Guide to Narrative Craft.* 8th ed. Boston: Longman, 2011.

Canetti, Elias. *Crowds and Power.* Trans. Carol Stewart. New York: Farrar Straus Giroux, 1962.

Carlson, Ron. *Ron Carlson Writes a Story.* St. Paul: Graywolf, 2007.

Chatman, Seymour. *Coming to Terms: The Rhetoric of Narrative in Fiction and Film.* Ithaca: Cornell University Press, 1990.

Corbett, Edward P. J. *Classical Rhetoric for the Modern Student.* 3rd ed. New York: Oxford University Press, 1990.

Cortazar, Julio. *Hopscotch.* Trans. Gregory Rabassa. New York: Avon, 1966.

Culler, Jonathan. *Literary Theory: A Very Short Introduction.* New York: Oxford University Press, 2000.

———. *Structuralist Poetics: Structuralism, Linguistics and the Study of Literature.* Ithaca: Cornell University Press, 1975.

Devitt, Amy J. *Writing Genres.* Carbondale: Southern Illinois University Press, 2004.

Di Nucci, Ezio. "Self-Sacrifice and the Trolley Problem." *Philosophical Psychology* 26.5 (2013): 662–72.

Eaglestone, Robert. *Doing English: A Guide for Literature Students.* 3rd ed. New York: Routledge, 2009.

Eco, Umberto. *The Role of the Reader: Explorations in the Semiotics of Texts.* Bloomington: Indiana University Press, 1979.

Edmundson, Mark. *Why Read?* New York: Bloomsbury, 2004.

Esrock, Ellen J. "Taking a Second Look: The Reader's Visual Image." *Second Thoughts: A Focus on Rereading.* Ed. David Galef. Detroit: Wayne State University Press, 1998. 152–66.

Firestein, Stuart. *Ignorance: How It Drives Science.* New York: Oxford University Press, 2012.

Fish, Stanley. *Is There a Text in This Class? The Authority of Interpretive Communities.* Cambridge: Harvard University Press, 1980.

Foucault, Michel. *Discipline and Punish: The Birth of the Prison.* 2nd ed. Trans. Alan Sheridan. New York: Vintage, 1991.

Freud, Sigmund. *The Freud Reader.* Ed. Peter Gay. Trans. James Strachey et al. New York: Norton, 1989.

Gallop, Jane. *The Deaths of the Author: Reading and Writing in Time.* Durham: Duke University Press, 2011.

Gardner, John. *The Art of Fiction: Notes on Craft for Young Writers.* New York: Knopf, 1984.

Gardner, John, and Lennis Dunlap. "The Modern Writer's Use of the Sketch, Fable, Yarn, and Tale." *The Forms of Fiction.* Ed. John Gardner and Lennis Dunlap. New York: Random House, 1962. 23–37.

Gilligan, Carol. *In a Different Voice: Psychological Theory and Women's Development.* Cambridge: Harvard University Press, 1982.

Harkin, Patricia. *Acts of Reading.* Upper Saddle River: Prentice Hall, 1999.

———. "The Reception of Reader-Response Theory." *College Composition and Communication* 56.3 (2005): 410–25.

Harris, Joseph. *Rewriting: How to Do Things with Texts.* Logan: Utah State University Press, 2006.

Hayles, N. Katherine. "How We Read: Close, Hyper, Machine." *ADE Bulletin* 150 (2010): 62–79.

Hesse, Douglas. "A Boundary Zone: First-Person Short Stories and Narrative Essays." *Short Story Theory at a Crossroads.* Ed. Susan Lohafer and Jo Ellyn Clarey. Baton Rouge: Louisiana State University Press, 1989. 85–105.

Hesse, Karen. *Out of the Dust.* New York: Scholastic, 1997.

Hogan, Patrick Colm. "The Multiplicity of Implied Authors and the Complex Case of *Uncle Tom's Cabin*." *Narrative* 20.1 (2012): 26–42.

Hughes, George. *Reading Novels.* Nashville: Vanderbilt University Press, 2002.

Irving, Washington. "Rip Van Winkle." *Concise Anthology of American Literature.* 5th ed. Ed. George McMichael et al. Upper Saddle River: Prentice Hall, 2001. 455–68.

Iser, Wolfgang. *The Act of Reading: A Theory of Aesthetic Response.* Baltimore: The Johns Hopkins University Press, 1978.

———. *The Implied Reader: Patterns of Communication in Prose Fiction from Bunyan to Beckett.* Baltimore: The Johns Hopkins University Press, 1974.

Janis, Irving L. *Groupthink: Psychological Studies of Policy Decisions and Fiascoes.* 2nd ed. Boston: Wadsworth, 1982.

Jehlen, Myra. "On How, to Become Knowledge, Cognition Needs Beauty." *Raritan* 32.1 (2012): 1–19.

Kaplan, Ulas, Caitlin E. Crockett, and Terrence Tivnan. "Moral Motivation in College Students through Multiple Development Structures: Evidence of Intrapersonal Variability in a Complex Dynamic System." *Motivation and Emotion* 38.3 (2014): 336–52.

Klaus, Carl H. *The Made-Up Self: Impersonation in the Personal Essay.* Iowa City: University of Iowa Press, 2010.

Kohlberg, Lawrence. "The Development of Children's Orientations toward a Moral Order: I. Sequence in the Development of Moral Thought." 1963. *Human Development* 51 (2008): 8–20.

Kurtzworth, Harry Muir. "How to Draw a Comic Strip." *The World Book Encyclopedia.* Vol. 3. Chicago: Field Enterprises Educational Corporation, 1962. 195.

Lanser, Susan S. "The Implied Author: An Agnostic Manifesto." *Style* 45.1 (2011): 153–60.

Lee, Alison. "Unfixing Meaning: Challenges of Poststructuralist Theory for Classroom Study." *Knowledge in the Making: Challenging Texts in the Classroom.* Ed. Bill Corcoran, Mike Hayhoe and Gordon M. Pradl. Portsmouth: Heinemann Boynton/Cook, 1994. 91–105.

Lerner, Melvin J. *The Belief in a Just World: A Fundamental Delusion.* New York: Plenum Press, 1980.

Le Tellier, Hervé. *Eléctrico W.* Trans. Adriana Hunter. New York: Other Press, 2012.

Levinson, Jerrold. *The Pleasures of Aesthetics: Philosophical Essays.* Ithaca: Cornell University Press, 1996.

"The Man in the Well." *This American Life.* Narr. Ira Sher. Prod. Ira Glass. PRI. WBEZ, Chicago, 21 July 1996. Radio.

March-Russell, Paul. *The Short Story: An Introduction.* Edinburgh: Edinburgh University Press, 2009.

May, Charles E. *The Short Story: The Reality of Artifice.* New York: Twayne, 1995.

Miller, Christopher. *American Cornball: A Laffopedic Guide to the Formerly Funny.* New York: Harper, 2013.

Murray, Donald M. "Internal Revision: A Process of Discovery." *Learning by Teaching: Selected Articles on Writing and Teaching.* Portsmouth: Boynton/Cook, 1982. 72–87.

Newkirk, Thomas. "Looking for Trouble: A Way to Unmask Our Readings." *College English* 46.8 (1984): 756–66.

Nodelman, Perry, and Mavis Reimer. *The Pleasures of Children's Literature.* 3rd ed. Boston: Allyn and Bacon, 2003.

Oatley, Keith. "Thinking Deeply in Reading and Writing." *The Edge of the Precipice: Why Read Literature in the Digital Age?* Ed. Paul Socken. Ithaca: McGill-Queen's University Press, 2013. 175–91.

Perry, Gina. *Behind the Shock Machine: The Untold Story of the Notorious Milgram Psychology Experiments.* New York: The New Press, 2013.

Phelan, James. *Living to Tell About It: A Rhetoric and Ethics of Character Narration.* Ithaca: Cornell University Press, 2005.

———. *Narrative as Rhetoric: Technique, Audiences, Ethics, Ideology.* Columbus: The Ohio State University Press, 1996.

———. "Narrative Theory, 1966–2006: A Narrative." *The Nature of Narrative: Fortieth Anniversary Edition, Revised and Expanded.* Ed. Robert Scholes, James Phelan, and Robert Kellogg. New York: Oxford University Press, 2006. 283–336.

Phelan, James, and Peter J. Rabinowitz. "Narrative as Rhetoric." *Narrative Theory: Core Concepts and Critical Debates*. Ed. David Herman et al. Columbus: The Ohio State University Press, 2012. 3–8.

———. "Narrative Worlds: Space, Setting, Perspective." *Narrative Theory: Core Concepts and Critical Debates*. Ed. David Herman et al. Columbus: The Ohio State University Press, 2012. 84–91.

Qualley, Donna. *Turns of Thought: Teaching Composition as Reflexive Inquiry*. Portsmouth: Boynton/Cook, 1997.

———. "Using Reading in the Writing Classroom." *Nuts and Bolts: A Practical Guide to Teaching College Composition*. Ed. Thomas Newkirk. Portsmouth: Boynton/Cook, 1993. 101–27.

Rabinowitz, Peter J. *Before Reading: Narrative Conventions and the Politics of Interpretation*. Columbus: The Ohio State University Press, 1987.

———. "Shakespeare's Dolphin, Dumbo's Feather, and Other Red Herrings: Some Thoughts on Intention and Meaning." *Style* 44.3 (2010): 342–64.

Rabinowitz, Peter J., and Michael W. Smith. *Authorizing Readers: Resistance and Respect in the Teaching of Literature*. New York: Teachers College, 1998.

Reid, Ian. *The Short Story*. London: Methuen, 1977.

Richards, I. A. *Practical Criticism: A Study of Literary Judgment*. New York: Harcourt Brace Jovanovich, 1929.

———. *Principles of Literary Criticism*. New York: Routledge, 2001.

Ronson, Jon. *So You've Been Publicly Shamed*. New York: Riverhead Books, 2015.

Rosenblatt, Louise M. *Literature as Exploration*. 5th ed. New York: MLA, 1995.

Salvatori, Mariolina, and Patricia Donahue. "Stories about Reading: Appearance, Disappearance, Morphing, and Revival." *College English* 75.2 (2012): 199–217.

Savarese, Ralph James, and Lisa Zunshine. "The Critic as Neurocosmopolite; Or, What Cognitive Approaches to Literature Can Learn from Disability Studies: Lisa Zunshine in Conversation with Ralph James Savarese." *Narrative* 22.1 (2014): 17–44.

Scarry, Elaine. "The Difficulty of Imagining Other Persons." *Human Rights in Political Transitions: Gettysburg to Bosnia*. Ed. Carla Hesse and Robert Post. New York: Zone Books, 1999. 277–309.

Scholes, Robert. "The Transition to College Reading." *Pedagogy* 2.2 (2002): 165–72.

Sher, Ira. "The Man in the Well." *Chicago Review* 41.4 (1995): 21–26.

Schwartz, Howard. "Kafka and the Modern Parable." *Imperial Messages: One Hundred Modern Parables*. Ed. Howard Schwartz. New York: Overlook, 1991. xxi–xxix.

Swirski, Peter. *Literature, Analytically Speaking: Explorations in the Theory of Interpretation, Analytic Aesthetics, and Evolution*. Austin: University of Texas Press, 2010.

Tatar, Maria. Introduction. *The Classic Fairy Tales*. Ed. Maria Tatar. New York: Norton, 1999. ix–xviii.

Tomlinson, Barbara. *Authors on Writing: Metaphors and Intellectual Labor*. New York: Palgrave Macmillan, 2005.

Troscianko, Emily T. "Reading Imaginatively: The Imagination in Cognitive Science and Cognitive Literary Theory." *Journal of Literary Semantics* 42.2 (2013): 181–98.

Tyson, Lois. *Critical Theory Today: A User-Friendly Guide.* 3rd ed. New York: Routledge, 2015.

Vandaele, Jeroen. "The Implied Author as an Ethical Buffer: An Argument from Translated and Censored Fiction." *Style* 48.2 (2014): 162–80.

Wark, Gillian R., and Dennis L. Krebs. "Gender and Dilemma Differences in Real-Life Moral Judgment." *Developmental Psychology* 32.2 (1996): 220–30.

Warner, Marina. *No Go the Bogeyman: Scaring, Lulling, and Making Mock.* New York: Farrar, Straus and Giroux, 1998.

Weissman, Gary. "The Virtue of Misreadings: Interpreting 'The Man in the Well.'" *College English* 73.1 (2010): 28–49.

Wimsatt, W. K. Jr., and M. C. Beardsley. "The Intentional Fallacy." *The Sewanee Review* 54.3 (1946): 468–88.

Wood, James. *How Fiction Works.* New York: Picador, 2008.

Wright, Austin M. "Recalcitrance in the Short Story." *Short Story Theory at a Crossroads.* Ed. Susan Lohafer and Jo Ellyn Clarey. Baton Rouge: Louisiana State University Press, 1989. 115–29.

Zunshine, Lisa. *Getting Inside Your Head: What Cognitive Science Can Tell Us about Popular Culture.* Baltimore: The Johns Hopkins University Press, 2012.

———. *Why We Read Fiction: Theory of Mind and the Novel.* Columbus: The Ohio State University Press, 2006.

INDEX

Abbott, H. Porter, 29, 45–46, 61–62, 144–45, 162–64, 184
adaptive reading, 163–64, 169
Adventures of Huckleberry Finn (Twain), 21, 190
allegory, 139–42, 149, 177–78, 197, 203
Allen, Graham, 106–7
Appleyard, J. A., 24–25, 59, 81–82, 110
Attridge, Derek, 118
author: as Author-God, 3, 109; as a constructive agent, 28, 109, 111, 119, 187; and narrator, 20–21, 38–39, 70–71; as an oracle, 111; as a reader, 119, 120, 122, 190–91, 194; romantic vision of, 190; as the source of meaning, 3, 24, 81–82; as unknowing, 115; as a writer, 27, 111, 115; as the writer's ghost, 107–8. *See also* death of the author; flesh-and-blood author; implied author; writer
authorial audience, 132–37, 138, 149, 161–64, 166, 169
authorial intention, 3, 19, 20–21, 24, 28, 108–11, 120 123, 133–34, 146–47, 153, 161–62, 181–82, 187, 190; and hypothetical intentionalism, 133; and retrospective intention, 127–28; of Sher, 112–15, 119–22, 117, 119–20, 125–28, 148, 143–44, 156, 171, 189; and unconscious intention, 126–28, 163. *See also* writerly choices
authorial reading, 28, 132–37, 156, 161, 162–64, 168–69, 176, 187

barefoot boy genre, 187–89
Baron-Cohen, Simon, 29, 41, 42
Barthes, Roland, 3, 4, 5–6, 7, 19, 23, 29, 38, 108–10, 153
Bartholomae, David, 69
"Bartleby the Scrivener" (Melville), 142, 179
Beardsley, Monroe C., 110–11, 144
belief in a just world, 68
Bennett, Andrew, 115, 187
Bettelheim, Bruno, 175
Blau, Sheridan, 14, 21, 23, 29, 86–87, 117
Booth, Wayne, 29, 144–45, 146–47
Boswell, Robert, 29, 116–17, 118
Brooks, Peter, 151–52, 158

215

Browning, Christopher, 82–83
Burns, Sarah, 187–88
Burroway, Janet, 29, 115–16, 118

Canetti, Elias, 89–91, 92, 94, 98, 103, 106
Carlson, Ron, 29, 116–19, 121, 122–25, 134, 137, 152, 185
Chatman, Seymour, 145
Chekhov, Anton, 23, 149–50
Chicago Review, 2, 137, 193
closed text, 37–38, 45
comic strip, 8–12, 13–14, 15, 129–30, 135–36, 154
composition studies, 1, 27, 29–30
confessional narrative, 157–58, 160–61, 173
Corbett, Edward P. J., 29, 64–65
Cortazar, Julio, 193, 198–99
creative writing, 15, 29–30, 115–18; and workshop, 195–96. See also writing, of fiction
Culler, Jonathan, 21–22, 30, 120, 123–24, 154, 166–67

dead father, 98–101, 103–4, 105, 108; and primal father, 98–99
death of the author, 3, 4, 19, 108–11, 115
Devitt, Amy J., 29, 153
Di Nucci, Ezio, 165
Donahue, Patricia, 27
Dunlap, Lennis, 140

Eaglestone, Robert, 2
Eco, Umberto, 37–38, 45
Edmundson, Mark, 105, 107–8, 109
Eléctrico W (Le Tellier), 201–2
Esrock, Ellen J., 6, 75–76
ethics, 2, 14, 38, 44, 88, 90, 146, 148, 165–69, 172–73; and acts or behavior, 91, 93–94, 119–20; of care, 88, 168; of justice, 88, 168. See also morality
evidentiary reasoning, 14–15, 50, 65, 182–83; and faulty reasoning, 64–66, 79

fable, 140, 141, 165, 198
fairy tale, 173–75, 178

"The Fall of the House of Usher" (Poe), 142
Firestein, Stuart, 23
Fish, Stanley, 26–27, 29, 180–84, 189
flesh-and-blood author, 3, 144, 146–48
Foucault, Michel, 29, 91–92, 94, 103, 105–6, 107
fraternal clan, 98–99, 103, 180
Freud, Sigmund, 29, 98–100, 103–4, 106, 108, 160; and Freudian, 129, 159, 175, 202

Gallop, Jane, 108–9
gaps and gap-filling, 17, 18, 37, 38, 39–40, 42, 45, 50, 62, 74, 79, 84, 94, 150–51, 167, 186–87
Gardner, John, 29, 115–16, 140
genre, 9, 10, 13–15, 22, 25, 28, 39, 65, 133–43, 152–53, 156, 158, 161, 166–67, 168–71, 173–74, 177, 180–81, 183, 187–89, 196, 197–98, 205, 207; and genre fiction, 137, 152–53
Gilligan, Carol, 29, 168–70
Glass, Ira, 39
Grandin, Temple, 41, 43
groupthink, 90

Harkin, Patricia, 27, 29, 39, 153–54
Harris, Joseph, 7–8, 25, 29, 123, 147, 181
Hayles, N. Katherine, 153
Heinz dilemma, 167–71, 181
Hemingway, Ernest, 138, 163
hermeneutic circle, 13, 139
Hesse, Douglas, 138–39
Hesse, Karen, 78–79, 107
Hogan, Patrick Colm, 145–46
Holland, Cecelia, 118
Hopscotch (Cortazar), 193, 198–99
Hughes, George, 134, 137

implied author, 144–48; and inferred author, 145–46
inexplicitly noncommittal, 76–77, 129
intentional fallacy, 110, 144
intentional reading, 162–64, 187
interpretive closure, 45–46, 176

intertextuality, 13–14, 79, 85, 106–7, 130, 187
Irving, Washington, 131–32, 134
Iser, Wolfgang, 16–17, 29, 37, 39, 62, 77, 185, 189

Janis, Irving L., 29, 90
Jehlen, Myra, 125
Joyce, James, 25, 149–50
Jung, Carl, 127, 157

Kafka, Franz, 139–40, 143, 198
Klaus, Carl H., 146
Kohlberg, Lawrence, 29, 167–71
Krebs, Dennis L., 166, 171

Lacan, Jacques, 29, 106, 126–27
Lanser, Susan S., 144, 145
Lee, Alison, 29, 71
Lee, Harper, 78
Lerner, Melvin J., 29, 68, 69
Le Tellier, Hervé, 201–2
Levinson, Jerrold, 29, 133–34
literary analysis, 1, 4, 22, 25, 28, 30, 65, 69, 108, 118, 154, 182. *See also* literary interpretation
literary competence, 166–67
literary interpretation: as collaborative, 17, 18, 25, 28–29, 80, 94, 164, 182, 185; as cumulative, 5, 25, 164, 182; as a genre, 14, 65, 180–81; goal of, 17–18, 22–23, 25–26; as open-ended, 5, 94–95, 130–31, 165; as rewriting, 7–8, 15, 26, 105; and the single right interpretation, 3, 13, 15–16, 23, 24, 46, 61, 77, 109–10, 131, 146; as storytelling, 14, 26; and uncertainty, 21–22, 45–46, 84–87, 110–11; as writing-based, 1, 4, 6, 14, 26, 30, 181. *See also* gaps; literary analysis; misreading; rewriting
literary studies, 1, 4, 23, 26–27, 29–30, 40, 105
literary theory, 12, 26–27, 29–30, 75–76, 105–6, 107, 108–9, 126–27, 158–59, 162, 182, 194, 196
literature: as a challenge to understanding, 184; humanizing function of, 2; and literary language, 20–22, 37, 59, 70 153–54, 155; and otherness, 19–22; teaching of, 1–4, 18–23, 30, 71–72, 80, 82, 86–87, 105–6, 108, 118, 132–33, 153, 162, 171, 185, 187, 196
Lord of the Flies (Golding), 52

"The Man in the Well" (Sher), 31–36; as archetypal, 37, 203; and the barefoot boy genre, 188–89; as a confessional narrative, 157–61; as a fairy tale, 173–75, 178; and gaps, 38, 42, 74; and mental imagery, 78–79, 96–97, 128–30; and mind reading, 42–43; minimalist style of, 37, 73, 96, 128, 141, 152, 176; as a modern parable, 139, 141, 142–44, 148, 156–58, 161; as a moral dilemma, 165–66, 171; narration of, 39, 42, 95, 142; as an open text, 37–38, 45; setting of, 95–96, 142, 188–89; and symbolism, 37, 59, 70, 73–74, 99, 130, 141, 142, 154–55, 159–61, 172–73, 178; teaching of, 2–4, 43–44, 71, 85, 94, 111, 112, 158, 185–87, 189; Weissman's misreadings of, 10, 50, 96–97, 128–30, 148, 172; writing of, 113–14, 192–93, 205. *See also* student responses to "The Man in the Well"
Mansfield, Katherine, 149–50
March-Russell, Paul, 140, 149
May, Charles E., 141–42, 149–50, 179
Melville, Herman, 142, 198
Milgram, Stanley, 82, 85–86, 89
mimetic, 14–15, 24, 59–60, 84, 123, 135, 141, 143, 177–78, 179–80; and the mimetic illusion, 15, 60, 143, 179
mindblindness, 41–43
mind reading, 40–44, 89, 123; and mind misreading, 40, 116
misreading, 2, 3–4, 13, 15–18, 23, 27, 37–80, 64–66, 131, 136, 139, 146, 176, 182–83, 186
mob mentality, 90–91
modern parable, 139–41, 143, 148, 156–58, 161, 177
moral competence, 166–67, 171
moral dilemma, 165–71
morality: of the children, 58–60, 63–65, 66–68, 73, 83–84, 88, 90–91, 93–94,

112–13, 127, 143, 148, 165, 166–67, 171–74, 178; enforced through fear, 88, 112, 119–20; and moral agency, 49; and moral development, 93–94, 98, 167–68; and moral understanding, 51, 58, 62, 148, 171–72; and moral of the story, 24, 44, 108, 115, 140–41, 165. *See also* ethics; moral competence; moral dilemma

Murray, Donald, 29, 118

Nabokov, Vladimir, 197
narrator: and character narrator, 21; and author, 20–21, 22, 38; as unreliable, 21. *See also* "The Man in the Well," narration of
New Criticism, 25, 30, 110, 144, 162
Newkirk, Thomas, 29, 86–87
Nodelman, Perry, 174–75

Oatley, Keith, 153
open text, 37–38, 45
Ordinary Men (Browning), 82–83, 89
Out of the Dust (Hesse), 78–79, 107
overreading, 61–64, 70, 71, 73, 74, 79, 97, 149, 169, 182–83

pacing, 120–21, 122, 124–25, 126, 191
Panopticon, 91–92, 94, 98, 99, 103, 106
parable, 140–41, 165. *See also* modern parable
paratext, 137
peer pressure, 90
Phelan, James, 14–15, 20–21, 28, 29, 84, 109, 123–24, 145, 179, 183–84, 206
plot, 24, 59, 121, 149–53, 154, 161, 194
Poe, Edgar Allan, 142
potential text, 17–18, 86, 107, 131, 161, 180, 187
primal horde, 98–99, 103, 106. *See also* fraternal clan
psychoanalysis, 157, 197; and Oedipal theory, 98, 159; and psychoanalytic theory, 29, 106, 159

Qualley, Donna, 1, 29, 67–68, 71, 126, 152, 189

Rabinowitz, Peter J., 21, 28, 29, 66, 120, 123–24, 132–39, 152–53, 157, 162–64, 176, 183, 186, 206
reader-response theory, 26–27, 29, 162
reading: the act of, 6, 62, 66, 79; developmental stages of, 24–25; as idiosyncratic, 182–83, 186; of fiction, 18–22, 40–41, 206–7; as a hypothetical complete reading, 6; and intertextuality, 106–7; literarily and literally, 39, 153–56; and mental imagery, 75–79, 128–30; as a metaphor for writing, 6; for plot, 151–52; and the reading problem, 18–22; as rule-governed, 135–37; as a social practice, 66, 124, 136, 137; teaching of, 21, 27, 86–87; and uncertainty, 21–22, 37, 40–41, 42, 44–46, 86–87, 117–18; as writing, 5–6; opposed to writing, 6–7, 64, 94. *See also* adaptive reading; authorial audience; authorial reading; intentional reading; mind reading; overreading; risk-averse reading; risky reading; symptomatic reading; underreading
recalcitrance, 183–85, 186
Reid, Ian, 140
Reimer, Mavis, 174–75
resistant text, 45–46, 184
reversal crowd, 89–94, 98, 103, 106, 180
rewriting: 7–8, 13, 17–18, 26, 46, 103, 105, 164, 182; of the comic strip, 11–12, 15, 129–30
rhetorical narrative theory, 29, 30, 109
Richards, I. A., 16–19, 30, 70, 76
"Rip Van Winkle" (Irving), 131–32, 134
risk-averse reading, 66–69, 71
risky reading, 67–69, 71, 126, 176
risky writing, 68–70
Ron Carlson Writes a Story (Carlson), 116–19, 121–25, 137, 152
Rosenblatt, Louise M., 61, 62, 70–71

Sacks, Oliver, 43
Salvatori, Mariolina, 27
Savarese, Ralph James, 41–42
Scarry, Elaine, 179
Scholes, Robert, 18–21, 28, 30, 162, 187

Schulz, Bruno, 198
Schwartz, Howard, 139–41
Sher, Ira, 2, 27–28, 38–39, 42, 60–61, 64, 71, 97, 106, 111–15, 117, 119–22, 125–29, 143–44, 147–50, 155–57, 160–61, 170–72, 179, 189, 190–207
short story: genre of, 134, 141–42; minimalist, 137, 138; modern, 149–50
Smith, Michael W., 20, 29, 186
Spicer, Jack, 191
student responses to "The Man in the Well," 2–4, 25–26, 28, 37, 38–39, 44–88, 90–91, 94, 97, 104, 111–12, 117, 121, 130, 139, 142, 143–44, 146, 150–51, 154–55, 158, 165, 166–67, 172–73, 174–83, 185–86, 189, 196, 202; Allison, 56, 57, 58, 63; Betty, 46–47, 49, 52, 70; Carla, 104; Cheryl, 56, 177–78; Eugene, 90; Isaac, 82, 83, 84–86, 87, 89; Jill, 60, 63; Jordan, 57, 58, 59, 63; Krista, 72–75, 76, 78–80, 107, 129, 186, 196; Langston, 47–48, 49, 53–55, 58, 64, 65, 66, 69; Melanie, 48–50, 55, 65–67, 70, 94; Morgan, 66–68; Robin, 83–86, 97; Ruth, 90, 91; Tara, 158–61; Victor, 52
superego, 98–99, 103–4, 105
Swirski, Peter, 12
symptomatic reading, 162–64, 187
synthetic, 14–15, 24, 25, 59–60, 84, 123, 135, 142–43, 178–80

Tatar, Maria, 173
teaching. *See* literature, teaching of; "The Man in the Well," teaching of
text: and Appleyard, 24–25, 59; as finished, 123, 147, 148; and Fish, 182–84; and Iser, 16, 17, 185; and Lee, 71; and Rosenblatt, 61, 71; and Swirski, 12; as readerly and writerly, 5–6, 38, 45, 109, 153; and work, 12–13. *See also* closed text; open text; potential text; resistant text
textual evidence, 3, 14, 15, 50, 61, 62, 71, 79, 104, 110, 112, 146, 148, 182–83, 187
textuality, 14, 84

thematic, 14, 24, 25, 84, 106, 123, 180
This American Life, 39, 137
To Kill a Mockingbird (Lee), 78
Tomlinson, Barbara, 29, 124, 186
Tom Sawyer (Twain), 188, 190
Trolley Problem, 165–66, 170
Troscianko, Emily T., 29, 76–77
Twain, Mark, 21, 188, 190
Tyson, Lois, 108

underreading, 61–63, 71, 74, 129

Vandaele, Jeroen, 146

Walser, Robert, 198
Wark, Gillian R., 166, 171
Warner, Marina, 174
Wimsatt, W. K., 110–11, 144
Wood, James, 4–6, 7
Wright, Austin M., 183–85
writer: author as, 27, 111; as unknowing, 115–16; and refusal to explain, 5, 116; reader as, 5, 27, 115
writerly choices, 120–21, 122–25, 131, 156, 187. *See also* authorial intentional
writing: the work of, 6, 26, 123, 124–25, 192; as a collective practice, 29, 124, 186; of critical writing, 7–8, 118, 185, 195; and discovery, 115, 117–19, 122, 124, 125, 128, 147, 194–95, 205; of fiction, 115–17, 118–9, 124, 137, 156, 191–92, 194–95, 204; as interpretation, 1, 4, 13, 26; as a metaphor, 4–7; as opposed to reading, 6–7, 94; as reading, 6; as rule-governed, 124, 135–36, 137; and seeing, 76; as a solitary practice, 26, 117, 124, 134, 185; and scholarship, 29–30; and uncertainty, 117–18, 123. *See also* creative writing; literary interpretation; rewriting; risky writing; writerly choices

Zimbardo, Philip, 85–86, 89
Zunshine, Lisa, 29, 40–43, 107

THEORY AND INTERPRETATION OF NARRATIVE
James Phelan, Peter J. Rabinowitz, and Robyn Warhol, Series Editors

Because the series editors believe that the most significant work in narrative studies today contributes both to our knowledge of specific narratives and to our understanding of narrative in general, studies in the series typically offer interpretations of individual narratives and address significant theoretical issues underlying those interpretations. The series does not privilege one critical perspective but is open to work from any strong theoretical position.

The Writer in the Well: On Misreading and Rewriting Literature
GARY WEISSMAN

Narrating Space / Spatializing Narrative: Where Narrative Theory and Geography Meet
MARIE-LAURE RYAN, KENNETH FOOTE, AND MAOZ AZARYAHU

Narrative Sequence in Contemporary Narratology
EDITED BY RAPHAËL BARONI AND FRANÇOISE REVAZ

The Submerged Plot and the Mother's Pleasure from Jane Austen to Arundhati Roy
KELLY A. MARSH

Narrative Theory Unbound: Queer and Feminist Interventions
EDITED BY ROBYN WARHOL AND SUSAN S. LANSER

Unnatural Narrative: Theory, History, and Practice
BRIAN RICHARDSON

Ethics and the Dynamic Observer Narrator: Reckoning with Past and Present in German Literature
KATRA A. BYRAM

Narrative Paths: African Travel in Modern Fiction and Nonfiction
KAI MIKKONEN

The Reader as Peeping Tom: Nonreciprocal Gazing in Narrative Fiction and Film
JEREMY HAWTHORN

Thomas Hardy's Brains: Psychology, Neurology, and Hardy's Imagination
SUZANNE KEEN

The Return of the Omniscient Narrator: Authorship and Authority in Twenty-First Century Fiction
PAUL DAWSON

Feminist Narrative Ethics: Tacit Persuasion in Modernist Form
KATHERINE SAUNDERS NASH

Real Mysteries: Narrative and the Unknowable
H. PORTER ABBOTT

A Poetics of Unnatural Narrative
EDITED BY JAN ALBER, HENRIK SKOV NIELSEN, AND BRIAN RICHARDSON

Narrative Discourse: Authors and Narrators in Literature, Film, and Art
PATRICK COLM HOGAN

An Aesthetics of Narrative Performance: Transnational Theater, Literature, and Film in Contemporary Germany
CLAUDIA BREGER

Literary Identification from Charlotte Brontë to Tsitsi Dangarembga
LAURA GREEN

Narrative Theory: Core Concepts and Critical Debates
DAVID HERMAN, JAMES PHELAN AND PETER J. RABINOWITZ, BRIAN RICHARDSON, AND ROBYN WARHOL

After Testimony: The Ethics and Aesthetics of Holocaust Narrative for the Future
EDITED BY JAKOB LOTHE, SUSAN RUBIN SULEIMAN, AND JAMES PHELAN

The Vitality of Allegory: Figural Narrative in Modern and Contemporary Fiction
GARY JOHNSON

Narrative Middles: Navigating the Nineteenth-Century British Novel
EDITED BY CAROLINE LEVINE AND MARIO ORTIZ-ROBLES

Fact, Fiction, and Form: Selected Essays
RALPH W. RADER. EDITED BY JAMES PHELAN AND DAVID H. RICHTER.

The Real, the True, and the Told: Postmodern Historical Narrative and the Ethics of Representation
ERIC L. BERLATSKY

Franz Kafka: Narration, Rhetoric, and Reading
EDITED BY JAKOB LOTHE, BEATRICE SANDBERG, AND RONALD SPEIRS

Social Minds in the Novel
ALAN PALMER

Narrative Structures and the Language of the Self
MATTHEW CLARK

Imagining Minds: The Neuro-Aesthetics of Austen, Eliot, and Hardy
KAY YOUNG

Postclassical Narratology: Approaches and Analyses
EDITED BY JAN ALBER AND MONIKA FLUDERNIK

Techniques for Living: Fiction and Theory in the Work of Christine Brooke-Rose
KAREN R. LAWRENCE

Towards the Ethics of Form in Fiction: Narratives of Cultural Remission
LEONA TOKER

Tabloid, Inc.: Crimes, Newspapers, Narratives
V. PENELOPE PELIZZON AND NANCY M. WEST

Narrative Means, Lyric Ends: Temporality in the Nineteenth-Century British Long Poem
MONIQUE R. MORGAN

Understanding Nationalism: On Narrative, Cognitive Science, and Identity
PATRICK COLM HOGAN

Joseph Conrad: Voice, Sequence, History, Genre
EDITED BY JAKOB LOTHE, JEREMY HAWTHORN, JAMES PHELAN

The Rhetoric of Fictionality: Narrative Theory and the Idea of Fiction
RICHARD WALSH

Experiencing Fiction: Judgments, Progressions, and the Rhetorical Theory of Narrative
JAMES PHELAN

Unnatural Voices: Extreme Narration in Modern and Contemporary Fiction
BRIAN RICHARDSON

Narrative Causalities
EMMA KAFALENOS

Why We Read Fiction: Theory of Mind and the Novel
LISA ZUNSHINE

I Know That You Know That I Know: Narrating Subjects from Moll Flanders *to* Marnie
GEORGE BUTTE

Bloodscripts: Writing the Violent Subject
ELANA GOMEL

Surprised by Shame: Dostoevsky's Liars and Narrative Exposure
DEBORAH A. MARTINSEN

Having a Good Cry: Effeminate Feelings and Pop-Culture Forms
ROBYN R. WARHOL

Politics, Persuasion, and Pragmatism: A Rhetoric of Feminist Utopian Fiction
ELLEN PEEL

Telling Tales: Gender and Narrative Form in Victorian Literature and Culture
ELIZABETH LANGLAND

Narrative Dynamics: Essays on Time, Plot, Closure, and Frames
EDITED BY BRIAN RICHARDSON

Breaking the Frame: Metalepsis and the Construction of the Subject
DEBRA MALINA

Invisible Author: Last Essays
CHRISTINE BROOKE-ROSE

Ordinary Pleasures: Couples, Conversation, and Comedy
KAY YOUNG

Narratologies: New Perspectives on Narrative Analysis
EDITED BY DAVID HERMAN

Before Reading: Narrative Conventions and the Politics of Interpretation
PETER J. RABINOWITZ

Matters of Fact: Reading Nonfiction over the Edge
DANIEL W. LEHMAN

The Progress of Romance: Literary Historiography and the Gothic Novel
DAVID H. RICHTER

A Glance Beyond Doubt: Narration, Representation, Subjectivity
SHLOMITH RIMMON-KENAN

Narrative as Rhetoric: Technique, Audiences, Ethics, Ideology
JAMES PHELAN

Misreading Jane Eyre: *A Postformalist Paradigm*
JEROME BEATY

Psychological Politics of the American Dream: The Commodification of Subjectivity in Twentieth-Century American Literature
LOIS TYSON

Understanding Narrative
EDITED BY JAMES PHELAN AND PETER J. RABINOWITZ

Framing Anna Karenina: Tolstoy, the Woman Question, and the Victorian Novel
AMY MANDELKER

Gendered Interventions: Narrative Discourse in the Victorian Novel
ROBYN R. WARHOL

Reading People, Reading Plots: Character, Progression, and the Interpretation of Narrative
JAMES PHELAN

www.ingramcontent.com/pod-product-compliance
Lightning Source LLC
Chambersburg PA
CBHW030136240426
43672CB00005B/149